Pocket
TOKYO

TOP SIGHTS • LOCAL LIFE • MADE EASY

Rebecca Milner

In This Book

QuickStart Guide

Your keys to understanding the city – we help you decide what to do and how to do it

Need to Know
Tips for a smooth trip

Neighbourhoods
What's where

Explore Tokyo

The best things to see and do, neighbourhood by neighbourhood

Top Sights
Make the most of your visit

Local Life
The insider's city

The Best of Tokyo

The city's highlights in handy lists to help you plan

Best Walks
See the city on foot

Tokyo' Best...
The best experiences

Survival Guide

Tips and tricks for a seamless, hassle-free city experience

Getting Around
Travel like a local

Essential Information
Including where to stay

Our selection of the city's best places to eat, drink and experience:

◎ **Sights**

✖ **Eating**

🍷 **Drinking**

✪ **Entertainment**

🔒 **Shopping**

These symbols give you the vital information for each listing:

☏ Telephone Numbers	👪 Family-Friendly
⊘ Opening Hours	🐾 Pet-Friendly
P Parking	🚌 Bus
⊖ Nonsmoking	⛴ Ferry
@ Internet Access	M Metro
🛜 Wi-Fi Access	S Subway
🥗 Vegetarian Selection	🚋 Tram
🍽 English-Language Menu	🚆 Train

Find each listing quickly on maps for each neighbourhood:

Bar Hemingway

16 🍷 Map p233, B2

Legend has it that Hemi
self, wielding a machine
rate this timber-pan
ered bar during
showpiece is a
en by Papa ar
town. Dress
s.com; Hôtel Rit
⊘6.30pm-2a

Lonely Planet's Tokyo

Lonely Planet Pocket Guides are designed to get you straight to the heart of the city.

Inside you'll find all the must-see sights, plus tips to make your visit to each one really memorable. We've split the city into easy-to-navigate neighbourhoods and provided clear maps so you'll find your way around with ease. Our expert authors have searched out the best of the city: walks, food, nightlife and shopping, to name a few. Because you want to explore, our 'Local Life' pages will take you to some of the most exciting areas to experience the real Tokyo.

And of course you'll find all the practical tips you need for a smooth trip: itineraries for short visits, how to get around, and how much to tip the guy who serves you a drink at the end of a long day's exploration.

It's your guarantee of a really great experience.

Our Promise

You can trust our travel information because Lonely Planet authors visit the places we write about, each and every edition. We never accept freebies for positive coverage, so you can rely on us to tell it like it is.

The Best of Tokyo 163

Tokyo's Best Walks

Tokyo's Best...

Survival Guide 187

QuickStart Guide

Welcome to Tokyo

Tokyo is a city forever reaching into the future, resulting in sci-fi streetscapes of crackling neon and soaring towers. Yet it is also a city steeped in history, where you can find traces of the shōgun's capital on the kabuki stage or under the cherry blossoms. It's a tapestry of sensorial madness unlike anywhere else in the world.

Shinjuku (p104)
MARC FERNANDEZ DIAZ/GETTY IMAGES ©

👁 Tokyo Top Sights

Tsukiji Central Fish Market (p34)

The world's largest fish market, where prized tuna are auctioned to the highest bidder, is Tokyo's most unique sight, and a rare peek into the working life of the city.

Meiji-jingū (p90)

Tokyo's most famous Shintō shrine is shrouded in woods. It's a peaceful haven that feels worlds away from the city, even though it is right in the thick of it.

Sensō-ji (p146)

The spiritual home of Tokyoites' ancestors, Sensō-ji was founded more than 1000 years before Tokyo got its start. Today the temple retains an alluring, lively atmosphere redolent of Edo (old Tokyo under the shōgun).

Sumō in Ryōgoku (p46)

Salt-slinging, belly-slapping and ritual are all part of the spectacle that is sumō, Japan's ancient, traditional sport. Catch a tournament at the national stadium in Ryōgoku or a morning practice session.

Kabuki (p36)

Kabuki, a form of stylised Japanese theatre, features stories from popular legend and an all-male cast in dramatic makeup and decadent costumes. See a performance at Kabuki-za, Tokyo's rebuilt kabuki theatre.

WILL ROBB / GETTY IMAGES ©

DEA / G. SOSIO / GETTY IMAGES ©

Roppongi Hills (p50)

This is no ordinary mall: it's a utopian micro-city with a world-class art museum. Love it or hate it, Roppongi Hills is integral to understanding the Tokyo of today, and possibly the Tokyo of tomorrow.

Tokyo National Museum (p130)

Japan's premier museum houses the world's largest collection of Japanese art and antiquities such as swords, gilded screens, kimonos and colourful *ukiyo-e* (wood-block prints).

Mt Fuji (p158)

Japan's national symbol is a perfect, snowcapped cone. On a clear day, you can catch a glimpse from atop a Tokyo skyscraper, but nothing compares to the thrill of seeing a sunrise from the summit.

Imperial Palace (p24)

Take a tour of the leafy grounds of the imperial family's residence, or content yourself to stroll along the ancient moat and climb an old castle keep in the garden.

CRAIG PERSHOUSE / GETTY IMAGES ©

TAKAU99 / GETTY IMAGES © ARCHITECT NIKKEN SEKKEI

Ōedo Onsen Monogatari (p156)

Bubbling hot springs piped from below Tokyo Bay fill the baths at Ōedo Onsen Monogatari, a combination of public bathhouse and theme park that is Japanese to the core.

Tokyo Sky Tree (p144)

Opened in 2012, Tokyo Sky Tree is among the world's tallest structures at 634m. Two observation decks present a stunning panorama of the greater Tokyo area and, if you're lucky, Mt Fuji.

Tokyo Local Life

Insider tips to help you find the real city

Get beyond the big ticket sights and see Tokyo from a local's point of view. Explore the city's bohemian enclaves and historical quarters, its fascinating subcultures, quirky shops, hip cafes and sublime nightlife.

Hanging out in Shimo-Kitazawa (p86)

▶ Bohemian culture
▶ Bars & pubs

This is a neighbourhood of snaking alleys, secondhand stores, coffee shops, raucous *izakaya* (Japanese-style pubs) and hole-in-the-wall bars. It's been a bastion of counterculture for decades, with a colourful street scene and a down-to-earth vibe. Leave the bustle behind and lose yourself in this pocket of Tokyo bohemia.

East Shinjuku at Night (p106)

▶ Colourful nightlife
▶ Late night eats

East Shinjuku, neighbour to strait-laced business district Nishi-Shinjuku, is Tokyo's largest, most off-the-wall nightlife district. Walk through crackling neon canyons piled high with bars, cabarets, karaoke parlours – even batting cages – then raise a glass (and slurp some noodles) in the collection of wooden shanties known as Golden Gai.

An Afternoon in Akihabara (p126)

▶ Pop culture
▶ Quirky shops & cafes

Akihabara is where much of Japan's *otaku* (geek) culture is born. It's an alternative universe of maid cafes (where the waitresses dress like french maids) and *rāmen* vending machines, anime collectibles and vintage video arcades. And you don't have to be a geek yourself to appreciate this fascinating subculture.

A Stroll Through Historic Yanaka (p134)

▶ Art galleries
▶ Hidden lanes

The rare neighbourhood to survive both the Great Kantō earthquake and the firebombing of WWII, Yanaka looks and feels like the Tokyo of 100 years ago. It's long been a favourite of artists and there are studios and galleries dotting the neighbourhood's winding lanes, in addition to boutiques and cafes.

Late night eating in Shinjuku

Akihabara's Electric Town

Other great places to experience the city like a local:

Tokyo Day Planner

Day One

Start the day in Harajuku with a visit to **Meiji-jingū** (p90), Tokyo's most famous Shintō shrine. Next stroll down nearby **Takeshita-dōri** (p93), a pedestrian alley famous for its wild teen fashions. Then make your way over to the neighbourhood's main drag, **Omote-sandō** (p94), to see some jaw-dropping contemporary architecture. Break for a lunch of dumplings at local favourite **Harajuku Gyōza Rō** (p95).

Take the subway to Roppongi and head for **Roppongi Hills** (p50), a fascinating city within the city and home to Tokyo's best contemporary art museum, **Mori Art Museum** (p51). Stop for sweeping views over the city from the adjacent observatory, **Tokyo City View** (p51), on the 52nd floor. If time permits, check out **Tokyo Midtown** (p55), home to the **Suntory Museum of Art** (p54) and **21_21 Design Sight** (p54).

From Roppongi, hop on the subway for Shinjuku, a neighbourhood known for its bustling crowds and cascades of neon. Have dinner at an *izakaya* (Japanese-style pub), such as **Donjaka** (p112), then explore the various nightlife options in **East Shinjuku** (p112). Make sure to raise a glass in **Golden Gai** (p112).

Day Two

Take the train to Ueno and spend an hour or two taking in the highlights of the **Tokyo National Museum** (p130). Give yourself another hour to check out the temples, shrines, flora and fauna in **Ueno-kōen** (p137), the city's oldest park. Then take a stroll through the old-fashioned, open-air market, **Ameya-yokochō** (p137),

From Ueno, it's a short walk to the wonderfully atmospheric restaurant **Hantei** (p139). After lunch, spend a couple of hours exploring **Yanaka** (p112), a historical neighbourhood beloved by artists. Then catch the train for Asakusa to visit the temple **Sensō-ji** (p146), the shrine **Asakusa-jinja** (p149) and the maze of old-world alleys that surround these two sights.

From Asakusa, you can walk or taxi over to the landmark **Tokyo Sky Tree** (p144), across the river, for night views over the city. Or instead, get a view of the tower from the **Asahi Sky Room** (p154). For dinner, splurge on premium grade beef at **Asakusa Imahan** (p153), followed by a nightcap at **Kamiya Bar** (p153), one of Tokyo's oldest bars.

Short on time?
We've arranged Tokyo's must-sees into these day-by-day itineraries to make sure you see the very best of the city in the time you have available.

Day Three

Take a taxi to arrive at the **Tsukiji Fish Market** (p34) by 5am to claim a spot in the visitor's gallery for the tuna auction; otherwise, arrive at 9am when the wholesalers' market opens to visitors. After exploring the market, grab a meal at **Daiwa Sushi** (p42). From Tsukiji it's an easy walk to **Hama-rikyū Onshi-teien** (p39), where you can stop for a break in the garden's teahouse, **Nakajima no Ochaya** (p43).

Take the train (or a taxi) from Shimbashi to stately **Tokyo Station** (p27), from where it's a short walk to the **Imperial Palace** (p24). Take the 1.30pm tour of the palace grounds (if you've booked ahead); otherwise visit the **Imperial Palace East Garden** (p25). From here, walk over to Ginza's stately boulevard **Chūō-dōri** (p39), with its grand department stores, such as **Mitsukoshi** (p44).

Spend the evening at Ginza's kabuki theatre **Kabuki-za** (p36); book ahead unless you plan to pick up last-minute, one-act tickets. It's the custom to eat a *bentō* (boxed meal) for dinner during intermission, or go for a late dinner at **Bird Land** (p42).

Day Four

If you're feeling ambitious, you can make a day-trip out to **Mt Fuji** (p112). Alternatively, if you're in the mood for some pampering, you can splash out on a lavish *kaiseki* (traditional haute cuisine) lunch at **Tofuya-Ukai** (p59) and then spend a few hours bath-hopping at **Ōedo Onsen Monogatari** (p112). Otherwise, take some time to explore some of Tokyo's more off-beat neighbourhoods, including **Akihabara** (p112), famous for its *otaku* (geek) culture, or **Naka-Meguro** (p67), known for its canal lined with hip cafes and boutiques.

In the late afternoon head to Shibuya to see the legendary intersection, **Shibuya Crossing** (p78), and its always-buzzing main drag **Center-gai** (p78). Then take the train to **Shimo-Kitazawa** (p112) and wander the tiny lanes of this bohemian neighbourhood.

Have dinner at **Shirube** (p87), an *izakaya* (Japanese-style pub) loved by locals, then settle into one of Shimo-Kitazawa's cosy bars, such as **Mother** (p87). If you've got energy to spare, return to Shibuya to take in the nightlife there. Hit up club **Womb** (p81) or karaoke parlour **Shidax Village** (p82), and dance and sing until dawn.

Need to Know

For more information,
see Survival Guide (p188)

Currency
Japanese yen (¥)

Language
Japanese

Visas
Citizens of 61 countries, including Australia, Canada, Hong Kong, Korea, New Zealand, Singapore, UK, USA and almost all European nations, do not require visas to enter Japan for stays of 90 days or fewer.

Money
Post offices and some convenience stores have international ATMs. Credit cards are accepted at major establishments, though it's best to have cash on hand.

Mobile Phones
Local SIM cards cannot be used in overseas phones and only 3G phones will work in Japan; rentals are available at the airport.

Time
Japan Standard Time (GMT plus nine hours)

Plugs & Adaptors
Plugs have two flat pins; electrical current is 100V. North American appliances will work; others will require an adaptor.

Tipping
Tipping is not common practice in Japan, though top-end restaurants will add a 10% service charge to your bill.

❶ Before You Go

Your Daily Budget

Budget less than ¥8000
▶ Dorm beds ¥3000
▶ Bowl of noodles ¥800
▶ Free sights and cheaper museums
▶ One-act tickets for kabuki ¥1000

Midrange ¥8000–¥20,000
▶ Double room in a business hotel ¥10,000
▶ Dinner and drinks at an *izakaya* (Japanese-style pub) ¥3500
▶ Mezzanine seats for kabuki ¥6000

Top End more than ¥20,000
▶ Double room in a four-star hotel ¥30,000
▶ Tasting course at a top sushi restaurant ¥20,000
▶ Best seats for kabuki ¥20,000

Useful Websites

▶ **Lonely Planet** (www.lonelyplanet.com/japan) Destination information, hotel bookings, traveller forum and more.

▶ **Go Tokyo** (www.gotokyo.org/en/index.html) Tokyo's official site covers sights, events and tours.

▶ **Metropolis** (http://metropolis.co.jp) Arts and entertainment listings.

Advance Planning

▶ **One month** Book tickets for kabuki, sumō and the Imperial Palace tour; make reservations at top-end restaurants; book your hotel now and you may lock in a better rate.

▶ **One week** Scan web listings for festivals, live music shows and exhibitions.

② Arriving in Tokyo

Narita Airport is 66km east of Tokyo; the more convenient Haneda Airport is on the city's southern edge. However, some flights to Haneda arrive in the middle of the night when a taxi (budget around ¥6000) is your only option.

✈ From Narita Airport

Destination	Best Transport
Marunouchi (Tokyo Station), Shinjuku, Shibuya	Narita Express
Ginza, Roppongi, Ebisu	Keisei Skyliner to Ueno, then subway (Hibiya Line)
Ueno	Keisei Skyliner
Asakusa	Keisei Skyliner to Ueno, then subway (Ginza Line)

✈ From Haneda Airport

Destination	Best Transport
Marunouchi (Tokyo Station), Ueno	Tokyo Monorail to Hamamatsuchō, then JR Yamanote Line
Ebisu, Shibuya, Shinjuku	Keikyū Line to Shinagawa, then JR Yamanote Line
Roppongi	Tokyo Monorail to Hamatsuchō, then subway (Ōedo Line from Daimon Station)
Ginza, Asakusa	Keikyū Line to Sengakuji, then subway (Asakusa Line)

🚄 From Tokyo Station

Tokyo Station, the *Shinkansen* (bullet train) terminus, is serviced by the JR Yamanote Line and the Marunouchi metro line. There are taxi ranks in front of both the Marunouchi Central and Yaesu Central exits.

③ Getting Around

Tokyo's public transport system – a tourist attraction in its own right – is excellent. It's a good idea to get a pre-paid Suica card (p192), which works on all trains and buses and means you won't have to worry about purchasing paper tickets.

🚃 Train

The rail network, which includes 13 subway lines (run by either Tokyo Metro or TOEI) and Japan Rail (JR) lines, will take you pretty much anywhere you need to go. It's the quickest and easiest way to get around, though it doesn't run between midnight and 5am. With a Suica pass you can transfer seamlessly between lines.

🚕 Taxi

Taxis only make economic sense if you've got a group of four; additionally, taxi drivers rarely speak English and know only major destinations. Still, they're your only option after midnight.

🚲 Bicycle

Bicycles are good for getting around quieter neighbourhoods where traffic is thinner; some guesthouses have bicycles to lend.

🚢 Boat

Tourist boats run up and down the Sumida-gawa; they're not cheap or efficient, but the views are lovely.

🚌 Bus

In central Tokyo, the train beats the bus 9.9 times out of 10 for efficiency.

🚗 Car

Considering the traffic, convoluted city layout, exorbitant parking rates and efficiency of the city's public transport, most Tokyoites don't even have drivers' licenses. We don't recommend driving here.

Tokyo Neighbourhoods

Iidabashi & Around (p118)
A controversial shrine, an atmospheric hill with old-world alleys and hidden restaurants, a traditional garden and the stadium of baseball's Yomiuri Giants.

Shibuya (p74)
The centre of Tokyo's youth culture looks like the set of a sci-fi flick, with a collection of giant TV screens, lurid fashion and crowds.

Shinjuku (p104)
Tokyo's biggest hub has the world's busiest train station, the city hall, a sprawling park, shopping and nightlife.

◉ *Meiji-jingū*

◉ *Imperial Palace*

Kabuki-za **◉**

Tsukiji Fish Market

◉ *Roppongi Hills*

Harajuku & Aoyama (p88)
Home to Tokyo's grandest Shintō shrine, this nexus of tradition and trends swarms with shoppers and luxury brand architecture.

◉ Top Sights

Meiji-jingū

Ebisu & Meguro (p64)
A collection of funky neighbourhoods, with stylish boutiques, unexpected museums and excellent restaurants and bars.

Ueno (p128)
Tokyo's most famous museum, plus temples, shrines and residential neighbourhoods where time seems to have stopped decades ago.

⊙ **Top Sights**

Tokyo National Museum

Tokyo Sky Tree & Asakusa (p142)
The traditional heart of Tokyo, a riverside district of ancient temples, old merchants' quarters and nostalgic restaurants and bars.

⊙ **Top Sights**

Tokyo Sky Tree

Sensō-ji

Tokyo National Museum

Sensō-ji ⊙

Tokyo Sky Tree ⊙

⊙ *Ryōgoku Kokugikan*

Imperial Palace & Marunouchi (Tokyo Station) (p22)
History meets modernity when the grounds of the Imperial Palace meet the skyscrapers of Marunouchi.

⊙ **Top Sights**

Imperial Palace

Tsukiji Fish Market & Ginza (p32)
Tokyo's classiest neighbourhood, with department stores, boutiques, gardens, teahouses and high-end restaurants.

⊙ **Top Sights**

Tsukiji Fish Market

Kabuki-za

Roppongi & Akasaka (p48)
Legendary for its nightlife, this forward-looking neighbourhood is also the place for cutting-edge art, architecture and design.

⊙ **Top Sights**

Roppongi Hills

Ōedo Onsen Monogatari

Worth a Trip

⊙ **Top Sights**

Ōedo Onsen Monogatari

Sumō at Ryōgoku Kokugikan

Mt Fuji

Explore
Tokyo

Worth a Trip

Shibuya Crossing (p78)
TOMML / GETTY IMAGES ©

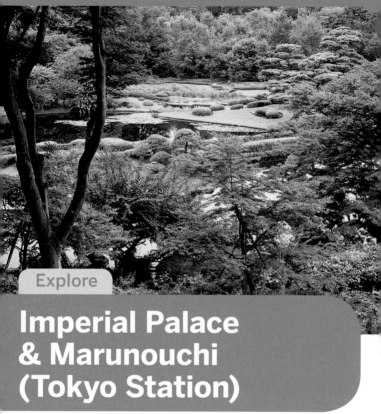

Explore

Imperial Palace & Marunouchi (Tokyo Station)

Marunouchi is the geographic centre of Tokyo and its top draw, the Imperial Palace, is the city's symbolic one. The neighbourhood is a high-powered business district with dozens of glossy skyscrapers on show. It's establishment Tokyo at its finest, with museums and architectural masterpieces, but also restaurants, bars and shops for the office workers who hold it all together.

The Sights in a Day

☀ Take the train to **Tokyo Station** (p27) to see the recently restored 100-year-old building, then head to the **Imperial Palace** (p24). A tour of the grounds begins at 10am (you'll need to book ahead), after which you can spend an hour exploring the **Imperial Palace East Garden** (p25). Next, stroll down elegant Marunouchi Naka-dōri to the **Mitsubishi Ichigōkan Museum** (p27), followed by lunch at **Cafe 1894** (p29) next door.

☀ In the afternoon, amble over to the architecturally impressive **Tokyo International Forum** (p27), and then to the **National Film Centre** (p27) for an exhibition on the history of Japanese cinema. Next, walk up Chūō-dōri, where grand old department stores like **Takashimaya** (p31) hold court. Make a detour to the colourful **Kite Museum** (p28), and make sure you don't miss **Nihombashi** (p27) – the bridge that marks the geographic centre of Tokyo.

☽ Marunouchi gets pretty quiet in the evenings, but there are small pockets of nightlife. Grab a casual dinner of grilled skewers at **Ishii** (p29) then go for drinks with a view at **So Tired** (p30), and look out over Tokyo Station from the terrace.

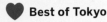

👁 Top Sights

Imperial Palace (p24)

♥ Best of Tokyo

Architecture

Tokyo International Forum (p27)

Takashimaya (p31)

Parks & Gardens

Imperial Palace East Garden (p25)

Galleries & Museums

Kite Museum (p28)

Food

Tokyo Rāmen Street (p28)

Nightlife & Live Music

So Tired (p30)

Getting There

🚉 **Train** The JR Yamanote Line stops at Tokyo Station and Yūrakuchō. Tokyo Station is also serviced by Narita Express and *shinkansen* (bullet trains), heading north and south.

Ⓢ **Subway** The Marunouchi Line runs through Tokyo Station. Several lines such as Marunouchi, Hanzōmon and Chiyoda Lines stop at Ōtemachi; Chiyoda Line continues to Nijūbashimae and Hibiya. The Ginza Line services Nihombashi and Kyōbashi.

Top Sights
Imperial Palace

The Imperial Palace, residence of Japan's emperor, occupies pride of place in the city centre. It also occupies the site where Edo-jō, the Tokugawa shōgun's castle, once stood. While the palace is closed to the public, visitors can take a free guided tour of the grounds. The Imperial Palace East Garden, open without reservation and also free, preserves some of the original castle masonry and is an attractive retreat from the bustle of downtown Tokyo.

皇居; Kōkyo

Map p26, A2

3213-1111

http://sankan.kunaicho.
go.jp/english/index.html

Chiyoda, Chiyoda-ku

admission free

Marunouchi Line to
Ōtemachi, exits C13b
or C8b

Imperial Palace

Don't Miss

Nijū-bashi & the Palace Moat

The original moat, dating to the Edo-jō period, wraps around the palace grounds. Even if you skip the tour, you can walk along the edge of the moat to see **Nijū-bashi**, one of Japan's most famous bridges, an elegant succession of stone arches used for formal ceremonies and receptions.

The Imperial Palace

The present palace, modern but traditional in style, was completed in 1968, replacing one built in 1888 and destroyed during WWII. If you take the guided tour, you'll walk past a few of the outer buildings, including the plaza where the public gathers on 2 January and 23 December for a rare public appearance by the imperial family.

Fujimi-yagura

The three-storey watch tower **Fujimi-yagura** (富士見櫓), whose name translates to Mt Fuji Keep, is one of the few remaining structures of the former castle. It was constructed in 1659 and is the highlight of the guided tour of the grounds. Another keep, **Fushimi-yagura** (伏見櫓), was supposedly relocated from Kyoto in the 17th century.

Imperial Palace East Garden

The **Imperial Palace East Garden** (東御苑; Kōkyo Higashi-gyoen; admission free; ⏰9am-4pm Nov-Feb, to 4.30pm Mar-Apr, Sep & Oct, to 5pm May-Aug, closed Mon & Fri year-round; 🚇Marunouchi Line to Ōtemachi, exit C10) is the only corner of the palace grounds open to the public without a reservation. You can see the massive stones used to build the castle walls and can climb on the ruins of one of the keeps. The entrance is via the gate **Ōte-mon** (大手門); take a token on arrival and return it at the end of your visit.

☑ **Top Tips**

▶ Tours, leaving from the Kikyō-mon gate, run twice daily from Monday to Friday (10am and 1.30pm), but only in the mornings from late July until the end of August.

▶ You must sign up in advance through the Imperial Household Agency's website: http://sankan.kunaicho.go.jp/english/index.html.

▶ The Imperial Palace East Garden is closed on Mondays and Fridays, so it's easier to book a tour on those days, but it means missing the garden.

▶ Be sure to snag a free English audio headset for the tour.

✖ **Take a Break**

Not far from Nijū-bashi, **Cafe 1894** (p29) does light lunches, coffee and cake.

Sushi restaurant **Numazu Uogashi** (p30) is a short walk from the Imperial Palace East Garden.

Sights

National Film Centre ARTS CENTRE

1 Map p26, D4

The National Film Centre is an archive of Japanese and foreign films affiliated with the National Museum of Modern Art. The 7th-floor gallery offers a concise history (in English) of Japanese cinema, including rare footage of some of the earliest films – when the actors were straight off the kabuki (a form of stylised Japanese theatre based on popular legends) stage – and vintage film memorabilia. (東京国立近代美術館フィルムセンター; www.momat.go.jp/english/nfc/index.html; 3-7-6 Kyōbashi, Chūō-ku; screenings adult/student ¥500/300, gallery only ¥200/70; ⊙gallery 11am-6.30pm Tue-Sat, check website for screening times; ☒Ginza Line to Kyōbashi, exit 1)

Tokyo International Forum ARCHITECTURE

2 Map p26, C4

Looking like a glass ship plying the urban waters, this convention centre is one of Tokyo's architectural marvels. Architect Rafael Viñoly won Japan's first international architecture competition with his design; the building was completed in 1996. Take the elevator to the 7th floor of the glass eastern wing to explore the catwalks. (東京国際フォーラム; 3-5-1 Marunouchi, Chiyoda-ku; admission free; ☒JR Yamanote Line to Yūrakuchō, central exit)

Nihombashi BRIDGE

3 Map p26, E2

The Imperial Palace is the city's symbolic centre, but this bridge, where Chūō-dōri crosses Nihombashi-gawa (Nihombashi River), is its geographic centre. All distance was measured from this point during the Edo period. The granite bridge is guarded with bronze lions, though you could walk past it without noticing, as it's now in the shadow of the city expressway. (日本橋; ☒Ginza Line to Mitsukoshimae, exits B5 or B6)

Tokyo Station BUILDING

4 Map p26, C3

Tokyo Station, at the heart of Marunouchi, turns 100 in 2014. The elegant red brick building was damaged during WWII and hastily rebuilt after. A lengthy renovation project, completed in 2012, saw it returned to its former height and glory, and its ornate domes restored. (東京駅; 1-9 Marunouchi, Chiyoda-ku)

Mitsubishi Ichigōkan Museum MUSEUM

5 Map p26, C3

The Mitsubishi Ichigōkan was the area's first office building, designed in 1894 by English architect Josiah Conder. The original is long gone but this faithful replica, housing an art gallery, opened in 2010. Exhibitions cover art – mostly European – from the time of the original structure's heyday. (三菱一号館美術館; http://mimt.jp/english; 2-6-2

KARIN SLADE / GETTY IMAGES © ARCHITECT: RAFAEL VIÑOLY

Tokyo International Forum (p27)

Marunouchi, Chiyoda-ku; admission ¥1500; ⏰10am-6pm Tue, Wed & Sun, to 8pm Thu-Sat; 🚇Chiyoda Line to Nijūbashimae, exit 1)

Take a Break Grab lunch or a coffee at **Cafe 1894** (opposite page) next door.

Kite Museum   MUSEUM

6 Map p26, E2

This tiny museum pays hommage to the Edo-dako (Edo-style kite), brilliantly coloured and decorated with imagery of folk heroes and warriors. It's above Taimeiken restaurant (たいめいけん). (凧の博物館; ☎3271-2465; www.tako.gr.jp/eng/museums_e/tokyo_e.html; 5th fl, 1-12-10 Nihombashi, Chūō-ku; adult/child ¥200/100; ⏰11am-5pm Mon-Sat; 🚇Ginza Line to Nihombashi, exit C5)

Eating

Tokyo Rāmen Street   RĀMEN $

7 🍽 Map p26, D3

Eight of Japan's famous *rāmen* shops operate mini-branches in a corner of Tokyo Station (in the basement on the Yaesu side). All of the major styles are represented, from *shōyu* (soy sauce base) to *tsukemen* (cold noodles served on the side). Good luck picking just one! (東京ラーメンストリート; www.tokyoeki-1bangai.co.jp/ramenstreet; basement fl, Tokyo Station; rāmen from ¥750; ⏰7.30am-10.30pm; 🚇JR Yamanote Line to Tokyo Station, Yaesu south exit)

Ishii

KUSHIYAKI $

8 ✗ Map p26, C2

Yakiton (grilled pork skewers) – rather than the more common *yakitori* (grilled chicken skewers) – is the speciality here. Ishii is done up like a retro, post-WWII food stand and is famous for using all of the pig (and we mean *all* of it). It's on the 5th floor of the Shin-Maru building; look for the lanterns out front. (い志井; 5th fl, Shin-Marunouchi Bldg, 1-5-1 Marunouchi, Chiyoda-ku; skewers from ¥140; ☺11am-2pm & 4pm-2am Mon-Sat, 11am-10pm Sun; ☒JR Yamanote Line to Tokyo, Marunouchi north exit; 🖐)

Cafe 1894

INTERNATIONAL $

Cafe 1894 (see **5** ◎ Map p26, C3) is a faithful replica of the bank – vaulted ceilings, chandeliers, elaborate woodwork – that was built here in 1894. At lunch, the restaurant serves tasty spreads, inspired by the exhibitions at the museum next door. (カフェ1894; 2-6-2 Marunouchi, Chiyoda-ku; lunch set from ¥1480, coffee ¥525; ☺11am-11pm Mon-Thu,

Understand

The Meiji Restoration

Following the shōgun (former military ruler) Tokugawa Ieyasu's decision to make Edo his capital in 1603, the most transformative event in Tokyo history was the Meiji Restoration.

For 250 years the Tokugawa shōguns kept Japan almost entirely isolated. Then, in 1853, the black ships under the command of US Navy Commodore Matthew Perry sailed into Tokyo Bay demanding that Japan open itself to foreign trade. Faced with the Americans' superior weaponry, the antiquated Tokugawa regime was powerless.

The humiliating acquiescence that followed fanned existing flames of anti-government sentiment, and a coalition of southern Japan *daimyō* (feudal lords) founded a movement (and army) to restore the emperor to power. The shōgun stepped down in 1867 and in 1868, following months of civil war, the 16-year-old Emperor Meiji was named head of state. Meiji moved the seat of imperial power from Kyoto to Edo, renaming the city Tokyo (Eastern Capital).

The Meiji Restoration had far-reaching social implications, as Japan opened up to the world and began to adopt technology as well as political and social ideas from the West. Marunouchi was established as the first business district in the modern sense, and a culture of white-collar workers in suit and tie commuting by streetcar grew up around it. Naturally, job opportunities – and the chance to join the emerging middle class – drew migrants from all the provinces.

Sat & Sun, to 2am Fri; Ⓜ Chiyoda Line to Nijūbashimae, exit 1)

Meal MUJI   DELI $

On the 2nd floor of the Yūrakuchō MUJI shop, this deli follows the brand's 'simpler is better' mantra with fresh, natural fare. Claim your seat, then head to the counter and point to your picks from the variety of hot and cold dishes (see 🔟 🔒 Map p26, C4). (☎5208-8241; www.muji.net/cafemeal/; 3-8-3 Marunouchi, Chiyoda-ku; meals from ¥780; ⏰10am-9pm; Ⓡ JR Yamanote Line to Yūrakuchō, Kyōbashi exit; ☺🍴)

Robata Honten   IZAKAYA $$

9 🍽 Map p26, B4

Alongside the train tracks and inside an old wooden building blackened by the years, this *izakaya* (Japanese version of a pub/eatery) has enough ambience that it needn't worry about the food. Fortunately, it does: filling, home-style dishes, a mix of Japanese

and Western, are served family-style, piled high in bowls on the counter – just point to what you want. (爐端本店; ☎3591-1905; 1-3-8 Yūrakuchō, Chiyoda-ku; dishes ¥1000-1500; ⏰5-11pm Mon-Sat; Ⓜ Ginza Line to Hibiya, exit A4)

Numazu Uogashi   SUSHI $$

 10 🍽 Map p26, C3

It may be in the lofty confines of the Marunouchi Building, but this friendly, workmanlike sushi shop feels like Tsukiji. Single serves are pretty expensive, but portions are generous and set lunches are a great deal. (沼津魚がし; ☎5220-5550; 6th fl, Marunouchi Bldg, 2-4-1 Marunouchi, Chiyoda-ku; sets ¥980-3300; ⏰11am-11pm Mon-Sat, to 10pm Sun; Ⓡ JR Yamanote Line to Tokyo Station, Marunouchi centre exit; 📖)

Drinking

So Tired   BAR

The best thing about this bar, on the 7th floor of the Shin-Maru Building, is that you can buy a drink at the counter and take it out to the terrace. The views aren't sky-high; instead you feel curiously suspended among the office towers, hovering over Tokyo Station below (see **8** 🍽 Map p26, C2). (☎5220-1358; www.heads-west.com/shop/so-tired.html; 7th fl, Shin-Marunouchi Bldg, 1-5-1 Marunouchi, Chiyoda-ku; ⏰11am-4am Mon-Sat, to 11pm Sun; Ⓡ JR Yamanote Line to Tokyo, Marunouchi north exit; 📖)

Ⓞ Local Life
Ōedo Antique Market

Twice a month treasure-hunters descend on the **Ōedo Antique Market** (大江戸骨董市; ☎6407-6011; www.antique-market.jp; 3-5-1 Marunouchi, Chiyoda-ku; ⏰9am-4pm 1st & 3rd Sun of month; Ⓡ JR Yamanote Line to Yūrakuchō, central exit) in the courtyard of Tokyo International Forum (p27). With around 250 vendors, it's the largest antique market in the country.

Bar Oak
BAR

11 Map p26, C3

Inside the newly renovated Tokyo Station Hotel, this bar feels like a relic from another era. Considering the dark wood panelling, a jazz piano soundtrack and black-tie bartenders, you'd expect the clientele to be wearing fedoras and furs. Naturally, the martinis (¥1100) are excellent. (バーオーク; 2nd fl, Tokyo Station Hotel, 1-9-1 Marunouchi, Chiyoda-ku; ⏱5pm-midnight; ☒JR Yamanote Line to Tokyo, Marunouchi south exit; 🄳)

Shopping

Muji
CLOTHING, HOMEWARES

12 Map p26, C4

Muji (short for Mujirushi) means no brand, though by now the label's simple, functional aesthetic is as iconic as any brand. This Yūrakuchō outpost is one of Tokyo's largest and carries clothes for men and women, homewares and its unbeatable line of travel accessories. (無印良品; www.mujiyurakucho.com; 3-8-3 Marunouchi, Chiyoda-ku; ⏱10am-9pm; ☒JR Yamanote to Yūrakuchō, Kyōbashi exit)

Takashimaya
DEPARTMENT STORE

13 Map p26, E3

Takashimaya's branch on New York's Fifth Ave is renowned for its cutting-edge Japanese-inspired interior, but the design of the Tokyo flagship store

Marunouchi District

(1933) tips its pillbox hat to New York's gilded age. Uniformed female elevator operators still announce each floor in high-pitched, sing-song voices. (高島屋; 2-4-1 Nihombashi, Chūō-ku; ⏱10am-8pm; ☒Ginza Line to Nihombashi, Takashimaya exit)

Tokyo Character Street
TOYS

14 Map p26, D2

On the basement level of Tokyo Station, some 15 Japanese TV networks and toy manufacturers operate shop after shop selling official toys, character goods, sweets and accessories. (東京キャラクターストリート; First Avenue, level B1, Tokyo Station; ⏱10am-8.30pm; ☒JR Yamanote Line to Tokyo Station, Yaesu exit)

TOSHIAKI ONO / A COLLECTIONRF / GETTY IMAGES ©

Explore

Tsukiji Fish Market & Ginza

Ginza is Tokyo's most polished neighbourhood, a fashion centre for more than a century, resplendent with department stores, galleries, gardens and teahouses. The city's kabuki theatre, Kabuki-za, is here, as are many of Tokyo's most celebrated restaurants. A short walk away is a luxury commercial centre of a different sort: Tsukiji Fish Market.

The Sights in a Day

☀ Get an early start – 5am if you want to catch the tuna auction – at **Tsukiji Fish Market** (p34). Budget two hours to explore the wholesale market (open 9 to 11am), with its diverse array of photogenic sea creatures, and the outer market, followed by an indulgent sushi meal at **Daiwa Sushi** (p42). Afterwards, walk down to the landscape garden **Hama-rikyū Onshi-teien** (p39) and have tea at **Nakajima no Ochaya** (p43).

☀ Spend the afternoon gallery-hopping and window-shopping in Ginza. Stroll along **Chūō-dōri** (p39), home to both grand department stores such as **Mitsukoshi** (p44), and high-street chains, including **Uniqlo** (p44). Then weave through the side streets to find galleries such as **Tokyo Gallery** (p40). In the late afternoon, see a kabuki performance at Tokyo's most famous theatre, **Kabuki-za** (p36).

☽ If you're at Kabuki-za, your dinner will be the elaborate *bentō* (boxed meal), traditionally eaten during intermission. Otherwise try **Bird Land** (p42) for some upmarket *yakitori* (skewered grilled chicken). Wind down the evening at **Aux Amis Des Vins** (p43), a cosy alley-side bistro with an excellent wine list.

◉ Top Sights

Tsukiji Central Fish Market (p34)

Kabuki-za (p36)

♥ Best of Tokyo

Parks & Gardens
Hama-rikyū Onshi-teien (p39)

Galleries & Museums
Tokyo Gallery (p40)

Food
Daiwa Sushi (p42)

Sushi Kanesaka (p42)

Bird Land (p42)

Narutomi (p40)

Shopping
Dover Street Market (p44)

Mitsukoshi (p44)

Getting There

🚃 **Train** The JR Yamanote Line stops at Shimbashi Station.

Ⓢ **Subway** Ginza, Hibiya and Marunouchi Lines stop at Ginza Station; Hibiya Line continues to Higashi-Ginza and Tsukiji, take the Ginza Line to Shimbashi and Ōedo Line to Shiodome and Tsukijishijō.

⚓ **Ferry** Tokyo Cruise water buses travel to Hama-rikyū Onshi-teien.

Top Sights
Tsukiji Central Fish Market

The world's biggest seafood market, moving an astounding 2400 tonnes of seafood a day and supplying Tokyo's top restaurants, has stood on its current spot since 1935, although it is slated to move to reclaimed land on Tokyo Bay in the spring of 2015. You'll find all manner of fascinating creatures passing through, but it is the *maguro* (bluefin tuna) that has emerged the star. Even if you don't arrive at dawn for the tuna auction, you can still get a flavour of the frenetic atmosphere of the market and feast your eyes (and camera) on the incredible array of fish.

築地市場; Tsukiji Shijō

Map p38, C4

3542-1111

www.tsukiji-market.or.jp

5-2 Tsukiji, Chūō-ku

closed Sun, most Weds

Ōedo Line to Tsukijishijō, exits A1 & A2

Market produce

Don't Miss

Tuna Auction

Bidding for prized *maguro* – which can sell for more than US$10,000 each – starts at 5am. Up to 120 visitors a day in two shifts are allowed to watch the auction from a gallery between 5.25am and 6.15am. It's first-come-first-served; register at 5am at the **Fish Information Center** (おさかな普及センター; Map p38, D4; 6-20-5 Tsukiji, Chūō-ku), near the market's Kachidoki-mon (gate).

Seafood Intermediate Wholesalers Area

Here you can see a truly global haul of sea creatures, from gloriously magenta octopi to gnarled turban shells. All are laid out for buyers in Styrofoam crates – it's a photographer's paradise. This part of the market opens to the public from 9am, and you'll want to get here as close to then as possible; by 11am most stalls are cleaning up.

Outer Market

The outer market, open roughly 5am to 2pm on market days, is where rows of vendors hawk related goods such as dried fish and seaweed, rubber boots and crockery. It's far more pedestrian friendly. It is also where you'll find the market's Shintō shrine, **Namiyoke-jinja** (波除神社), whose deity protects seafarers.

Forklifts & Handcarts

Tsukiji is a working market, and you need to exercise caution to avoid getting in the way. Forklifts and handcarts perform a perfect high-speed choreography not accounting for the odd tourist. Don't come in large groups, with small children or in nice shoes, and definitely don't touch anything you don't plan to buy.

☑ Top Tips

▶ In addition to regular market holidays, the tuna auction may close to visitors during busy periods (such as December and January). Check out the calendar for details (www.tsukiji-market.or.jp/tukiji_e.htm).

▶ The line to register for the tuna auction starts forming before 5am; to make sure you get in get here by 4.30am (or 4am on Saturdays). Public transportation doesn't start up early enough, so you'll have to take a taxi or hang out nearby all night.

▶ Get a map at the **Tourist Information Center** (TIC; Map p38, D3; 5-2 Tsukiji, Chūō-ku; ⊗8am-2pm) inside the Outer Market.

✕ Take a Break

Get a caffeine kick at **Yonemoto Coffee** (米本珈琲; Map p38, D3; 4-11-1 Tsukiji, Chūō-ku; coffee ¥250; ⊗6am-4pm Mon-Sat; ⊠Hibiya Line to Tsukiji, exit 1).

Go for sushi breakfast at **Daiwa Sushi** (p42).

Top Sights
Kabuki-za

Dramatic, intensely visual kabuki is Japan's most recognised art form. It developed during the reign of the shōgun and was shaped by the decadent tastes of Edo's increasingly wealthy merchant class – resulting in the breathtaking costumes and elaborate stagecraft that characterise the form. Kabuki-za is Tokyo's kabuki theatre. Established in 1889, the theatre reopened after a lengthy reconstruction in 2013. The new building, designed by architect Kuma Kengō, is a blend of traditional elegance and modern sensibilities, with scarlet and gold throughout.

歌舞伎座

⊙ Map p38, C2

☎ 3545-6800

www.kabuki-bito.jp/eng

4-12-15 Ginza, Chūō-ku

tickets ¥4000–20,000, single-act tickets ¥800–2000

🚊 Hibiya Line to Higashi-Ginza, exit 3

Kabuki-za

Don't Miss

The Actors

Kabuki actors train from childhood and descendants of the great Edo-era actors still grace the stage, as sons follow their fathers into the *yago* (kabuki acting house). These stars enjoy a celebrity on par with screen actors; some have earned the status of 'living treasure'. Only men appear in kabuki, and actors who specialise in portraying women are called *onnagata*.

The Fans

At pivotal moments enthusiastic fans shout out the name of the *yago* of the actor – an act called *kakegoe*.

The Plays

During several centuries, kabuki has developed a repertoire of popular themes, such as famous historical accounts, the conflict between love and loyalty and stories of love-suicide. A full kabuki performance comprises of several acts, usually from different plays, so you should get a sampling of various themes and styles.

The Visual Impact

There is no pretense of reality in kabuki; it's ruled by aesthetics and plays to the senses rather than the intellect. Kabuki has been likened to a moving wood-block print, and when the actors pause in dramatic poses – called *mie* – the whole stage really does look fit to be framed.

The Stage Design

The kabuki stage employs a number of unique devices, such as the *hanamichi* (the walkway that extends into the audience), which is used for dramatic entrances and exits. Naturally the best seats are those that line the *hanamichi*.

☑ Top Tips

▶ If you purchased a ticket online, look for the ticket dispensers in front of the theatre and in the basement passage from the subway station. Just insert the credit card you used to purchase the ticket.

▶ Arrive 30 minutes before the start of the show to allow time to pick up an earphone guide and a *bentō*. The earphone recording begins 10 minutes before each act, with background information about the play.

✕ Take a Break

During intermission (usually 30 minutes), it's tradition to eat a *bentō* at the theatre. Order one in advance to eat at the restaurant **Hanakago** (はなかご; ☎ 3545-6820; bentō ¥2100-3500) on the 3rd floor or purchase one (around ¥1000) to eat at your seat from any of the concession stands inside the theatre or in the basement passage.

For reviews see	
◉ Top Sights	p34
◎ Sights	p39
✖ Eating	p40
✚ Drinking	p43
◉ Entertainment	p44
🛍 Shopping	p44

400 m
0.2 miles

Ⓜ Hatchōbori

HATCHŌBORI

Shin-Ōhashi-dōri

SHINTOMI

TSUKIJI

Shintomi-chō

CHŪŌ-KU

KACHIDOKI

Tokyo Cruise Route

Ⓜ Tsukiji

Kachidoki-bashi

Kachidoki-mon

Sumida-gawa (Sumida River)

Ⓜ Hatchōbori

Ginza-itchōme

Shōwa-dōri

Kabuki-za

Ⓜ Ginza Ⓜ 24

Ginza Maronnier-dōri

Koyanagi

Gallery ◎ 5

Matsuya-dōri

Chūō-dōri

Higashi-Ginza

Tsukiji Outer Market

Ⓜ Tsukijishijō

Tourist Information Center

Ⓜ Tsukiji

Fish Information Center

i Information Center

◉ Tsukiji Fish Market

✖ 10 13

✖ 6

Shuto Expwy No1

Tokyo Cruise

Tsukiji-gawa

25

GINZA

Namiki-dōri

Namiki-dōri

Ⓜ Hibiya Yūrakuchō Ⓡ

Harumi-dōri

Sony Building ◎ 3

Miyuki-dōri

Sukibayashi-dōri

12 16 2 27

Ginza 26 23 6

Chūō-dōri

11 20

Tokyo Gallery ◎ 14

Shiseido 7 Gallery 18

4

Minato-dōri

Ⓜ Shimbashi

Ⓜ Shimbashi

Ⓜ Shimbashi

Ⓜ Shiodome

Shiodome

Hama-rikyū Onshi-teien

✖ 17

◎ 1

Kaigan-dōri

To Haneda

HIBIYA

Hibiya-dōri

Hibiya-kōen

◎ 8

21

UCHISAIWAI-CHŌ

Uchisaiwaichō

Sotobori-dōri

SHIMBASHI

Sights

Hama-rikyū Onshi-teien GARDEN

 Map p38, B4

Once the horse stables and hunting ground of the Tokugawa clan, the family of shōgun who ruled from Tokyo, this gorgeous garden features manicured hills set below the imposing business district towers next door. A complimentary audio guide uses satellite technology to detect your location within the garden and automatically narrates interesting facts and stories. (浜離宮恩賜庭園; Detached Palace Garden; www.tokyo-park.or.jp/park/format/index028.html; 1-1 Hama-rikyū-teien, Chūo-ku; adult/child ¥300/free; ◷9am-5pm; ℝÕedo Line to Shiodome, exit A1)

Take a Break Wrap your hands around a bowl of *matcha* (powdered green tea) at **Nakajima no Ochaya** (p43).

Chūō-dōri STREET

2 Map p38, C2

Chūō-dōri (Centre Avenue) runs through the heart of Ginza and is lined with grand department stores and glittering luxury boutiques – offering the city's best window-shopping. On weekend afternoons a stretch of it is closed to car traffic, creating what the Japanese call *hokōsha-tengoku* or 'pedestrian paradise'. (中央通り; ℝGinza Line to Ginza, exit A3)

Take a Break The terrace at **Le Cafe Doutor Ginza** (ル・カフェドトール銀座4丁目本店; Map p38, B1; 1st & 2nd fl, San'ai Bldg 5-7-2 Ginza, Chūo-ku; ◷8am-11pm; ℝGinza Line to Ginza, exit A1) is perfect for people-watching.

Sony Building SHOWROOM

3 Map p38, B1

Come here to play around with yet-to-be-released Sony gadgets and gizmos,

---

Understand
Trendsetting Ginza

In the 1870s, Ginza was the first neighbourhood in Tokyo to modernise; welcoming Western-style brick buildings, the city's first department stores, gas lamps and other harbingers of globalisation – and it's been a fashion centre ever since. In the 1920s, *moga* (modern girls) cut their hair short, wore trousers and walked arm-in-arm with *mobo* (modern boys) through Ginza.

Today, other shopping districts rival Ginza in opulence, vitality and popularity, but it retains a distinct snob value: all the major international fashion houses have lavish boutiques here. Ginza also remains the launching pad for foreign brands making their debut in Japan: McDonalds (1971), Starbucks (1996) and H&M (2008) all opened their first shops in the neighbourhood.

including the latest cameras. There's a duty free shop on the 4th floor that sells international models of popular products, too. (ソニービル; 📞3573-2371; www.sonybuilding.jp; 5-3-1 Ginza, Chūō-ku; admission free; ⏰11am-7pm; 🚇Ginza, Hibiya, Marunouchi line to Ginza, exit B9)

Tokyo Gallery
ART GALLERY

4 🎯 Map p38, B2

Tokyo Gallery collaborates with the Beijing–Tokyo Art Project, and shows challenging, often politically pointed works by Japanese and Chinese artists. (東京画廊; 📞3571-1808; www.tokyo-gallery.com; 7th fl, 8-10-5 Ginza, Chūō-ku; admission free; ⏰11am-7pm Tue-Fri, to 5pm Sat; 🚇JR Yamanote Line to Shimbashi, Ginza exit)

Gallery Koyanagi
ART GALLERY

5 🎯 Map p38, C1

Exhibits include works from serious heavy hitters from Japan and abroad, such as Sugimoto Hiroshi, Marlene Dumas and Olafur Eliasson. Enter from the alley behind Bank of Tokyo-Mitsubishi. (ギャラリー小柳; 📞3561-1896; www.gallerykoyanagi.com; 8th fl, 1-7-5 Ginza, Chūō-ku; ⏰11am-7pm Tue-Sat; 🚇Ginza Line to Ginza, exit A9)

Ginza Graphic Gallery
ART GALLERY

6 🎯 Map p38, B2

This graphic design showcase celebrates the best in print, from retrospectives of influential designers to suggestions of what's to come. (ギンザ・グラフィック・ギャラリ

ー; 📞3571-5206; www.dnp.co.jp/gallery/ggg; 7-7-2 Ginza, Chūō-ku; admission free; ⏰11am-7pm Tue-Fri, to 6pm Sat; 🚇Ginza Line to Ginza, exit A2)

Shiseido Gallery
ART GALLERY

7 🎯 Map p38, B2

An ever-changing selection of up-and-coming artists from around the globe fill this high-ceiling space. (資生堂ギャラリー; 📞3572-3901; www.shiseido.co.jp/e/gallery/html; Basement fl, 8-8-3 Ginza, Chūō-ku; admission free; ⏰11am-7pm Tue-Sat, to 6pm Sun; 🚇JR Yamanote Line to Shimbashi, Ginza exit)

Hibiya-kōen
PARK

8 🎯 Map p38, A1

Leafy Hibiya Park has pleasant strolling paths and something in bloom nearly year-round. The dogwood trees were originally a gift from the United States in 1915, in exchange for the cherry trees presented by Japan to Washington DC in 1912. (日比谷公園; Hibiya-kōen, Chiyoda-ku; admission free; 🚇Hibiya Line to Hibiya, exits A10 & A14)

Eating

Narutomi
SOBA $

9 🍴 Map p38, C3

At stylish Narutomi all the *soba* (buckwheat noodles) are hand cut, and you can watch the chefs at work in the open kitchen. Try the *gobō ten seiro* (ごぼう天せいろ; cold soba noodles served in a bamboo basket

TRAVELASIA / GETTY IMAGES ©

Traditional restaurant, Tsukiji Central Fish Market (p34)

with burdock tempura; ¥1155). There's a vertical white sign out front and plain white curtains over the door. (成富; ☎5565-0055; http://narutomi-soba.net/; 8-18-6 Ginza, Chūō-ku; noodles ¥840-1890; ⏰11.30am-3pm Mon-Sat & 5pm-9pm Mon-Fri; 🚃Hibiya Line to Higashi-Ginza, exit 6)

Tenfusa

TEMPURA $

10 🍴 Map p38, C4

Raw isn't the only way to eat seafood at Tsukiji: Tenfusa, delightfully off the tourist radar, does tempura dishes that are popular with market workers. The *ō-ebi anago tendon* (大エビ穴子天井; ¥1300) comes with a huge prawn and an even larger slice of *anago* (salt-water eel). (天房; Bldg 6, 5-2-1 Tsukiji,

Chūō-ku; meals from ¥1100; ⏰6.30am-2pm; 🚃Ōedo Line to Tsukijishijō, exit A2)

Ginza Bairin

TONKATSU $

11 🍴 Map p38, B2

Cheap and cheerful *tonkatsu* (とんかつ; deep-fried pork cutlet) is the name of the game at this salaryman favourite in the heart of Ginza, in business since 1927. Look for the plastic food models in the window. (銀座梅林; www.ginzabairin.com; 7-8-1 Ginza, Chūō-ku; meals from ¥980; ⏰11.30am-8.45pm; 🚃Ginza Line to Ginza, exit A2; ♿🍴)

Manneken

BAKERY $

12 🍴 Map p38, C2

Participate in Tokyoites' favourite pastime – waiting in line – at this bustling

Top Tip

Tsukiji Market Sushi

Tsukiji's Outer Market has dozens of eateries. If you don't have the patience to wait for a seat at **Daiwa Sushi** there are plenty of other good places to try. Any place drawing a crowd is a safe bet, or look to where the workers, in their rubber boots, are heading. The World Wildlife Fund lists bluefin tuna as an endangered fish, and reports of over-fishing continue, so if you'd prefer to refrain, tell the sushi chef: *Maguro nuki de onegaishimasu* (hold the tuna, please).

Belgian waffle stand. They taste as good as they smell, and come in unusual seasonal flavours such as *murasaki imo* (紫芋; purple sweet potato). (マネケン; www.manneken.co.jp; 5-7-19 Ginza, Chūō-ku; waffles from ¥150; ⏰11am-10pm; 🚇Ginza Line to Ginza, exit B3;)

Daiwa Sushi

SUSHI $$

13 Map p38, C4

This is one of Tsukiji's most famous sushi counters and waits of more than an hour are commonplace. Trust us, it's worth it. The standard set is a solid bet and includes *chū-toro* (中トロ; medium-grade tuna) and *uni* (ウニ; sea urchin roe); there's a picture menu, too. Though the staff may be too polite to say so, you're expected to eat and run. (大和寿司; 🕿3547-6807; Bldg 6, 5-2-1 Tsukiji, Chūō-ku; sushi set ¥3500;

⏰5am-1.30pm Mon-Sat, closed occasional Wed; 🚇Ōedo Line to Tsukijishijō, exit A2;)

Sushi Kanesaka

SUSHI $$$

14 Map p38, B2

Tucked away below street level (marked by a small, square lantern), this sushi superstar is the workshop of the eponymous master chef who slices through premium pieces of fresh fish with a surgeon's precision. If you're contemplating a sushi splurge during your time in Tokyo, this is the place to do it. But book ahead – there are only twenty seats. (鮨かねさか; 🕿5568-4411; www.sushi-kanesaka.com; basement fl, 8-10-3 Ginza, Chūō-ku; lunch/dinner course from ¥5000/20,000; ⏰11.30am-1pm & 5-10pm Mon-Fri, to 9pm Sat & Sun; 🚇JR Yamanote Line to Shimbashi, Ginza exit;)

Bird Land

YAKITORI $$$

15 Map p38, C1

This suave basement bar turns out gourmet grilled chicken from free-range heirloom birds. Chefs in whites behind a U-shaped counter dispense *yakitori* in all shapes, sizes, colours and organs, supplemented with chunks of pâté and other refined nibbles. The set menu offers a good variety, and everything goes with the excellent wine list. Enter beneath Suit Company. (バードランド; 🕿5250-1081; http://ginza-birdland.sakura.ne.jp/; 4-2-15 Ginza, Chūō-ku; dishes ¥150-1200, set meals ¥6000-8000; ⏰5pm-9.30pm Tue-Sat; 🚇Ginza Line to Ginza, exit C6; 📷)

Drinking

Cha Ginza
TEAHOUSE

16 Map p38, B2

For a modern take on the ancient tea ceremony, head to the rooftop of this sleek urban teahouse, where perfect bowls of *matcha* are prepared before your eyes. *Sencha* (green leaf tea) is served inside on the 2nd floor. Order a tea set (cup of tea and Japanese sweet) from the shop on the ground floor; there's usually someone here who speaks English. (茶・銀座; http://www.uogashi-meicha.co.jp/shop/ginza/; 5-5-6 Ginza, Chūō-ku; tea set ¥500; ⏰11am-7pm Tue-Sun; 🚇Ginza Line to Ginza, exit B3)

Nakajima no Ochaya
TEAHOUSE

17 Map p38, C4

This beautiful teahouse from 1704 stands elegantly along a cedar bridge in the middle of Hama-rikyū Onshi-teien. It's the ideal spot to contemplate the very faraway 21st century beyond the garden walls over a cup of *matcha*. (中島の御茶屋; http://www.tokyo-park.or.jp/park/format/restaurant028.html; 1-1 Hama-rikyū Onshi-teien, Chūō-ku; tea set ¥500; ⏰9am-4.30pm; 🚇Ōedo Line to Shiodome, exit A1; 🏠)

Cafe de l'Ambre
CAFE

18 Map p38, B3

The sign over the door here reads 'coffee only' but, oh, what a selection!

In business since 1948, l'Ambre specialises in aged beans from all over the world, which the owner still roasts himself by the front window. (カフェ・ド・ランブル; ☎3571-1551; www.h6.dion.ne.jp/~lambre; 8-10-15 Ginza, Chūō-ku; coffee from ¥650; ⏰noon-10pm Mon-Sat, to 7pm Sun; 🚇Ginza Line to Ginza, exit A4; 🏠)

Aux Amis des Vins
WINE BAR

19 Map p38, C1

Even when it rains, the plastic tarp comes down and good wine is drunk alleyside. The enclosed upstairs seating area is warm and informal, and you can order snacks or full *prix-fixe* dinners to go with your wine. A solid selection of wine comes by the glass (¥800) or by the bottle. (オザミデヴァン; ☎3567-4120; 2-5-6 Ginza, Chūō-ku; ⏰5.30pm-2am Mon-Fri, noon-midnight Sat; 🚇Yūrakuchō Line to Ginza-itchōme, exits 5 & 8)

Ginza Lion
BEER HALL

20 Map p38, B2

An institution, the Lion was one of Japan's first beer halls when Yebisu beer rose to popularity during the early Meiji period. This fantastically kitsch incarnation dates to 1934. Come for the atmosphere – skip the food. (銀座ライオン; www.ginzalion.jp; 7-9-20 Ginza, Chūō-ku; ⏰11.30am-11pm; 🚇Ginza Line to Ginza, exit A4; 🏠)

Entertainment

Takarazuka Gekijō
TRADITIONAL THEATRE

21 Map p38, B1

The all-female Takarazuka Gekijō revue, goes back to 1914, but is still wildly popular with a mostly female audience who come to swoon over actresses in drag. If you love camp, this is for you. The musicals are in Japanese, but English synopses are available. (宝塚劇場; ☎5251-2001; http://kageki.hankyu.co.jp/english/index.html; 1-1-3 Yūrakuchō, Chiyoda-ku; tickets ¥3500-11,000; 🚇Hibiya Line to Hibiya, exits A5 & A13)

Shopping

Mitsukoshi
DEPARTMENT STORE

22 Map p38, C1

One of Ginza's grande dames, Mitsukoshi is the quintessential Tokyo department store, and it gleams after a recent renovation. The homewares department on the 8th floor has beautiful made-in-Japan crockery and chopsticks and the *depachika* (basement food hall) is peerless. The tax refund counter is on the 2nd floor mezzanine. (三越; www.mitsukoshi.co.jp; 4-6-16 Ginza, Chūō-ku; ⏰10am-8pm; 🚇Ginza Line to Ginza, exits A7 & A11)

Dover Street Market Ginza
FASHION

A department store as envisioned by Kawakubo Rei (of Comme des Garçons), DSM (see 23 Map p38, B2) has seven floors of avant-garde brands, including several Japanese labels and everything in the Comme des Garçons line-up. The quirky installations alone make it worth the visit. (DSM; ☎6228-5080; http://ginza.doverstreetmarket.com; 6-9-5 Ginza, Chūō-ku; ⏰11am-8pm Sun-Thu, to 9pm Fri & Sat; 🚇Ginza Line to Ginza, exit A2)

Uniqlo
CLOTHING

23 Map p38, B2

Uniqlo made its name with inexpensive, well-made basics that are tweaked with style – designers such as Jil Sander and Jun Takahashi have participated in recent capsule collections. This enormous, 12-storey outpost offers everything in the Uniqlo cannon, from socks to coats. Check out the T-shirts on the 11th floor and the limited edition items on the 12th floor. (ユニクロ; www.uniqlo.com; 5-7-7 Ginza, Chūō-ku; ⏰11am-9pm; 🚇Ginza Line to Ginza, exit A2)

🔍 Local Life
Namiki-dōri

Narrow **Namiki-dōri** (Map p38, C1) is Tokyo's most exclusive nightlife strip, where velvet drapes blot out the windows and elegant women dressed in kimono wait on company execs and politicians in members-only bars and clubs. Stroll through in the evening and you might catch a glimpse of this secretive world.

Itōya

ARTS & CRAFTS

24 🔒 Map p38, C1

Floor after floor of stationery-shop love await visitors to this century-old purveyor of fountain pens and paper-bound luxuries. Itoya also stocks traditional *washi* (fine Japanese handmade paper) and *furoshiki* (wrapping cloths). (伊東屋; 2-7-15 Ginza, Chūo-ku; ☺10.30am-8pm Mon-Sat, to 7pm Sun; 🚇Ginza Line to Ginza, exit A13)

Ginza Hands

MISCELLANEOUS

25 🔒 Map p38, C1

Ginza Hands deals in *zakka* – miscellaneous goods to improve your life – including all sorts of home and beauty products, stationery and gadgets. Head to the 9th floor for a collection of the latest must-haves, be they mobile phone accessories or character goods. (銀座ハンズ; ☎3538-0109; http://ginza.tokyu-hands.co.jp/; 5th-9th fl, Marronnier Gate, 2-2-14 Ginza, Chūo-ku; ☺11am-9pm; 🚇JR Yamanote to Yūrakuchō, Kyōbashi exit)

Natsuno

HOMEWARES

26 🔒 Map p38, B2

Shelf after shelf of *hashi* (chopsticks) in wood, lacquer, even gold leaf, line the walls of this tiny shop on a Ginza side street, alongside plenty of *hashi-oki* (chopstick rests) to match. Prices run from a few hundred yen to ¥10,000. Sister shop Konatsu on the 6th floor sells adorable tableware for

Chūo-dōri (p39)

kids. (夏野; 6-7-4 Ginza, Chūo-ku; ☺10am-8pm Mon-Sat, to 7pm Sun; 🚇Ginza Line to Ginza, exit B3)

Mikimoto

JEWELLERY

27 🔒 Map p38, C2

Mikimoto was founded in 1893 by the self-made Mikimoto Kōkichi. At an early age he became fascinated with pearl divers and later developed the cultured pearl, building Mikimoto into the most famous of Tokyo's pearl shops. (ミキモト; ☎3535-4611; www.mikimoto.com/jp; 4-5-5 Ginza, Chūo-ku; ☺11am-7pm; 🚇Ginza Line to Ginza, exit A9)

◉ Top Sights
Sumō at Ryōgoku Kokugikan

Getting There

🚇 Take the JR Sōbu Line to Ryōgoku and use the west exit; the stadium is a two-minute walk away.

🚇 The Toei Ōedo Line also stops at Ryōgoku.

Travellers who visit Tokyo in January, May or September should not miss the opportunity to attend a Grand Tournament at Ryōgoku Kokugikan – 15-day tournaments at the national sumō stadium. Nevermind if you're a sports fan or not, ancient sumō is just as captivating for its spectacle and ritual. Ringside tickets cost ¥14,300, but reserved arena seats start from ¥2100. Same-day unreserved seats can be bought from the stadium box office for only ¥1500. During the rest of the year, you can catch the big boys in action at one of the neighbourhood stables.

Sumō wrestlers, Ryōgoku Kokugikan

Don't Miss

The Ritual

Sumō was originally part of a ritual prayer to the gods for a good harvest. While it has obviously evolved, it remains deeply connected to Japan's Shintō tradition. You'll see a roof suspended over the *dōyo* (ring) that resembles that of a shrine. Before bouts, *rikishi* (wrestlers) rinse their mouths with water and toss salt into the ring – both are purification rituals.

Makuuchi Entering the Ring

Things really pick up at 3.45pm when the *makuuchi* (top-tier) wrestlers perform their ceremonial entrance, wearing colourful, embroidered aprons. This is followed by the grand entrance of the *yokozuna* – the top of the top – complete with sword-bearing attendants.

The Yokozuna

In order to achieve this highest rank a wrestler must win two consecutive tournaments and be considered, in the eyes of the Sumō Association, to embody certain traditional values. The *yokozuna* wrestle in the final, most exciting, bouts of the day. You'll also see portraits of past champions hanging around the stadium and at the Sumō Museum attached to the stadium.

Nearby: Arashio-beya

If you're not visiting during a tournament, you can watch an early morning practice at **Arashio Stable** (荒汐部屋; Arashio-beya; ☎3666-7646; www. arashio.net; 2-47-2 Hama-chō, Nihombashi, Chūō-ku; admission free; ◷7.30am-10am; ⎗Toei Shinjuku Line to Hamachō, exit A2), one of many stables where wrestlers sleep, eat and train. See the website for information about visiting and etiquette.

両国国技館; Ryōgoku Sumō Stadium

☎3623-5111

www.sumo.or.jp/eng/ ticket/index.html

1-3-28 Yokoami, Sumida-ku

◷tournaments Jan, May & Sep

☑ Top Tips

▶ On the last days of the tournament, you'll need to get in line by 6am to score a same-day ticket.

▶ Rent a radio (¥100, ¥2000 deposit) to hear the action in English.

✖ Take a Break

Wrestlers eat *chanko-nabe*, a protein-rich stew. You can try it at **Chanko Kaijō** (ちゃんこ会場; chanko-nabe ¥250; ◷noon-4pm), in the stadium's basement, or at **Hana no mai** (花の舞; 1-3-20 Yokoami, Sumida-ku; chanko-nabe ¥980-2980; ◷11.30am-2pm & 4pm-midnight; ⎗JR Sōbu Line to Ryōgoku, west exit), next to JR Ryōgoku Station.

Explore

Roppongi & Akasaka

Roppongi is Tokyo's most exciting neighbourhood. Once notorious for low-brow nightlife, Roppongi is now wallowing in sophistication, with the shops, restaurants and museums to prove it. Must-sees include the future-forward microcity, Roppongi Hills, and its contemporary art museum, Mori Art Museum. But Roppongi hasn't given up its nightlife crown – it remains one of the best places to party in Asia.

The Sights in a Day

☀ Start the day in Shiba-kōen, taking the subway to Akebane-bashi. Situated on the edge of this leafy park is **Zōjō-ji** (p56), one of Tokyo's most important temples. This is also where you'll spot red-and-white **Tokyo Tower** (p55), which offers views over the city. Then settle in for a long, leisurely lunch of Japanese haute cuisine at **Tofuya-Ukai** (p59).

☀ Take a cab to **Tokyo Midtown** (p55) in Roppongi. Wander through the halls and garden, taking in an exhibition at **21_21 Design Sight** (p54) or the **Suntory Museum of Art** (p54). Then walk over to **Roppongi Hills** (p50) – the neighbourhood's other city within the city. Budget at least an hour or two for the **Mori Art Museum** (p51), timing your visit for sundown cocktails at **Mado Lounge** (p60).

☽ Have dinner at one of Roppongi's lively *izakaya* (Japanese-style pub), such as **Jōmon** (p58) or **Gonpachi** (p58). Then pick your pleasure from the neighbourhood's overwhelming nightlife options: Will you bar hop? Dance till dawn? Catch a show or sing your heart out at karaoke? Don't worry, it's possible to pick more than one.

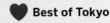

👁 Top Sights

Roppongi Hills (p50)

💜 Best of Tokyo

Temples & Shrines
Zōjō-ji (p56)

Galleries & Museums
Mori Art Museum (p51)

National Art Center Tokyo (p54)

Food
Tofuya-Ukai (p59)

Jōmon (p58)

Shopping
Souvenir from Tokyo (p63)

Nightlife & Live Music
SuperDeluxe (p59)

Pink Cow (p60)

Mado Lounge (p60)

Festa Iikura (p60)

Getting There

S Subway The Hibiya and Ōedo Lines both stop at Roppongi. The Hibiya Line is most convenient for Roppongi Hills; the Ōedo Line for Tokyo Midtown. The Hibiya Line continues to Kamiyachō; the Ōedo Line goes to Akebane-bashi. The Chiyoda Line services Nogizaka and Akasaka.

Top Sights
Roppongi Hills

A mall like you've never seen before, Roppongi Hills, completed in 2003, sprawls across more than 11 hectares and is home to the city's most exciting contemporary art museum, Mori Art Museum, a sky-high observatory, shops galore, dozens of restaurants and even a formal garden. It's imposing, upmarket and polarising – an architectural marvel, a grand vision realised or a crass shrine to conspicuous consumption? Explore the towers and corridors of this urban maze and decide for yourself, but you can't understand contemporary Tokyo without stopping here.

六本木ヒルズ

◉ Map p52, C5

www.roppongihills.com/en

Roppongi 6-chōme, Minato-ku

🕘 11am-11pm

🚇 Hibiya Line to Roppongi, exit 1

Mori Art Museum

Don't Miss

Mori Art Museum

Perched on the 52nd and 53rd floors of Mori Tower, the **Mori Art Museum** (森美術館; www.mori. art.museum; 52nd fl, Mori Tower, Roppongi Hills, 6-10-1 Roppongi, Minato-ku; adult/student/child ¥1500/1000/500; ⏰10am-10pm Wed-Mon, to 5pm Tue; 🚇Hibiya Line to Roppongi, exit 1) is Tokyo's top contemporary art museum. There's no permanent exhibition; instead original shows introduce major local and global artists and movements. Recent exhibitions have included the works of Chinese artist and dissident Ai Weiwei and native son Aida Makoto.

Tokyo City View

Admission to the Mori Art Museum is shared with **Tokyo City View** (東京シティビュー; 📞6406-6652; www.roppongihills.com/tcv/en; ⏰10am-11pm Mon-Thu & Sun, to 1am Fri & Sat), the observatory that wraps itself around the 52nd floor. From this 250m-high vantage point, you can see 360-degree views of the never-ending city. Weather permitting, you can also pop out to the rooftop **Sky Deck** (52nd fl, Mori Tower; additional ¥300; ⏰11am-8pm) for open-air views.

Public Art

The open-air plaza near the street entrance is the lucky home of one of Louise Bourgeois' giant *Maman* spider sculptures. It has an amusing way of messing with the scale of the buildings, especially in photos. There are other sculptural wonders scattered around the complex, too.

Mohri Garden

This traditional landscaped garden, when juxtaposed with the gleaming towers, creates a fascinating study of luxury then and now. Look for the cherry trees in spring.

☑ Top Tips

▶ Unlike most museums, Mori Art Museum is open late – until 10pm everyday except Tuesdays.

▶ Keep an eye out for events, especially in the summer, at Roppongi Hills Arena, an open-air space nestled in the middle of the complex.

▶ In winter months, look for beautiful illuminations along Keiyakizaka-dōri, on the southern edge of the complex.

▶ Keep in mind that Roppongi Hills, including the Mori Art Museum, can get crowded on weekends.

✕ Take a Break

Mado Lounge (p60), on the same floor of Mori Tower as the Mori Art Museum, has fabulous views over the city.

Tired of sophistication? The wonderfully lowbrow **Chinese Cafe 8** (p58), across the street from Roppongi Hills, has the answer for that.

A B C D

1 Jingū Kyūjō
(Jingū Stadium)

Icho-Namiki

Gaien-higashi-dōri

Jingū-gaien

N 0   400 m
0   0.2 miles

Aoyama-dōri
31

Aoyama-itchōme M

Prince Chichibu
Memorial
Rugby Stadium

TV
Broadcasting
Centre

2 M Gaienmae

16

Nogi-
jinja 8

Nogizaka M

MINAMI-
AOYAMA

Aoyama-reien
(Aoyama
Cemetery)

Aoyama-bochi-dōri (Cherry St)

3
3 21_21 Design Sight
Suntory   Midtown
Museum of Art 2   Garden
27   Tokyo Midtown
5
National Art   11
1 Center Tokyo   ROPPONGI

Roppongi M   Roppongi
Crossing
25
23   10
22 M
Roppongi

4 Aoyama-
kōen

Seijōki-dōri

26
Piramide
Building   18
9
14

Gaien-nishi-dōri

13
Shuto Expwy No 3

24   19 $ Roppongi
17   Hills
12   29   TV
Asahi
21   Keyaki-zaka
TV Asahi-dōri   Azabu-jūban-dōri

5 **For reviews see**

◉	Top Sights	p50
◉	Sights	p54
✕	Eating	p56
🍷	Drinking	p59
✪	Entertainment	p61
🔒	Shopping	p63

NISHI-AZABU   MOTO-
AZABU

ABU
JŪBA

E Hitotsugi-dōri Sotobori-dōri Tamachi-dōri

F **NAGATACHŌ**

National Diet Building

G Kokkaimae Garden (Japanese Style)

H Tokyo Metropolitan Police Department

1

Akasaka-dōri

Kokkai-gijidōmae Ⓜ

Ministry of Foreign Affairs

Kasumigaseki Ⓜ

Kasumigaseki

asaka Ⓜ

Roppongi-dōri

Ⓜ Tameike-sannō

KASUMIGASEKI

2

AKASAKA

Ⓜ Toranomon

Sotobori-dōri

Shuto Expwy No 3

TORANOMON

Toranomon Hospital

Ⓜ

Ark Hills

Hotel Ōkura

4 ◉
Musée Tomo

Sakurada-dōri

🔒 **30**

Atago-dōri

3

Roppongi-dōri

Roppongi-itchōme Ⓜ

Shuto Expwy No 2

Ⓜ Kamiyachō

4

aien-higashi-dōri

32 🔒

Azabu Post Office ✉

🚻 **20**

Onarimon Ⓜ

SHIBA KŌEN

AZABUDAI

Sakurada-dōri

6 ◉ Tokyo Tower

5

Azabu-Jūban

HIGASHI-AZABU

15 ✕

7 ◉
Zōjō-ji

Shiba-kōen

Sights

National Art Center Tokyo
MUSEUM

1 ⊙ Map p52, C3

Designed by Kurokawa Kishō, this architectural marvel is the country's largest exhibition space. Opened in 2007 it has no permanent collection, although shows have included international blockbusters and the annual Japan Media Arts Festival. It's also worth visiting for the undulating glass facade, cafes atop giant inverted cones and excellent gift shop. (国立新美術館; ☑5777-8600; www.nact.jp; 7-22-1 Roppongi, Minato-ku; admission varies by exhibition, building admission free; ☺10am-6pm Wed, Thu & Sat-Mon, to 8pm Fri; ☒Chiyoda Line to Nogizaka, exit 6)

Take a Break Go for lunch at **Brasserie Paul Bocuse Le Musée** (p59), in the museum atrium.

Suntory Museum of Art
MUSEUM

2 ⊙ Map p52, D3

From the time of its original opening in 1961, the Suntory Museum of Art has been a champion of lifestyle art. Rotating exhibitions focus on the beauty of useful things: Japanese ceramics, lacquerware, dyeing, weaving and such. Its new Tokyo Midtown digs by architect Kuma Kengō are at turns understated and breathtaking. (サントリー美術館; ☑3479-8600; www.suntory.com/sma; 4th fl, Tokyo Midtown, 9-7-4 Akasaka, Minato-ku; admission varies; ☺10am-6pm Sun-Thu, to 8pm Fri & Sat; ☒Ōedo Line to Roppongi, exit 8)

21_21 Design Sight
MUSEUM

3 ⊙ Map p52, D3

Contemporary and often genre-bending exhibitions on art, architecture and design are held in this graceful bunker designed by Andō Tadao. It's on the grounds of Tokyo Midtown. Check the website for workshops and talk events. (21_21デザインサイト; ☑3475-2121; www.2121designsight.jp; Tokyo Midtown, 9-7-6 Akasaka, Minato-ku; adult/child ¥1000/free; ☺11am-8pm Wed-Mon; ☒Chiyoda Line to Nogizaka, exit 3)

Musée Tomo
MUSEUM

4 ⊙ Map p52, G3

Perhaps Tokyo's most elegant museum, Musée Tomo is named for Kikuchi Tomo, whose collection of contemporary Japanese ceramics wowed in Washington and London before being exhibited in Tokyo. Exhibitions change every few months; the displays are always beautifully laid out, with informative exhibition notes. (智美術館; ☑5733-5131; www.musee-tomo.or.jp; 4-1-35 Toranomon, Minato-ku;

Top Tip

Art Triangle Roppongi

Roppongi has three big art museums: **Mori Art Museum** (p51), **Suntory Museum of Art** and the **National Art Center Tokyo** that are known collectively as Roppongi Art Triangle. Show your ticket stub from any one museum to get discounted admission at the others.

Tokyo Tower

admission varies; ⏰11am-6pm Tue-Sun;
🚇Hibiya Line to Kamiyachō, exit 4B)

Tokyo Midtown LANDMARK

5 📍 Map p52, D3

Tokyo Midtown is an upscale shopping centre and then some: its ultramodern towers have offices, residences and several museums, in addition to sophisticated boutiques, restaurants and bars. It's worth a visit just for the Japanese modern interior: escalators ascend alongside man-made waterfalls of rock and glass and bridges are lined with backlit *washi* (Japanese handmade paper). (東京ミッドタウン; www.tokyo-midtown.com/en; 9-7 Akasaka, Minato-ku; ⏰11am-11pm; 🚇Ōedo Line to Roppongi, exit 8)

Take a Break Treat yourself to a *matcha* parfait at **Kyō Hayashi-ya** (p56).

Tokyo Tower TOWER

6 📍 Map p52, G5

It might look like a garish Eiffel Tower rip-off, but to Tokyoites, Tokyo Tower remains a symbol of the city's post-WWII rebirth. At 333m and finished in 1958, Tokyo Tower is 13m taller than the French tower that inspired its design. Lifts whisk visitors up to the main observation deck at 150m; there's another 'special' deck at 250m. (東京タワー; www.tokyotower.co.jp/english; 4-2-8 Shiba-kōen, Minato-ku; adult/child main observation deck ¥820/460, special observation deck ¥600/400; ⏰observation deck 9am-10pm; 🚇Ōedo Line to Akabanebashi, Akabanebashi exit; 👶)

Zōjō-ji
BUDDHIST TEMPLE

7 🎯 Map p52, G5

One of the most important temples of the Jōdō (Pure Land) sect of Buddhism, this is also the former funerary temple of the Tokugawa regime, and the tombs of six shōgun stand out back. Zōjō-ji is best viewed at dusk when Tokyo Tower lights the grounds from behind. (増上寺; www.zojoji.or.jp/en/index.html; Shiba-kōen, Minato-ku; admission free; ⏰dawn-dusk; 🚇Ōedo Line to Akabanebashi, Akabanebashi exit)

Nogi-jinja
SHINTŌ SHRINE

8 🎯 Map p52, C3

This shrine honours General Nogi, hero of the Russo–Japanese War. Hours after Emperor Meiji's funeral procession, Nogi and his wife committed ritual suicide (Nogi disemboweled himself, his wife slit her throat). Nogi's residence is on the same grounds. (乃木神社; 8-11-27 Akasaka, Minato-ku; ⏰9am-5pm; 🚇Chiyoda Line to Nogizaka, exit 1)

Piramide Building
ART GALLERY

9 🎯 Map p52, D4

Just next to Roppongi Hills, this building – yes, with a Louvre-style pyramid in the courtyard – houses several galleries under one roof, including a branch of influential photography gallery Taka Ishii. Gallery-hoping is a joy here when they hold collective opening nights. (ピラミデビル; 6-6-9 Roppongi , Minato-ku; admission varies; ⏰opening hours vary; 🚇Hibiya Line to Roppongi, exit 1A)

Eating

Tsurutontan
NOODLES $

10 🍴 Map p52, D4

Huge bowls of *udon* (thick wheat noodles) are the speciality at this popular all-night joint. Go for simple (topped with seaweed or pickled plum), exotic (*udon* carbonara) or filling (*tsuruton zanmai*: topped with fried tofu, tempura and beef). Look for the samples out front. (つるとんたん; 3-14-12 Roppongi, Minato-ku; udon ¥680-1800; ⏰11am-8am; 🚇Hibiya Line to Roppongi, exit 5; 🥢📖)

Kyō Hayashi-ya
SWEETS $

11 🍴 Map p52, D3

Decadent parfaits, with layers of *matcha* jelly, *anko* (sweet red bean paste) and fresh cream are served along with pots of earthy tea at this elegant teahouse inside Tokyo Midtown. (京はやしや; www.kyo-hayashiya.com/midtown.html; Basement fl, Galleria, Tokyo Midtown, 9-7-3 Akasaka, Minato-ku; dessert ¥560-1260; ⏰11am-9pm; 🚇Ōedo Line to Roppongi, exit 8; 🥢📖)

Tokyo Curry Lab
CURRY $

Under Tokyo Tower (see **6** 🎯 Map p52, G5), this space station–like restaurant specialises in the curiously addictive Japanese dish *kare-raisu* (curry rice). There are personal TVs at each seat and hilariously illustrated placemats (you'll see). (東京カレーラボ; 2nd fl, Tokyo Tower, 4-2-8 Shiba-kōen, Minato-ku; meals ¥1000-1350; ⏰11am-10pm; 🚇Hibiya Line to Kamiyachō, exit 1; 📖)

Understand

Roppongi Hills & Tokyo Development

A New Mall is Born

When Roppongi Hills opened in 2003, it was more than just another shopping mall. It was an ambitious prototype for what could be the future of Tokyo. It took developer Mori Minoru no fewer than 17 years to acquire the land and to construct this labyrinthine kingdom. He envisioned improving the quality of urban life by centralising home, work and leisure into a utopian microcity. The design team included a cast of international visionaries, such as megamall mastermind Jon Jerde and Pritzker Prize winner Fumihiko Maki.

Up-market boutiques and restaurants occupy the lower floors. One gleaming office building stretching 53 storeys high assumes the centre: at the top, a contemporary art museum. There is a hotel (the Grand Hyatt), a movie theatre, several residential blocks and a formal garden.

Foreign investment banks and leading IT companies quickly signed up for office space, and Roppongi was positioned as the centre of the new economy – an alternative to Marunouchi, a bastion of traditional (read: old-fashioned) business culture. The nouveau riche who lived, worked and played at Roppongi Hills were christened *Hills-zoku* ('Hills tribe') by the media and their lavish lifestyles were splashed across the tabloids.

The Roppongi Hills Effect

Similar projects appeared in succession: Shiodome Shio-site (2004), Tokyo Midtown (2005) and Akasaka Sacas (2008). However, Roppongi Hills and its ilk have proved polarising: conceived during the economic bubble of the late '80s and early '90s and unveiled in harder times, the luxury and exclusivity that such developments project seem out of step with today's lingering economic malaise. It didn't help that Lehman Brothers had an office in Roppongi Hills.

Still, there is no doubt that Roppongi Hills turned the neighbourhood around: once known primarily for its sleazy nightlife, Roppongi now attracts families who come for the cinema, museum and shops. Ten years on, Roppongi Hills remains a popular date spot for young professionals, and made a perfectly ordinary pastime out of knocking back drinks – in a suit and tie or heels – at the mall.

Chinese Cafe 8

CHINESE $

12 Map p52, C5

This all-night eatery is a Roppongi landmark, known for its cheeky decor, Peking Duck served at any hour, and abrupt service (in that order). (中国茶房8; ☑5414-5708; www.chinesecafe8.com; 2nd fl, 3-2-13 Nishi-Azabu, Minato-ku; dishes from ¥780; ◔24hr; ◮; ℝHibiya Line to Roppongi, exit 3; ◮◨)

Gonpachi

IZAKAYA $$

13 Map p52, B5

Gonpachi is a Tokyo institution, serving charcoal-grilled skewers plus tempura, noodles etc. Cavernous by local standards, it looks like an Edo-era night market on the inside and a feudal villa on the outside. (And if it looks vaguely familiar, that's because the restaurant inspired the set for one of the epic fight scenes in the movie Kill Bill). (権八; ☑5771-0170; www.gonpachi.jp/nishiazabu; 1-13-11 Nishi-Azabu, Minato-ku; skewers ¥180-1500, lunch sets weekday/weekend from ¥800/2050; ◔11.30am-3.30pm; ℝHibiya Line to Roppongi, exit 1; ◮◨)

Jōmon

IZAKAYA $$

14 Map p52, D4

Slide the wooden door open to find a cosy kitchen with bar seating and rows of ornate *shōchū* (liquor) jugs lining the wall. Skewers of grilled meat and vegetables are the speciality here, from straight up divine (top grade beef) to ingeniously delicious

TRAVELASIA / GETTY IMAGES © ARCHITECT: KISHO KUROKAWA

National Art Center Tokyo (p54)

(bacon-wrapped quail eggs). The restaurant is almost directly across from the Family Mart; book ahead on weekends. (ジョウモン; ☑3405-2585; www.teyandei.com; 5-9-17 Roppongi, Minato-ku; skewers ¥150-1600; ☺6pm-5am; 🚇Hibiya Line to Roppongi, exit 3; 🔳)

Brasserie Paul Bocuse Le Musée
FRENCH $$

Dine on fine French food atop an inverted cone in the atrium of the National Art Center Tokyo (see**1** ◉ Map p52, C3). House specialities include duck terrine and pan-fried scallops with risotto – all suprisingly reasonable given the location and the name on the marquee. (ブラッスリー ポール・ボキューズ ミュゼ; ☑5770-8161; www.paulbocuse.jp/eng/musee/index.html; 3rd fl, National Art Center Tokyo, 7-22-2 Roppongi, Minato-ku; lunch/dinner set menu from ¥2000/3500; ☺11am-9pm Sat-Mon, Wed, Thu, to 10pm Fri; 🚇Chiyoda Line to Nogizaka, exit 6; 🔳)

Tofuya-Ukai
KAISEKI $$$

15 🍴 Map p52, G5

One of the city's most impressive restaurants, Tofuya-Ukai has only private rooms, all of which overlook a beautiful, manicured garden. The *kaiseki* (Japanese haute cuisine) courses feature delicate, handmade tofu served a variety of ways, but may also include sashimi and grilled fish; considering the spread, it's excellent value. Enquire when booking about vegetarian courses; reserve well in advance. (とうふ屋うかい; ☑3436-1028; www.ukai.co.jp; 4-4-13

Shiba-kōen, Minato-ku; lunch/dinner set menu from ¥5500/8400; ☺11am-10pm; 🚇Toei Ōedo Line to Akabanebashi, exit 8; 🔳🔳)

Kikunoi
KAISEKI $$$

16 🍴 Map p52, D2

This Kyoto-based, nationally famous *kaiseki* restaurant serves exquisitely prepared seasonal dishes that are as beautiful as they are delicious (which earned Kikunoi two Michelin stars). Kikunoi's Chef Murata has also written a book in English on *kaiseki*, and the staff helpfully use it to explain the dishes. Reservations necessary. (菊乃井; ☑3568-6055; http://kikunoi.jp; 6-13-8 Akasaka, Minato-ku; lunch/dinner course from ¥5250/15,750; ☺lunch seating noon-1pm, dinner seating 5pm-8pm; 🚇Chiyoda Line to Akasaka, exit 6)

Drinking

SuperDeluxe
LOUNGE

17 🍷 Map p52, C4

This groovy basement performance space, also a cocktail lounge and club of sorts, stages everything from hula-hoop gatherings to literary evenings. Whatever is happening, you're guaranteed to run into an interesting mix of creative types from Tokyo and beyond. Check the website for event details. It's in an unmarked brown-brick building by a shoe-repair shop. (スーパー・デラックス; ☑5412-0515; www.super-deluxe.com; Basement fl, 3-1-25 Nishi-Azabu, Minato-ku; admission varies; 🚇Hibiya Line to Roppongi, exit 1B; 🔳)

Pink Cow

BAR

18 Map p52, D4

The Pink Cow is a funky, friendly place to hang out, with excellent California-style food and reasonably-priced wines by the glass. It's a hub for the artsy expat community – with events such as indie film screenings, writers' salons and burlesque nights – and a good bet if you're in the mood to mix with a creative crowd. (ピンクカウ; www.thepinkcow.com; Basement fl, Roi Bldg, 5-5-1 Roppongi, Minato-ku; ⊙5pm-late Tue-Sun; ☒Hibiya Line to Roppongi, exit 3; 📷)

Mado Lounge

LOUNGE

19 Map p52, C4

The views are stunning from the floor to ceiling windows of this swank, dimly-lit lounge bar on the 52nd floor of Mori Tower. You have to pay admission to the Mori Art Museum and/or Tokyo City View to take the elevator this high, so it makes sense to visit after hitting the museum. (マドラウンジ; ☎3470-0052; www.ma-do.jp; 52nd fl, Mori Tower, Roppongi Hills, 6-10-1 Roppongi, Minato-ku; ⊙11am-5pm & 6pm-1am, to 11pm Sun; ☒Hibiya Line to Roppongi, exit 1C)

Festa Iikura

KARAOKE

20 Map p52, F5

Kill two *tori* with one stone and savour some sushi while singing your heart out. In addition to having the best food of any karaoke joint in town, Festa Iikura has excellent service and complimentary costume rentals. It's the perfect place to bust out into *My Sharona* that we know you've been practising... (フェスタ飯倉; ☎5570-1500; www.festa-iikura.com; 3-5-7 Azabudai, Minato-ku; 3hr room & meal plan from ¥3000; ⊙5pm-5am Mon-Sat; ☒Hibiya Line to Kamiyachō, exit 2)

Muse

CLUB

21 Map p52, B5

This catacomb-like underground space, which looks like something out of a Tim Burton film, has two dance floors playing house and hip-hop, plenty of sofas and a billiard table. Muse draws a mix of locals and foreigners and really picks up after midnight. The cover charge is usually less on weekday nights; ID required. (ミューズ; ☎5467-1188; www.muse-web.

Local Life

Nishi-Azabu

A world away from the brashness of Roppongi, Nishi-Azabu is a so-phisticated playground for Tokyo's rich and famous. Many bars have a strict members-only policy, but fortunately not **These** (テーゼ; Map 52, B4; ☎5466-7331; www.these-jp.com; 2-15-12 Nishi-Azabu, Minato-ku; cover charge ¥500, drinks ¥1000; ⊙7pm-4am, to 2am Sun; ☒Hibiya Line to Roppongi, exit 3). Nicknamed the 'library bar' (and pronounced *tay*-zay), These is full of nooks and crannies, cosy sofas, and, yes, shelves of books. Look for the torches out front; reservations recommended.

com; B1 fl, 4-1-1 Nishi-Azabu, Minato-ku; admission women/men incl 2 drinks free/¥3000; 🕑9pm-late Mon-Fri, from 10pm Sat & Sun ; 🚇Hibiya Line to Roppongi, exit 3; 📶)

Geronimo
BAR

22 🚇 Map p52, D4

Love it or hate it, this shot bar at Roppongi Crossing is a neighbourhood institution. If someone bangs the drum (and it happens more often than you'd think) he or she buys a round of shots for the whole bar – which means if you get lucky you can drink here all night for very little. (ジェロニモ; 🕿3478-7449; www.geronimoshotbar.com; 2nd fl, 7-14-10 Roppongi, Minato-ku; 🕑6pm-6am Mon-Fri, from 7pm Sat & Sun; 🚇Hibiya Line to Roppongi, exit 4; 📶)

Lovenet
KARAOKE

23 🚇 Map p52, D4

Lovenet looks like what you'd get if a karaoke parlour mated with a love hotel. The most outrageous of its themed rooms is the Aqua Suite, complete with a large Jacuzzi. (ラブネット; 🕿5771-5511; www.lovenet-jp.com; 7-14-4 Roppongi, 3rd fl, Hotel Ibis, Minato-ku; suites per hr ¥2400-25,000; 🕑6pm-5am; 🚇Hibiya Line to Roppongi, exit 4A)

Heartland
BAR

24 🚇 Map p52, C4

Named for the house beer from Kirin, Heartland is a chic, easygoing watering hole at the base of Roppongi Hills'

Top Tip

Play It Safe

Pickpocketing is rare in Tokyo, but if it is going to happen, it will happen in Roppongi. Note that shadier bars have been known to overcharge credit cards; drink spiking has also been reported. Be particularly wary of places that employ street touts.

West Tower. It's very popular with the professional expats who work nearby, and is for many *the place* to begin a night in Roppongi. (ハートランド; 🕿5772-7600; www.heartland.jp; 6-10-1 Roppongi, Minato-ku; 🚇Hibiya Line to Roppongi, exit 3; 📶)

Entertainment

Abbey Road
LIVE MUSIC

25 ⭐ Map p52, D4

Abbey Road is, appropriately, the home of the Parrots, who reproduce a variety of Beatles' hits with uncanny accuracy. They perform several nights a week – check the website for their schedule and set list. Advance bookings are recommended; it's table seating and you can order food here along with drinks. (アビーロード; 🕿3402-0017; www.abbeyroad.ne.jp; Basement fl, 4-11-5 Roppongi, Minato-ku; admission ¥1900-2300; 🕑6-11.30pm Mon-Sat; 🚇Hibiya Line to Roppongi, exit 4A)

GREG ELMS / GETTY IMAGES ©

Roppongi Hills (p50)

Alfie
JAZZ

26 Map p52, D4

One of Tokyo's finest jazz venues, Alfie is an intimate space with soft amber lighting, two tiers of table seating and a loyal following. It's almost exclusively local talent on the stage here, meaning Alfie is a lot more reasonable then some of the bigger jazz venues around town. (アルフィー; ☎3479-2037; http://homepage1.nifty.com/live/alfie; 5th fl, 6-2-35 Roppongi, Minato-ku; admission ¥3000-4000; ☺shows 8pm Mon-Sat, 7pm Sun; 📵Hibiya Line to Roppongi, exit 1)

Billboard Live
LIVE MUSIC

27 Map p52, C3

This glitzy amphitheatre-like space in Tokyo Midtown plays host to major foreign talent – along the lines of Burt Bacharach or Sérgio Mendes, rather than the latest pop star. Japanese jazz, soul and rock groups make appearances here, too. (ビルボードライブ東京; ☎3405-1133; www.billboard-live.com; 9-7-4 Akasaka, 4th fl, Tokyo Midtown, Minato-ku; ☺5.30-9.30pm Mon-Fri, 5-9pm Sat & Sun; 📵Hibiya Line to Roppongi, Tokyo Midtown exit)

Kingyo
CABARET

28 Map p52, D4

By a cemetery off Roppongi's main drag, cheeky Kingyo puts on a glitzy, colourful cabaret of *nyū hāfu* (transsexual) and drag queen performers who revel in social critique. Look for the yellow sign showing a *kingyo* (goldfish) kissing a penis. (金魚; ☎3478-3000; www.kingyo.co.jp; 3-14-17 Roppongi, Minato-ku; admission from ¥3500; ☺shows 7.30pm & 10pm Tue-Sun; 📵Hibiya Line to Roppongi, exit 3)

Toho Cinemas Roppongi Hills
CINEMA

29 Map p52, C5

Toho's nine-screen multiplex has the biggest screen in Japan, as well as luxurious reclining seats and internet booking up to two days in advance for reserved seats. All-night screenings take place on nights before holidays.

(TOHOシネマズ六本木ヒルズ; https://hlo.tohotheater.jp/net/schedule/009/TNPI2000J01.do; 6-10-2 Roppongi, Minato-ku; adult ¥1800-3000, child ¥1000, 1st day of month & women on Wed ¥1000; ⏱10am-midnight Sun-Wed, to 5am Thu-Sat; 🚇Hibiya Line to Roppongi, exit 1C)

Shopping

Souvenir From Tokyo   SOUVENIRS

Tokyo's favourite homegrown designers have contributed a selection of bits and bobbles to this gift shop in the basement of the National Art Center Tokyo (see **1** ◉ Map p52, C3). The original, 'only-in Tokyo' totes, teas and homewares make excellent souvenirs. (スーベニアフロムトーキョー; www.souvenirfromtokyo.jp; Basement fl, National Art Center Tokyo, 7-22-2 Roppongi, Minato-ku; ⏱10am-6pm Sat-Mon, Wed, Thu, to 8pm Fri; 🚇Chiyoda Line to Nogizaka, exit 6)

Japan Sword   ANTIQUES

30 🔒 Map p52, G3

Japan Sword sells the genuine article: antique swords and samurai helmets dating from the Edo period and modern creations from living treasure artisans. The second-floor gallery is one of the rare places where real swords are displayed without glass casing. The staff speak English and can arrange the necessary paperwork for export. Convincing replicas are sold here, too. (日本刀剣; ☎3434-4324; www.japansword.co.jp; 3-8-1 Toranomon,

Top Tip

Tokyo Tower View

From Roppongi Crossing, head east on Gaien-higashi-dōri for a view of Tokyo Tower (p55).

Minato-ku; ⏱9.30am-6pm Mon-Fri, to 5pm Sat; 🚇Ginza Line to Toranomon, exit 2)

Japan Traditional Crafts   CRAFTS

31 🔒 Map p52, C1

Supported by the Japanese Ministry of Economy, Trade and Industry, this shop showcases crafts from around Japan, including lacquerwork boxes and earthy pottery. The emphasis is on high-end goods, but you can find beautiful things in all price ranges here. (全国伝統的工芸品センター; http://kougeihin.jp/en/top; 8-1-22 Akasaka, Minato-ku; ⏱11am-7pm Mon-Sat; 🚇Ginza Line to Aoyama-itchōme, exit 4)

Nuno   TEXTILES

32 🔒 Map p52, E4

The gorgeous, innovative fabrics on display here are interlaced with feathers and *washi*. They've appeared in a number of art exhibitions around the world, including one held at New York's Museum of Modern Art. Nuno is one of a handful of design shops clustered inside the Axis Building. (布; ☎3582-7997; www.nuno.com; Basement fl, Axis Bldg, 5-17-1 Roppongi, Minato-ku; ⏱11am-7pm Mon-Sat; 🚇Hibiya Line to Roppongi, exit 3)

Explore

Ebisu & Meguro

Ebisu – named for the beer Yebisu that was once brewed here – and Meguro represent Tokyo on a more human scale. There's a smattering of small, but significant, museums, such as the Tokyo Metropolitan Museum of Photography, plus excellent restaurants and bars. Nearby, the fashionable residential neighbourhoods Daikanyama and Naka-Meguro are resplendent with stylish boutiques and cafes.

The Sights in a Day

 Start the day in Ebisu and spend the morning at Yebisu Garden Place, taking in an exhibition at the **Tokyo Metropolitan Museum of Photography** (p67) and touring the **Beer Museum Yebisu** (p67). Then join the local office workers in the queue at **Afuri** (p69) for a bowl of *rāmen*.

After lunch, walk up Komazawa-dōri to chic neighbourhood **Daikanyama** (p67), about 15 minutes away, for some shopping. Stop for a coffee (and some people-watching) at **Sign** (p70). Then continue to **Naka-Meguro** (p67), Daikanyama's artsy little sister, and stroll along the canal lined with boutiques and cafes. Alternatively, take the train one station from Ebisu to Meguro and visit the **Institute for Nature Study** (p68), **Tokyo Metropolitan Teien Art Museum** (p68) and the shops along Meguro-dōri that make up the **Meguro Interior Shops Community** (p72).

If you're in Meguro, have dinner at **Tonki** (p69). Otherwise, return to Ebisu in the evening and hit up one of the stalls in **Ebisu-yokochō** (p69), and then hit the bar scene, starting at **Buri** (p70).

 Best of Tokyo

Parks & Gardens
Institute for Nature Study (p68)

Galleries & Museums
Tokyo Metropolitan Museum of Photography (p67)

Beer Museum Yebisu (p67)

Eating
Tonki (p69)

Ebisu-yokochō (p69)

Ouca (p69)

Shopping
Okura (p72)

Meguro Interior Shops Community (p72)

Nightlife & Live Music
Buri (p70)

Unit (p72)

Getting There

Train The JR Yamanote Line stops at Ebisu and Meguro. The Tōkyu-Tōyōko Line runs from Shibuya to Daikanyama and Naka-Meguro.

S Subway The Fukutoshin Line continues on the Tōkyu-Tōyōko Line after Shibuya; the Hibiya Line stops at Ebisu and Naka-Meguro; the Nambaku and Mita Lines stop at Meguro and Shirokanedai.

For reviews see

⊙	Sights	p67
⊗	Eating	p69
⊖	Drinking	p70
✪	Entertainment	p72
🔒	Shopping	p72

Sights

Tokyo Metropolitan Museum of Photography
MUSEUM

1 Map p66, C3

This is the city's top photography museum, with excellent changing exhibitions of both international and Japanese photographers. Ticket prices are based on how many exhibits you see (there are usually three going on at once). Take the Sky Walk from the station to **Yebisu Garden Place**; the five-storey museum is on the right towards the back. (東京都写真美術館; ☎3280-0099; www.syabi.com; 1-13-3 Mita, Meguro-ku; admission ¥500-1650; ◷10am-6pm Tue, Wed, Sat & Sun, to 8pm Thu & Fri; ℝJR Yamanote Line to Ebisu, east exit)

Take a Break Grab a coffee at **Cafe Bis** (カフェ・ビス; coffee ¥350; ◷11am-6pm), on the museum's 1st floor.

Beer Museum Yebisu
MUSEUM

2 Map p66, C3

This is the site of the original Yebisu brewery (1889). Inside you'll find a gallery of photographs and antique signage that documents the rise of Yebisu, and beer in general, in Japan. Skip the tour (¥500; in Japanese only) and head for the tasting salon where you can sample four kinds of beer. (エビスビール記念館; ☎5423-7255; www.sapporoholdings.jp/english/guide/yebisu; 4-20-1 Ebisu, Shibuya-ku; admission free; ◷11am-7pm Tue-Sun; ℝJR Yamanote Line to Ebisu, east exit)

Yamatane Museum of Art
MUSEUM

3 Map p66, C1

This exceptional collection of *nihonga* (Japanese-style paintings) includes some 1800 works from the Meiji Restoration and onwards, of which a small selection is displayed at any one time. Two names to look for: Hayami Gyoshū (1894–1935), whose *Dancing Flames* is an important cultural property; and Okumura Togyū (1889–1990), whose *Cherry Blossoms at Daigo-ji Temple* is a masterpiece in pastel colours. (山種美術館; ☎5777-8600; www.yamatane-museum.or.jp; 3-12-36 Hiroo, Shibuya-ku; adult/student/child ¥800/free, special exhibits extra; ◷10am-5pm Tue-Sun; ℝJR Yamanote Line to Ebisu, west exit)

Naka-Meguro
NEIGHBOURHOOD

4 Map p66, A2

Known to locals as Nakame, Naka-Meguro doesn't look like much when you exit the station. But cross the street with the tracks overhead and in one block you'll hit the Meguro-gawa, a tree-lined canal flanked by stylish cafes, restaurants and boutiques. Nakame is a favourite haunt (and home) of fashion, art and media types, whose tastes are reflected here. (中目黒; ℝHibiya Line to Naka-Meguro)

Daikanyama
NEIGHBOURHOOD

5 Map p66, A2

Daikanyama is a shopping district that favours small boutiques, quiet streets

SAPPORO HOLDINGS LTD ©

Beer Museum Yebisu (p67)

and a wealthy, impeccably dressed clientele (occasionally walking impeccably dressed dogs). Not everything here is outrageously priced though, and the neighbourhood can be an excellent place to discover still-under-the-radar Japanese designers. (代官山; Tōkyū Tōyoko Line to Daikanyama)

Institute for Nature Study PARK

6 Map p66, D4

What would Tokyo look like left to its own natural devices? Since 1949 this park, affiliated with the Tokyo National Museum, has let the local flora go wild. There are wonderful walks through its forests, marshes and ponds, making this one of Tokyo's most appealing – yet least known – getaways. (自然教育園; Shizen Kyōiku-en;

3441 -7176; www.ins.kahaku.go.jp; 5-21-5 Shirokanedai, Meguro-ku; adult/child ¥300/ free; ⏰9am-4.30pm Tue-Sun Sep-Apr, to 5pm Tue-Sun May-Aug, last entry 4pm year-round; Namboku Line to Shirokanedai, exit 1)

Tokyo Metropolitan Teien Art Museum MUSEUM

7 Map p66, D4

Inside a beautiful art deco structure that was once a princely estate, the Teien Museum hosts mostly exhibitions of decorative arts. It began a comprehensive renovation project in 2011 and plans to re-open sometime in 2014; check the website for updates. (東京都庭園美術館; www.teien-art-museum.ne.jp; 5-21-9 Shirokanedai, Minato-ku; admission varies; ⏰10am-6pm, closed 2nd & 4th Wed each month; Namboku Line to Shirokanedai, exit 1)

Meguro Parasitological Museum

MUSEUM

8 Map p66, B5

One for fans of the grotesque: this small museum was established in 1953 by a doctor concerned by the increasing number of parasites he was encountering in postwar conditions. The centrepiece is an 8.8m-long tapeworm found in the body of a 40-year-old Yokohama man. (目黒寄生虫館; ☎3716-1264; http://kiseichu.com/; 4-1-1 Shimo-Meguro, Meguro-ku; admission free; ◷10am-5pm Tue-Sun; ☐2 or 7 from Meguro Station to Ōtori-jinja-mae, ☒JR Yamanote Line to Meguro, west exit)

Eating

Tonki

TONKATSU $

9 ⊗ Map p66, C5

There are two things on the menu here: *rosu-katsu* (fatty loin cutlet) and *hire-katsu* (lean fillet cutlet). Sit at the counter to watch the perfectly choreographed chefs breading, frying and garnishing the tender morsels. Look for a white sign and *noren* (doorway curtains) across sliding doors. (とんき; 1-2-1 Shimo-Meguro, Meguro-ku; meals ¥1800; ◷4-11pm Wed-Mon, closed 3rd Mon of month; ☒JR Yamanote Line to Meguro, west exit; ☺🖵)

Afuri

RĀMEN $

10 ⊗ Map p66, C2

Hardly your typical surly *rāmen-ya* (*rāmen* shop), Afuri has upbeat young cooks and a hip industrial interior. The unorthodox menu might draw eye-rolls from purists, but house specialities including *yuzu-shio rāmen* (egg noodles in a light, salty broth flavoured with *yuzu*, a type of citrus, peel) draw queues at lunch. (あふり; 1-1-7 Ebisu, Shibuya-ku; noodles from ¥750; ◷11am-5am; ☒JR Yamanote Line to Ebisu, east exit; ☺🖵)

Ouca

ICE CREAM $

11 ⊗ Map p66, C2

This ice cream shop uses natural ingredients to whip up only-in-Japan flavours such as *kuro-goma* (black sesame), *yomogi* (mugwort) and *shio konbu* (salted kelp). (櫻花; 1-6-6 Ebisu, Shibuya-ku; ice cream from ¥380; ◷11am-11.30pm or until sold out; ☒JR Yamanote Line to Ebisu, east exit)

Chano-ma

JAPANESE $

12 ⊗ Map p66, A3

By day, Chano-ma is a laid-back cafe with a popular deli lunch special. By

Local Life
Ebisu-yokochō

A retro arcade **Ebisu-yokochō** (恵比寿横町; Map 66, C2; www.ebisu-yokocho.com; 1-7-4 Ebisu, Shibuya-ku; dishes ¥500-1500; ◷5pm-late; ☒JR Yamanote Line to Ebisu, east exit) is full of colourful counters dishing up everything from *okonomiyaki* (savoury pancake) to grilled scallops and sushi. It's lively all evening, and often until the early morning. Look for the rainbow-coloured sign marking the entrance.

Top Tip

Meguro-dōri Buses

Tōkyū buses 2 and 7 depart from outside Meguro Station and run down Meguro-dōri, stopping at Otori-jinja-mae – the closest stop for the Meguro Parasitological Museum (p69) and also the starting point for exploring the Meguro Interior Shops Community (p72). At any point along Meguro-dōri you can catch a bus heading back to Meguro Station. A single ride costs ¥210. Drop your coins in the slot next to the driver (or swipe your Suica card, see p192); exit through the rear doors.

night, it's a chilled-out lounge where you can sip cocktails by candlelight. It's in a very narrow building across the street from Naka-Meguro Station. (チャノマ; 1-22-4 Kami-Meguro, Meguro-ku; lunch set & mains from ¥880; ☉noon-2am Sun-Thu, to 4am Fri & Sat; ℝHibiya Line to Naka-Meguro; ✈🎫)

Ganko Dako
STREET FOOD **$**

 13   Map p66, B5

This street stall dishes out steaming hot *tako-yaki* (grilled octopus dumplings), topped with everything from kimchi to Worcestershire sauce. It's located, unfortunately, across from the Meguro Parasitological Museum; nonetheless, Ganko Dako draws them in – check out the celebrity signings on the wall. (頑固蛸; 3-11-6 Meguro,

Meguro-ku; tako-yaki ¥500; ☉11am-1am; ℝJR Yamanote Line to Meguro, west exit)

Sign
INTERNATIONAL **$**

 14   Map p66, A2

Right outside Daikanyama Station, with a terrace and picture windows, Sign is perfectly poised for prime people watching. Despite the hip decor, the menu is full of classic Japanese comfort foods such as *omu raisu* (rice topped with a soupy omelette and demi-glace sauce). (サイン; 19-4 Daikanyama-cho, Shibuya-ku; mains ¥980-1680; ☉11am-11pm; ℝTōkyū Tōyoko Line to Daikanyama; 🎫)

Ippo
IZAKAYA **$$**

 15   Map p66, C2

This mellow joint specialises in simple pleasures: fish and sake (there's an English sign out front that says just that). There's only a counter and a few tables, so groups should call ahead; staff speak English. Follow the wooden stairs under a ball of cedar fronds (a traditional symbol for a sake brewery). (一歩; ☎3445-8418; 2nd fl, 1-22-10 Ebisu, Shibuya-ku; mains from ¥800-1500; ☉6pm-3am; ℝJR Yamanote Line to Ebisu, east exit)

Drinking

Buri
BAR

 16   Map p66, B2

Buri means super in Hiroshima dialect and this popular *tachinomi-*

ya (standing bar) draws a boisterous, fun-loving crowd. Generous quantities of sake (more than 50 varieties; ¥750) are served semi-frozen, like slushies in colourful jars – super, indeed! (ぶり; ☑3496-7744; www.buri-group.com; 1-14-1 Ebisu-nishi, Shibuya-ku; ⊙5pm-3am; ⊠JR Yamanote Line to Ebisu, west exit;)

Nakame Takkyū Lounge   LOUNGE

17 Map p66, A3

Takkyū (table tennis) is serious sport in Japan, but this lounge draws a hip young crowd rather than real players (though some are suprisingly good!). It's in an apartment building (the one in back) to the right of a parking garage; ring the doorbell for entry. (中目卓球ラウンジ; 1-3-13 Kami-Meguro, 2nd fl, Lion House Naka-Meguro; admission ¥500; ⊙7pm-2am Mon-Sat; ⊠Hibiya Line to Naka-Meguro)

Kinfolk Lounge   LOUNGE

18 Map p66, A2

Sip mojitos under wooden rafters in this dim, moody lounge run by custom bicycle makers Kinfolk. From Naka-Meguro Station, cross Yamate-dōri and the river, then take the first left. It's a few minutes' walk on the left, up a rickety metal staircase above a restaurant. (キンフォーク; ☑5499-8683; http://www.kinfolklife.com/tokyo/; 2nd fl, 1-11-1 Kami-Meguro, Meguro-ku; ⊙6pm-midnight; ⊠Hibiya Line to Naka-Meguro;)

Ebisu Tachinomiya   BAR

19 Map p66, B2

This old-school *tachinomi-ya* serves inexpensive *yakitori* (grilled chicken skewers) and *chūhai* (cocktails made with *shōchū*, a distilled grain liquor). Try the *kingyō*, a *chūhai* spiked with chilli peppers and *shisō* (perilla) leaves. There are seats on the 2nd floor. (恵比寿立呑屋; ☑3791-4194; www.tachinomi-ya.com; 1-1-6 Ebisu-minami, Shibuya-ku; drinks from ¥390; ⊙5pm-1am, to midnight Sun ; ⊠JR Yamanote Line to Ebisu, west exit)

What the Dickens!   PUB

20 Map p66, B2

This British pub is a long-time favourite of down-to-earth expats and cosmopolitan Japanese. The beer and pub grub are well up to scratch and local bands play nightly. It has an unlikely location inside a building that looks like adobe decorated with a mosaic of a hummingbird. (ワット・ザ・ディッキンズ; ☑3780-2099; www.whatthedickens.jp; 4th fl, 1-13-3 Ebisu-nishi, Shibuya-ku; ⊙5pm-late Tue-Sat, to midnight Sun; ⊠JR Yamanote Line to Ebisu, west exit;)

Tableaux Lounge   LOUNGE

21 Map p66, A2

With quilted leather banquettes, bookshelves, a grand piano and glittering chandeliers, Tableaux goes for glamour of a different age. There's an extensive wine and cigar list, and live music nightly. Unless sitting at the bar, there's a ¥1050 cover charge. (タブローズラ ウンジ; ☑5489-2202; www.lounge.tableaux. jp; Basement fl, Sunroser Daikanyama Bldg, 11-6 Sarugaku-chō, Shibuya-ku; drinks from ¥1050; ⏲7pm-4am Mon-Sat, to midnight Sun; 🚉Tōkyū Tōyoko Line to Daikanyama; 🏮)

Entertainment

Unit   LIVE MUSIC

22 ⭐ Map p66, A2

This subterranean club often has two shows: live music in the evening and a DJ-hosted event after hours. Bookings include Japanese indie bands and over-seas artists making their Japan debut. In stylish Daikanyama, Unit isn't as grungy (or as smoky) as other Tokyo live music houses. (ユニット; ☑5459-8630; www.unit-tokyo.com; 1-34-17 Ebisu-nishi, Shibuya-ku; admission ¥2500-5000; 🚉Tōkyū Tōyoko Line to Daikanyama)

Liquid Room   LIVE MUSIC

23 ⭐ Map p66, C2

Some of the world's greatest perform-ers have graced the stage at Liquid Room, from the Flaming Lips and Sonic Youth to Linton Kwesi Johnson. This is an excellent place to see an old favourite or find a new one, but you'll have to buy tickets as soon as they go on sale. (リキッドルーム; ☑5464-0800; www.liquidroom.net; 3-16-6 Higashi, Shibuya-ku; 🚉JR Yamanote Line to Ebisu, west exit)

Shopping

Okura   FASHION, ACCESSORIES

24 🔒 Map p66, A2

Almost everything in this enchant-ing shop is dyed a deep indigo blue. There are some beautiful items, though unfortunately most aren't cheap. The shop looks like a rural house, with worn wooden floorboards and white-washed walls. Note: there's no sign out the front, but look for the traditional building. (オクラ; 20-11 Sarugaku-chō, Shibuya-ku; ⏲11.30am-8pm, 11am-8.30pm Sat & Sun; 🚉Tōkyū Tōyoko Line to Daikanyama)

Kamawanu   CRAFT

25 🔒 Map p66, A2

Kamawanu specialises in *tenugui* (dyed rectangular cloths of thin cot-

Local Life
Meguro Interior Shops Community

Tokyo's interior-design district, **Meguro Interior Shops Commu-nity** (ミスク; MISC; Map 66, A5;http:// misc.co.jp/; Meguro-dōri; dJR Yamanote Line to Meguro, west exit), has dozens of shops stretched out along 3km of Meguro-dōri. Here you can buy modernist wonders, high kitsch, antiques and everything in between. Even if you're not planning to buy anything it's interesting to poke around and imagine what Tokyo's concrete box apartments might look like on the inside. Note that many stores close on Wednesdays.

ton), which can be used as tea towels, handkerchiefs or gift wrap (the list goes on; they're surprisingly versatile). There are more than 200 different patterns available here with motifs from traditional to modern. Turn down the little street to the right of the post office, and look for a traditional building. (かまわぬ; www.kamawanu.co.jp; 23-1 Sarugaku-chō, Shibuya-ku; ⏰11am-7pm; 🚃Tōkyū Tōyoko Line to Daikanyama)

Daikanyama T-Site
BOOKS

26 🔒 Map p66, A2

This stylish shrine to the printed word earned a World Architecture Festival award for the designers, Klein Dytham Architecture. There's a decent selection of books on Japan in English, as well as international magazines, art tomes and a whole floor of music. With two in-house cafes, it's as much a hangout as it is a bookshop. (代官山T-SITE; http://tsite.jp/daikanyama/; 17-5 Sarugaku-chō, Shibuya-ku; ⏰7am-2am; 🚃Tōkyū Tōyoko Line to Daikanyama)

Unlimited by Limi Feu
FASHION

27 🔒 Map p66, B1

Designed by the daughter of fashion legend Yohji Yamamoto, Limi Feu creations are voluminous, dark and street smart. This is the brand's outlet store, with items from past seasons at serious markdowns. The discounts aren't marked, but if you show interest in something, the sales clerk will arrive with a calculator to show you what a bargain it would be. (アンリミ

THOMAS PICKARD / GETTY IMAGES ©

Rāmen noodles

テッド・バイ・リミフゥ; ☎3463-6324; www.limifeu.com; 7-4 Daikanyama-chō, Shibuya-ku; ⏰noon-9pm; 🚃Tōyoko Line to Daikanyama)

Kapital
FASHION

28 🔒 Map p66, B3

Kapital represents another side of Tokyo fashion, a world away from the city's pop image. The brand has a cult following for its premium denim, dyed a dozen times the traditional way, earthy knits and lushly patterned scarves. (キャピタル; ☎5725-3923; http://kapital.jp/; 2-20-2 Ebisu, Shibuya-ku; ⏰11am-8pm; 🚃JR Yamanote Line to Ebisu, west exit)

Explore

Shibuya

Shibuya hits you over the head with its sheer presence: its omnipresent flow of people, glowing video screens and pure exuberence. This is the beating heart of Tokyo's youth culture, where the fashion is loud, the street culture vivid and the nightclubs run until dawn. Nowhere else says 'Welcome to Tokyo' better than this, and the neighbourhood is a must-see for anyone interested in Tokyo pop culture.

The Sights in a Day

☀ Step out of Shibuya Station and you'll immediately encounter the madness of **Shibuya Crossing** (p78). Before making your way across what is quite possibly the world's busiest intersection, pay your respects to the loyal dog, **Hachikō** (p78). Then head east to the new **Shibuya Hikarie** (p78) building to see Shibuya's sophisticated side. There are galleries on the 8th floor and views over the neighbourhood from the 11th floor. Have lunch at **d47 Shokudō** (p79) on the 6th floor.

☀ After lunch, return to the thick of things and explore Shibuya's central drag, **Center-gai** (p78). There are several worthwhile shops around here, including **Tōkyū Hands** (p84) and **Parco** (p85), also home to the pop culture showcase that is the **Parco Museum** (p78). Be sure to take a peek into teen fashion trend machine **Shibuya 109** (p84).

☾ For dinner, feast on fresh seafood at **Kaikaya** (p80). Shibuya is known for its nightlife, and live music in particular: catch a concert at **Club Quattro** (p83) or **Shibuya O-East** (p83). If you've got energy in reserves, hit one of Shibuya's nightclubs such as **Womb** (p81) and dance until the trains start running again at dawn.

 Best of Tokyo

Food
d47 Shokudō (p79)

Sushi-no-Midori (p80)

Shopping & Markets
Tōkyū Hands (p84)

Sister (p84)

Nightlife & Music
Womb (p81)

Beat Cafe (p81)

Club Quattro (p83)

Nonbei-yokochō (p83)

Sound Museum Vision (p81)

Pop Culture
Shibuya Crossing (p78)

Shibuya 109 (p84)

Getting There

🚃 **Train** The JR Yamanote, Tōkyū Tōyōko and Keiō Inokashira Lines stop at Shibuya.

Ⓢ **Subway** The Ginza, Hanzōmon and Fukutoshin Lines all stop at Shibuya.

A
B
C
D

1

KAMIYAMA-CHŌ

Inokashira-dōri

NHK Broadcast Center and Studio Park

JINNAN

18

Kamiyama Shōtengai

Kōen-dōri

UDAGAWA-CHŌ

26

2

30

27
6
12

Parco
Museum

20

23

SHŌTŌ

8
34

15

32

22

Bunkamura

5

9

Center-gai

3

3
28

Center-gai

$

13

21

Shibuya Crossing

1

29

17

Hachikō Statue

DŌGENZAKA

Keiō Shibuya

24

Shibuya Mark City

14

11

16

MARUYAMA-CHŌ

10

4

5

Dōgenzaka

Shuto Expwy No 3

Tamagawa-dōri

25 *Cerulean Tower Tōkyū Hotel*

Bunkamura-dōri

KITA-AOYAMA

United Nations University

Meiji-dōri

33

Miyashita-kōen

31

Mitake-kōen

SHIBUYA-KU

Nonbei-yokochō

Shibuya Post Office

Shibuya

Miyamasu-zaka

Shibuya

Aoyama-dōri

4 Shibuya Hikarie

7

Shibuya

Tōkyū Shibuya

Shibuya-gawa

Meiji-dōri

For reviews see	
◉ Sights	p78
✖ Eating	p79
◍ Drinking	p81
✿ Entertainment	p83
🔒 Shopping	p84

0   200 m
0   0.1 miles

Sights

Shibuya Crossing
STREET

1 Map p76, D4

Rumoured to be the world's busiest, this intersection in front of Shibuya Station is known as the Scramble. It's a spectacle of giant video screens, neon and people coming from all directions at once. Up to a thousand cross with every light change, yet still manage to dodge each other with a practiced, nonchalant agility. (渋谷交差点; 🚃 JR Yamanote Line to Shibuya, Hachikō exit)

Hachikō Statue
MONUMENT

2 Map p76, D4

Hachikō, an Akita dog, belonged to a professor who lived near Shibuya Station. The professor died in 1925, but the dog continued to show up and wait at the station for his master until his own death 10 years later. The story became legend and a small statue was erected at the station plaza in the dog's memory. (ハチ公像; Hachikō Plaza; 🚃 JR Yamanote Line to Shibuya, Hachikō exit)

Center-gai
STREET

3 Map p76, D3

This pedestrian street is Shibuya's main artery. It's lined with all the places local teens and twenty-somethings love, including fast-food joints and fast-fashion boutiques, and you'll see the neighbourhood's colourful, bleached-hair denizens hanging out here day and night. (センター街; Sentā-gai; 🚃 JR Yamanote Line to Shibuya, Hachikō exit)

Shibuya Hikarie
CULTURAL BUILDING

4 Map p76, F4

This gleaming, 34-floor tower, completed in 2012, threatens to bring grown-up sophistication to youthful Shibuya. The lower floors are filled with shops and restaurants, but the 8th (🕐 11am-8pm) floor has two worthwhile exhibition spaces: one curated by the influential Tomio Koyama Gallery and another, the d47 Museum, which showcases crafts from around Japan's 47 prefectures. The 11th floor lounge has good views. (渋谷ヒカリエ; 📞 5468-5892; www.hikarie.jp; 2-21-1 Shibuya, Shibuya-ku; 🕐 10am-9pm; 🚃 JR Yamanote Line to Shibuya, east exit)

Bunkamura
ARTS CENTRE

5 Map p76, B3

Bunkamura means culture village, and this was Japan's first cross-cultural centre. There's an art museum, with changing exhibitions that swing both east and west, and an art-house cinema, Le Cinema. (文化村; 📞 3477-9111; www.bunkamura.co.jp; 2-24-1 Dōgenzaka, Shibuya-ku; admission varies; 🕐 museum open 10am-7pm, to 9pm Fri & Sat, closed between exhibitions; 🚃 JR Yamanote Line to Shibuya, Hachikō exit)

Parco Museum
MUSEUM

6 Map p76, C2

In line with the neighbourhood vibe, this small museum inside the Parco department store features exhibitions with a pop-culture flavour. (パルコミュージアム; 📞 3477-5873; www.parco-art.

TOM BONAVENTURE / GETTY IMAGES ©

Center-gai

com/web/museum; 3rd fl, Parco Part 1, 15-1 Udagawa-chō, Shibuya-ku; admission from ¥300; ⊙10am-9pm; 📵JR Yamanote line to Shibuya, Hachikō exit)

Eating

d47 Shokudō
SHOKUDŌ $

7 🍴 Map p76, F4

There are 47 prefectures in Japan and d47 serves a changing line-up of *teishoku* (set meals) that evoke the specialities of each one. Strangely, only the prefecture names are on the menu in English, so you'll have to take a chance on wherever strikes your fancy. (d47食堂; www.hikarie8.com/d47shokudo/about.shtml; 6th fl, Shibuya

Hikarie, 2-21-1 Shibuya, Shibuya-ku; meals ¥950-1680; ⊙11am-11pm; 📵JR Line to Shibuya, east exit; 🍴)

Nabezō
SHABU-SHABU $

8 🍴 Map p76, C3

Here's one for when you're really hungry: diners get a bubbling tabletop pot of broth and 90 minutes to dunk as much beef or pork as they like into it. Though it's a chain, Nabezō gets points for including a vegie bar with plenty of greens and mushrooms. (鍋ぞう; ☎3461-2941; www.nabe-zo.com; 6th fl, Beam Bldg, 31-2 Udagawa-chō, Shibuya-ku; meals from ¥1980; ⊙11.30am-3pm, 5-11pm Mon-Fri, 11.30am-11pm Sat & Sun; 📵Yamanote Line to Shibuya, Hachikō exit, 🍴)

Understand
Love Hotels

Rubuho ('love hotels' for amorous encounters) aren't just for the sleazy. Sky-high residential rents mean many young people live at home in cramped quarters until marriage; consequently, love hotels have become a crucial part of modern courtship rituals. They're notorious for their crazy decor – intended to evoke distant palaces or exotic islands – though these days, Tokyoites prefer a look that resembles an ordinary hotel.

Dōgenzaka has one of the largest collections of love hotels in the city, so much so that's it's been nicknamed 'Love Hotel Hill'. There are many night-clubs and concert venues around here, too. If you're travelling as a couple, a night in a *rubuho* can be a cheap alternative to a business hotel: an all-night 'stay' starts from ¥6000 (a three-hour daytime 'rest' goes for about ¥4000).

Viron
BAKERY $

 Map p76, C3

A fantastic French bakery (it apparently imports the flour from the motherland), Viron serves up sandwiches and quiches to take away – or you can take 'em upstairs to the pleasant cafe. (☎5458-1770; 33-8 Udagawa-chō, Shibuya-ku; sandwiches ¥525-1050; ⏰9am-10pm; ☒JR Yamanote Line to Shibuya, Hachikō exit)

Kaikaya
SEAFOOD $$

 Map p76, A5

The chef here is passionate about the sea and Kaikaiya is his attempt to bring the beach to Shibuya. Everything on the menu is caught in nearby Sagami Bay. It's a boisterous, popular place; reservations are recommended. From Dōgenzaka, turn right after the police box and the restaurant, with a red awning, is on your right. (開花屋; ☎3770-0878; www.kaikaya.com; 23-7 Maruyama-chō,

Shibuya-ku; lunch from ¥780, dishes ¥680-2500; ⏰11.30am-2pm & 5.30-11.30pm Mon-Fri, 5.30-11.30pm Sat & Sun; ☒Yamanote Line to Shibuya, Hachikō exit; ☻▣)

Sushi-no-Midori
SUSHI $$

 Map p76, D4

Sushi-no-Midori, famed for being excellent value, almost always has a line. Don't let the wait put you off; service is quick and the generous sushi sets are worth it. Look for the signs pointing to the Mark City complex inside Shibuya Station, near the Inokashira Line. (寿司 の美登利; 4th fl, Mark City, 1-12-3 Dōgenzaka, Shibuya-ku; sets from ¥2100; ⏰11am-10pm Mon-Fri, to 9pm Sat & Sun; ☒JR Yamanote Line to Shibuya, Hachikō exit; ☻▣)

Den Rokuen-Tei
ASIAN $$

 Map p76, D2

Modern twists on seasonally changing Japanese *izakaya* (traditional pub) dishes are served at this relaxed, stylish perch on the top of Parco 1. In the warmer months, the best seats are on the open-air terrace. (デンロクエンテイ; ☎6415-5489; 8th fl, Parco Part 1, 15-1 Udagawa-chō, Shibuya-ku; ◎11am-midnight; 🚇JR Yamanote line to Shibuya, Hachikō exit)

Za Watami
IZAKAYA $$

13 Map p76, D3

This *izakaya* chain is ubiquitous for a reason: it's exceedingly reasonable and has a huge menu covering all the classics, including *sashimi moriawase* (assorted raw fish), *yakitori* (grilled chicken skewers) and *gyōza* (dumplings). Expect a lively, young crowd. It's above the Softbank store and has a picture menu. (坐・和民; www.watami-foodservice.jp/watami; 6th-8th fl, Kiyama Bldg, 27-4 Udagawa-chō, Shibuya-ku; dishes from ¥300; ◎5pm-5am; 🚇JR Yamanote Line to Shibuya, Hachikō exit; ➲📖)

Drinking

Womb
CLUB

14 Map p76, B4

Womb's state-of-the-art sound system, enormous mirror ball and frenetic laser lighting go perfectly with the house and techno music played here. Though it draws more diehard music fans than scene chasers, Womb's four floors still get jammed at weekends. Photo ID is required. (ウーム; ☎5459-0039; www.womb.co.jp; 2-16 Maruyama-chō, Shibuya-ku; admission varies; ◎11pm-late; 🚇JR Yamanote Line to Shibuya, Hachikō exit)

Beat Cafe
BAR

15 Map p76, C3

It's all about the music at this shabby bar on Center Gai, run by an indie music promoter. Join an eclectic mix of local and international regulars who swig beers (¥650) and chat beats under the watchful eyes of taxidermic elk. Sister club Echo downstairs has a small dance floor and a groovy jumble-sale decor. (www.facebook.com/beatcafe; 3rd fl, 33-13 Udagawa-chō, Shibuya-ku; ◎7pm-5am; 🚇JR Yamanote line to Shibuya, Hachikō exit)

Sound Museum Vision
CLUB

16 Map p76, C4

Tokyo's newest club, opened in 2011, is a cavernous space with four dance floors. With a sleek modern interior and not so much of a cruisy vibe, Vision is downright classy for this side of Shibuya. A solid line-up of international DJs plays mostly house and techno. Bring ID. (☎5728-2824; www.vision-tokyo.com; Basement fl, 2-10-7 Dōgenzaka, Shibuya-ku; admission ¥3000-4000; ◎Events from 10pm; 🚇JR Yamanote line to Shibuya, Hachikō exit)

Shibuya Oiran
BAR

17 Map p76, B4

You can't miss this siren of a bar, with its bright red facade, the colour of *a torii* (the entrance gate of a Shintō shrine) and geisha lips. Conveniently located near the clubs, Oiran is the perfect place to start the night. It's

TOM BONAVENTURE / GETTY IMAGES ©

Shibuya Crossing (p78)

a *tachinomi-ya* (standing-only pub), though some of the original cocktails are designed to knock you off your feet (the 'Crazy Hachibei': sake and Jagermeister). (しぶや花魁; http://oiran. asia; 2-22-6 Dōgenzaka, Shibuya-ku; cocktails from ¥600; ⏰6pm to late; 🚃JR Yamanote Line to Shibuya, Hachikō exit; 📵)

Craftheads
BAR

18 🚻 Map p76, D1

One of the players in Tokyo's growing craft beer scene, Craftheads always has an interesting line up of local and imported brews on tap. It's a well-lit, smoke-free place where beer takes precedence over ambience, and a hangout

for the local, er, craft heads. Keep your eyes peeled for the sign leading down to the basement stairs. (クラフトヘッズ; 📞6416-9474; http://craftheads.jp/ craftheads/Welcome.html; Basement fl, 1-13-10 Jinnan, Shibuya-ku; ⏰5pm-midnight Tue-Fri, 3pm-midnight Sat, 3pm-10pm Sun; 🚃JR Yamanote Line to Shibuya, Hachikō exit; 📶🚭📵)

Shidax Village
KARAOKE

19 🚻 Map p76, E2

Topped by a massive red neon sign, Shidax outshines all the other karaoke joints in the neighbourhood. Rooms are spacious and make a stab at being stylish. (シダックスビレッジ; 📞3461-9356; http://yoyaku.sdx.co.jp/ pc/shopinfo_64030.html; 1-12-13 Jinnan, Shibuya-ku; per 30min Mon-Thu ¥540, Fri-Sun ¥590, 3hr room & meal plan from ¥2500; ⏰11am-5am; 🚃JR Yamanote Line to Shibuya, Hachikō exit)

Attic Room
CAFE

20 🚻 Map p76, C2

With dark wood and vintage armchairs, this peaceful haven offers coffee, cocktails and a respite from Shibuya's omnipresent crowds. It's a little tricky to find, but look for the old corner building near Tōkyū Hands department store. (アティックルーム; 📞5489-5228; http://www.atticroom.jp/ shops/index.html; 4th fl, Yamato Bldg, 31-1 Udagawa-chō, Shibuya-ku; coffee from ¥450; ⏰noon-midnight Tue-Sun, from 5pm Mon; 🚃JR Yamanote Line to Shibuya, Hachikō exit)

Ruby Room
CLUB

21 🚇 Map p76, C3

This tiny, sparkly gem of a cocktail lounge hosts both DJ and live-music events. It's an appealing spot for older kids hanging out in Shibuya and draws a laid-back international crowd. Some weekday events are free. (ルビールーム; ☎3780-3022; www.rubyroomtokyo. com; 2nd fl, 2-25-17 Dōgenzaka, Shibuya-ku; admission incl 1 drink ¥1500; ⏰8pm-late; 🚃JR Yamanote Line to Shibuya, Hachikō exit)

Entertainment

Club Quattro
LIVE MUSIC

22 ⭐ Map p76, C3

This venue feels like a concert hall, but it's actually more along the lines of a slick club. Though there's no explicit musical focus, emphasis is on rock and roll and world music, and the quality is generally high. Expect a more varied, artsy crowd than the club's location – near Sentā-gai in Shibuya – might lead you to expect. (クラブクアトロ; ☎3477-8750; www. club-quattro.com; 32-13-4 Udagawa-chō, Shibuya-ku; admission ¥3000-4000; 🚃JR Yamanote Line to Shibuya, Hachikō exit)

Cinema Rise
CINEMA

23 ⭐ Map p76, D2

This long-running independent cinema screens a mix of foreign and domestic art-house films and documentaries, though naturally the subtitles are only in Japanese. On Tuesdays, the first of the month and for the last show on Sunday evenings, tickets are only ¥1000; flash an international student ID anytime and get in for ¥1000. (シネマライズ; ☎3464-0051; www.cinemarise.com; 13-17 Udagawa-chō, Shibuya-ku; adult/student/child ¥1800/1500/1000; ⏰11am-11pm; 🚃JR Yamanote Line to Shibuya, Hachikō exit)

Shibuya O-East
LIVE MUSIC

24 ⭐ Map p76, B4

Shibuya O-East is the big mama of several related venues forming a compound of clubs up Love Hotel Hill. With its sheer size, this house draws bigger-name international and domestic acts. You'll encounter everything from J-Pop to indie here, plus mini-festivals that can introduce curious audiophiles to a whole slew

> **Q Local Life**
> ### Nonbei-yokochō
> A narrow nightlife strip along the JR tracks, **Nonbei-yokochō** is a collection of old wooden buildings that predates pretty much everything else in Shibuya. It's worthwhile just to stroll through. If you fancy a drink, check out teeny-tiny **Tight** (タイト; Map 76, E3; www.tight-tokyo. com; 2nd fl, 1-25-10 Shibuya, Shibuya-ku; drinks from ¥500; ⏰Mon-Sat 6pm-2am, to midnight Sun; 🚃JR Yamanote Line to Shibuya, Hachikō exit) – named for the tight fit around the bar. It has a big picture window in front.

of new bands and DJs. (渋谷オーイースト; ☑5458-4681; www.shibuya-o.com; 2-14-8 Dōgenzaka, Shibuya-ku; 圓JR Yamanote Line to Shibuya, Hachikō exit)

Jz Brat
LIVE MUSIC

25 ⭐ Map p76, D5

Billed as a jazz house, this intimate, upscale venue, with room for 100, actually boasts a more varied line-up, including pop, latin and even hip-hop. It's mostly local acts, which accounts for the reasonable ticket prices. Bonus: it's in the swank Cerulean Tower Tōkyū Hotel. (ジェイゼットブラット; ☑5728-0168; www.jzbrat.com; 2nd fl, Cerulean Tower Tōkyū Hotel, 26-1 Sakuragaokachō, Shibuya-ku; admission ¥3000-5000; 圓JR Yamanote Line to Shibuya, south exit)

Uplink
CINEMA

26 ⭐ Map p76, B2

Day and night Uplink screens quirky independent films (domestic and foreign) in a tiny art-house cinema with comfy chairs. (アップリンク; www.uplink.co.jp; 2nd fl, 37-18 Udagawa-chō, Shibuya-ku; 圓JR Yamanote Line to Shibuya, Hachikō exit)

Shopping

Tōkyū Hands
DEPARTMENT STORE

27 🔒 Map p76, C2

This DIY and *zakka* (miscellaneous goods) store has eight fascinating floors of everything you didn't know

you needed. It's perfect for souvenir hunting – surely someone you know needs reflexology slippers, right? (東急ハンズ; ☑5489-5111; http://shibuya.tokyu-hands.co.jp; 12-18 Udagawa-chō, Shibuya-ku; 圓JR Yamanote Line to Shibuya, Hachikō exit)

Sister
FASHION

28 🔒 Map p76, D3

This is one of the best places in the city to discover hot new Japanese designers. The sales clerks are painfully stylish, but surprisingly nice: they'll happily help you put together an enviable outfit from the shop's collection of new and vintage. Look for the Fake Tokyo banners out front. (シスター; ☑5456-9892; www.faketokyo.com; 2nd fl, 18-4 Udagawa-cho, Shibuya-ku; ⏱noon-10pm; 圓JR Yamanote Line to Shibuya, Hachikō exit)

Shibuya 109
FASHION

29 🔒 Map p76, D3

See all those dolled-up teens walking around Shibuya? This is where they shop. Nicknamed *marukyū*, this cylindrical tower houses dozens of small boutiques, each with its own carefully styled look (and loud competing music). Even if you don't intend to buy anything, you can't understand Shibuya without making a stop here. (渋谷109; Ichimarukyū; ☑3477-5111; http://www.shibuya109.jp/en/top; 2-29-1 Dōgenzaka, Shibuya-ku; ⏱10am-9pm; 圓JR Yamanote Line to Shibuya, Hachikō exit)

Parco
DEPARTMENT STORE

30 🔒 Map p76, D2

Parco stretches over several buildings, but the Parco 1 building has the best boutiques. They get edgier as you ascend: look for fun Japanese labels such as Hysteric Glamour and Merci Beaucoup on the 3rd and 4th floors. Menswear is on the 5th floor. There's also an excellent bookshop in the basement. (パルコ; ☎3464-5111; www.parco-shibuya.com; 15-1 Udagawa-chō, Shibuya-ku; ⏰10am-9pm; 🚃JR Yamanote Line to Shibuya, Hachikō exit)

Tower Records
BOOKS

31 🔒 Map p76, E2

Tower Records Japan became independent just before the American chain went bankrupt, and this enormous Shibuya branch is still going strong. It's Japan's largest record store with an extensive collection of... everything. (タワーレコード; ☎3496-3661; 1-22-14 Jinnan, 7F, Tower Records Bldg; ⏰10am-11pm; 🚃JR Yamanote line to Shibuya, Hachikō exit)

Loft
DEPARTMENT STORE

32 🔒 Map p76, D3

Loft is an emporium of cute homewares and accessories. Check out the candy-coloured stationery and travel goods on the first two floors. (ロフト; ☎3462-3807; www.loft.co.jp; 21-1 Udagawa-chō, Shibuya-ku; ⏰10am-9pm; 🚃JR Yamanote Line to Shibuya, Hachikō exit)

⬭ Local Life
Record Shops in Udagawa-chō

One of the many little neighbourhoods that make up Shibuya, **Udagawa-chō** is famous among DJs and record collectors for its cluster of music shops. You can find all sorts of genres (and obscurities here), generally in good condition. **Manhattan Records** (マンハッタンレコード; Map 76, C2; ☎3477-7166; http://manhattanrecords.jp; 10-1 Udagawa-chō, Shibuya-ku; ⏰noon-9pm; 🚃JR Yamanote line to Shibuya, Hachikō exit) is a good place to start.

Aquvii
ACCESSORIES

33 🔒 Map p76, E2

Come see what the cool kids are wearing (and making) at this showcase for quirky, made-in-Tokyo accessories and other oddities from local designers. (アクヴィ; ☎6427-1219; 6-19-16 Jingūmae, Shibuya-ku; ⏰noon-8pm; 🚃JR Yamanote Line to Shibuya, Hachikō exit)

Recofan
MUSIC

34 🔒 Map p76, C3

With a huge selection of used CDs, including folk, soul, J-pop and world music, you could easily lose half a day in here. (レコファン; ☎5454-0161; www.recofan.co.jp; 4th fl, Shibuya Beam Bldg, 31-2 Udagawa-chō, Shibuya-ku; ⏰11.30am-9pm; 🚃JR Yamanote line to Shibuya, Hachikō exit)

Local Life
Hanging out in Shimo-Kitazawa

The narrow streets of 'Shimokita' are barely passable by cars, meaning a streetscape like a doll-house version of Tokyo. It's been a favourite haunt for generations of students and there's a lively street scene all afternoon and evening, especially on weekends. If hippies – not bureaucrats – ran Tokyo, the city would look a lot more like Shimo-Kitazawa.

Getting There

🚈 The Keiō Inokashira Line connects Shibuya with Shimo-Kitazawa; the Odakyū Line connects Shinjuku with Shimo-Kitazawa.

❶ Explore an old market

Take the north exit from Shimo-Kitazawa Station and look right for an entrance to a **covered market**. This former post-WWII black market now houses stalls selling sundries and edibles. It's set to be demolished in a few years despite fierce local resistance.

❷ Check out Shimokita Garage Department

Head up the hill parallel to the train tracks, turn right and you'll see **Shimokita Garage Department** (東洋百貨店; 2-25-8 Kitazawa, Setagaya-ku; ⏰noon-8pm; 🚉Odakyū Line to Shimo-Kitazawa, north exit), a covered market with colourful murals at the entrance. With stalls of DIY accessories and used clothing, it's like a flea market with treasures galore.

❸ Go vintage shopping

The bohemian vibe translates to a love of vintage clothing. **Haight & Ashbury** (2nd fl, 2-37-2 Kitazawa, Setagaya-ku; ⏰noon-10pm; 🚉Odakyu Line to Shimo-Kitazawa, north exit), the neighbourhood's best secondhand store, has everything to re-enact any theatrical number, from the goatherd scene in *The Sound of Music* to the opening of *Cabaret*.

❹ Stop for espresso

Turn right onto Ichibangai for an espresso considered by many to be Tokyo's best, at **Bear Pond Espresso** (📞5454-2486; www.bear-pond.com; 2-36-12 Kitazawa, Setagaya-ku; espresso ¥300-700; ⏰10.30am-6pm Wed-Mon; 🚉Odakyū line to Shimokitazawa, North exit). Espresso is only served until 1pm Thursday to Monday.

❺ Shop at Village Vanguard

Cross the tracks and look right for **Village Vanguard** (ヴィレッジ・ヴァンガード; 2-10-15 Kitazawa, Setagaya-ku; ⏰10am-midnight; 🚉Odakyu Line to Shimo-Kitazawa, south exit), an irreverent pop culture emporium crammed with magazines, music, gadgets and toys.

❻ Walk down Azuma-dōri

Azuma-dōri epitomises Shimokita's south side, with bars, live music, retro street signs and low-slung buildings. Don't miss the mural that turns the elevated rail line into an ancient temple.

❼ Eat at Shirube

Shirube (汁べゑ; 📞3413-3785; 2-18-2 Kitazawa, Setagaya-ku; dishes ¥580-880; ⏰5.30pm-midnight Mon-Thu & Sun, to 2am Fri & Sat; 🍴; 🚉Keiō Inokashira Line to Shimo-Kitazawa, south exit) is a rowdy, local *izakaya* (Japanese-style pub). The menu mixes classic dishes and inventive fusion ones, with seating around an open kitchen. Book ahead on weekends and don't miss the *aburi saba* (blowtorch-grilled mackerel).

❽ Go for a drink at Mother

Mother (マザー; 📞3412-5318; www.rock-mother.com/index.html; 5-36-14 Kitazawa, Setagaya-ku; ⏰6pm-2am; 🚉Keiō Inokashira Line to Shimo-Kitazawa) is a classic Shimo-Kitazawa bar, with a funky decor, soundtrack from the '60s and '70s and tasty pan-Asian food and cocktails.

Explore

Harajuku
& Aoyama

Harajuku is one of Tokyo's biggest draws, both for its stately shrine, Meiji-jingū, and its street fashion. The boutique-lined boulevard Omote-sandō is a must-see for fans of contemporary architecture. Harajuku also has several excellent art museums and you can spend a rewarding day bouncing between the traditional and the modern while indulging in the area's excellent restaurants, cafes and boutiques.

The Sights in a Day

☀ Get an early start and beat the crowds to **Meiji-jingū** (p90), Tokyo's most famous Shintō shrine. Then join the teenage fashion parade down **Takeshita-dōri** (p93). Make a worthwhile detour to the **Ukiyo-e Ōta Memorial Art Museum** (p93), before breaking for lunch at local favourite **Harajuku Gyōza Rō** (p95).

☀ Spend the afternoon making your way down the boutique-lined boulevard **Omote-sandō** (p94), gawking at the impressive architecture. Duck into the alleyways of Ura-Hara, to see some off-the-wall fashions and to take a peak into the equally off-the-wall **Design Festa** (p95). Grab a coffee at one of the neighbourhood's many cafes, such as **Omotesando Koffee** (p99). Leave yourself an hour to explore the galleries of the **Nezu Museum** (p93) at the far end of Omote-sandō, in Aoyama.

☾ Watch the sunset over a glass of wine at **Two Rooms** (p99), then treat yourself to a dinner of inventive *kaiseki* (Japanese haute cuisine) at underground **Agaru Sagaru Nishi Iru Higashi Iru** (p99). If you have energy left over, go shake a tail feather with the fashion crowd at **Le Baron** (p100).

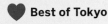

👁 **Top Sights**
Meiji-jingū (p90)

♥ **Best of Tokyo**

Parks & Gardens
Yoyogi-kōen (p94)

Galleries & Museums
Ukiyo-e Ōta Memorial Art Museum (p93)

Eating
Agaru Sagaru Nishi Iru Higashi Iru (p99)

Sentō & Onsen
Shimizu-yu (p95)

Shopping & Markets
Laforet (p102)

Nightlife & Live Music
Two Rooms (p99)

Pop Culture
KiddyLand (p101)

Getting There

🚃 **Train** The JR Yamanote Line stops at Harajuku; the JR Sōbu Line stops at Sendagaya.

Ⓢ **Subway** Chiyoda & Fukutoshin Lines stop at Meiji-jingū-mae. Chiyoda, Ginza & Hanzōmon Lines stop at Omote-sandō.

Top Sights
Meiji-jingū

Tokyo's grandest Shintō shrine is dedicated to the Emperor Meiji and Empress Shōken. Emperor Meiji's reign (1868–1912) coincided with the country's transformation from an isolationist, feudal state to a modern nation. Constructed in 1920, the shrine was destroyed in WWII air raids and rebuilt in 1958; however, unlike many of Japan's postwar reconstructions, Meiji-jingū has an authentic feel. The shrine occupies only a small fraction of the sprawling forested grounds, which contain 120,000 trees collected from around Japan.

明治神宮

⊙ Map p92, A2

www.meijijingu.or.jp

1-1 Yoyogi Kamizono-chō, Shibuya-ku

admission free

⊙ dawn-dusk

🚊 JR Yamanote Line to Harajuku, Omote-sandō exit

Meiji-jingū

Don't Miss

The Gates

Towering *torii* (gates) mark the entrance to the shrine and sacred space. The largest gate, created from a 1500-year-old Taiwanese cypress, stands 12 metres high. Along the path you'll also see rows of decorative sake barrels – gifts to the shrine (and a favourite of photographers).

The Font

Approaching the main shrine, the *temizuya* (font) is on the left. Shintō places a premium on purity, so visitors perform a cleansing ritual. Use the dipper to pour water over your left hand, then your right (without letting the water drip back into the pool). Fill your left hand with water and rinse out your mouth. Rinse your left hand a final time.

The Main Shrine

The main shrine is made of cypress from the Kiso region of Nagano. To make the customary offering, toss a coin – five-yen coins are considered the luckiest – into the box, bow twice, clap your hands twice, say a prayer if you like and bow again. Clapping is said to attract the gods' attention.

Meiji-jingū-gyoen

Meiji-jingū-gyoen (明治神宮御苑; Inner Garden; admission ¥500; 🕑9am-4.30pm) is a landscaped garden on the grounds of the shrine that once belonged to a feudal estate. When the grounds passed into imperial hands, the emperor himself designed the iris garden to please the empress. The entrance is on the right, about half-way down the path to the main shrine.

☑ Top Tips

▶ Every day at 8am and 2pm a priest strikes a large drum as part of a ritual offering of food to the deities enshrined here. This is the best time to visit.

▶ If you're lucky, you may also catch a traditional wedding procession – just try not to get in the way.

▶ You'll likely attract guards if you get your camera out too close to the main shrine. The rule of photo-taking here is this: if there's a roof over your head, it's a no-go.

✗ Take a Break

At the entrance to the shrine, overlooking the wooded path, **Mori no Terrace** (杜のテラス; Map p93, A3; 1-1 Yoyogi Kamizono-chō, Shibuya-ku; coffee ¥280; 🕑9am-4.30pm) serves coffee, pastries and ice cream.

Purveyor of delicious dumplings, **Harajuku Gyōza Rō** (p95), is a 10-minute walk away.

Shuto Expwy No 4

A **B** **C** **D**

★ 29

Tokyo
Metropolitan
Gymnasium

National
Stadium

Jingū-
gaien

Ⓜ Kita-sandō

0 ———— 400 m
0 ———— 0.2 miles

SENDAGAYA

Meiji-
kōen

◉ **Meiji-
jingū**

Meiji-
jingū
Kaikan

Meiji-dōri

Kita-sandō

Gaien-nishi-dōri

★ 2

Minami-sandō

★ 16

21 ◉
1 ◉ Takeshita-dōri

Takeshita-dōri

Tōgō-
jinja

Design
Festa
19 ✕
7 ◉

6 ◉

Ukiyo-e Ōta
Harajuku Ⓜ Memorial
Museum of Art

Watari Museum
of Contemporary
Art (Watari-Um)

Bell
Commons Ⓜ
Bldg Gaienma

Yoyogi- 5 ◉
kōen

Laforet
Museum
Harajuku

2 ◉
37 🅐
8 🅐

Ⓜ
Meiji-
jingū-mae

Ura-
Hara

Killer-dōri

Gaien-nishi-dōri

JINGŪMAE

HARAJUKU

38 🅐

Ⓜ Meiji-jingū-mae

33 🅐
32 ✕
23 🅐
24 🅐
11 ✕
15 ✕
36 🅐

22 🅐

12 🅐

26
🅐

Omote-Sandō
Hills

**KITA-
AOYAMA**

10 ◉
Shimizu-yu

Cat Street

Omote-sandō

27
🅐

13 ✕

Omote-
sandō
4 🅐

18 ✕ Ⓜ Omote-sandō

**MINAMI-
AOYAMA**

JINNAN

★ 31

34
🅐

**MINAMI-
AOYAMA**

25 🅐

17 ✕

20 🅐
9 ◉

Spiral
Building

35 🅐

Nezu
Museum
3 ◉

United
Nations
University

14 ✕

Aoyama-dōri

30 ★

Kottō-dōri

For reviews see	
◉ Top Sights	p90
◉ Sights	p93
✕ Eating	p95
🅐 Drinking	p99
★ Entertainment	p100
🅐 Shopping	p101

Sights

Takeshita-dōri
STREET

1 ⊙ Map p92, B3

The famous fashion subculture bazaar where aspiring *goth-lolis* (Gothic Lolitas) come to shop. The narrow alley is a pilgrimage site for teens and the pedestrian traffic can be intense, especially on weekends. (竹下通り; 🚊JR Yamanote Line to Harajuku, Takeshita exit)

Ukiyo-e Ōta Memorial Museum of Art
MUSEUM

2 ⊙ Map p92, B3

Pad quietly in slippers to view the first-rate collection of *ukiyo-e* (woodblock prints) amassed by Ōta Seizo, former head of the Toho Life Insurance Company. A small selection of the collection, numbering more than 10,000 prints and including works by masters such as Hokusai and Hiroshige, are arranged in changing, thematic exhibitions. (浮世絵太田記念美術館; 📞3403-0880; www.ukiyoe-ota-muse.jp; 1-10-10 Jingūmae, Shibuya-ku; adult ¥700-1000, child free; ⊙10.30am-5.30pm Tue-Sun, closed 27th to end of month; 🚊JR Yamanote Line to Harajuku, Omote-sandō exit)

Nezu Museum
MUSEUM

3 ⊙ Map p92, D5

This recently renovated museum offers a striking blend of old and new: a renowned collection of Japanese, Chinese and Korean antiquities in a gallery space designed by contemporary architect Kuma Kengō. Select items are displayed in manageable monthly exhibitions. (根津美術館; 📞3400-2536; www.nezu-muse.or.jp; 6-5-1 Minami-Aoyama, Minato-ku; adult/student/child ¥1000/800/free, special exhibitions ¥200 extra; ⊙10am-5pm Tue-Sun; 🚊Ginza Line to Omote-sandō, exit A5)

Take a Break Nezu Café (coffee ¥600; ⊙10am-5pm) is an attractive glass box in the garden behind the museum.

Understand
Harajuku Style
━━━━━━━━━━━━━━━━━━━━━━━━━━━━

Harajuku is the city's living catwalk. It's also that rare place in Japan where unconventionality is rewarded: a country girl can get off a train, get a job at a local boutique and – with enough moxie and sartorial innovation – find herself on the pages of a national magazine within a year. Clerks and hair stylists set the trends in Harajuku, not the fashion glossies, as photographers from street fashion magazines and websites stalk the neighbourhood looking for the next big thing. Every time someone declares Harajuku dead, another trend is born, inspiring a whole nation of teens.

Torii (shrine gate), Yoyogi-kōen

Omote-sandō STREET

4 Map p92, C4

The Champs-Élysées of Tokyo, Omote-sandō is a regal boulevard lined with trees and upscale fashion houses. Many designer boutiques come in designer buildings, and Omote-sandō is one of the best places in the city to see contemporary architecture. See p164 for our walking tour. (表参道; Ginza Line to Omote-sandō)

Yoyogi-kōen PARK

5 Map p92, A3

If it's a warm weekend afternoon you can count on a crowd around the grassy expanse of Yoyogi-kōen; revellers and noisemakers of all stripes, from hula-hoopers to African drum circles to a group of retro greasers dancing around a boom box. (代々木公園; JR Yamanote Line to Harajuku, Omote-sandō exit)

Watari Museum of Contemporary Art (Watari-Um) MUSEUM

6 Map p92, C3

Progressive and often provocative, this museum was built in 1990 to a design by Swiss architect Mario Botta. Exhibits range from retrospectives of established art-world figures (such as Yayoi Kusama and Nam June Paik) to graffiti and landscape artists. Some exhibitions spill onto the surrounding streets. (ワタリウム美術館; ☎3402-3001; www.watarium.co.jp; 3-7-6 Jingūmae, Shibuya-ku; adult/student ¥1000/800; ⏰11am-7pm Tue & Thu-Sun, to 9pm Wed; Ginza Line to Gaienmae, exit 3)

Take a Break Artsy **On Sundays Cafe** (coffee ¥500; ⏱11am-8pm) is inside the gift shop.

Design Festa

ART GALLERY

7 ◎ Map p92, C3

Design Festa has been a leader in Tokyo's fringe art scene for more than a decade. The building itself is worth a visit – inside are a dozen small galleries rented out by artists, who are usually hanging out nearby. (デザインフェスタ; ☎3479-1442; www.designfesta-gallery.com; 3-20-2 Jingūmae, Shibuya-ku; admission free; ⏱11am-7pm; 🚉JR Yamanote Line to Harajuku, Takeshita exit)

Take a Break Funky *okonomiyaki* (pancake) restaurant **Sakura-tei** (p98) is just out back.

Laforet Museum Harajuku

MUSEUM

8 ◎ Map p92, B3

After browsing the art-as-streetwear on the floors of Laforet department store below, check out art-as-art upstairs. Small film festivals, art installations and launch parties are held here regularly. (ラフォーレミュジアム原宿; ☎3475-3127; www.lapnet.jp/index.html; 6th fl, Laforet Bldg, 1-11-6 Jingūmae, Shibuya-ku; admission free; ⏱11am-8pm; 🚉JR Yamanote line to Harajuku, Omote-sandō exit)

Spiral Building

ARCHITECTURE

9 ◎ Map p92, C5

Its asymmetrical, geometric shape may not look sinuous from the outside, but the Spiral Building's name will make sense on entry. Inside, the 1st-floor gallery holds changing exhibitions and the 2nd-floor shop has homewares, jewellery and other stylishly designed loot. (スパイラルビル; ☎3498-1171; www.spiral.co.jp; 5-6-23 Minami-Aoyama, Minato-ku; admission free; ⏱11am-8pm; 🚉Ginza Omote-sandō, exit B1)

Shimizu-yu

BATHHOUSE

10 ◎ Map p92, D4

Not all *sentō* (public bathhouses) are historical relics – Shimizu-yu has ultra-modern, white-tile tubs, jet baths and a sauna. Its location means the baths are routinely filled with young shoppers, perhaps transitioning to a night out, in addition to the local grandmas. (清水湯; ☎3401-4404; http://shimizuyu.jp/; 3-12-3 Minami-Aoyama, Minato-ku; admission ¥450; ⏱noon-midnight Mon-Thu, to 11pm Sat & Sun; 🚉Ginza Line to Omote-sandō, exit A4)

Eating

Harajuku Gyōza Rō

GYŌZA $

11 🍴 Map p92, B4

Gyōza (dumplings) are the only thing on the menu, but there are no complaints from the regulars queuing for their fix. Have them *sui* (boiled) or *yaki* (pan-fried), with or without *niniku* (garlic) or *nira* (chives) – they're delicious. Expect to wait on weekends. (原宿餃子楼; 6-4-2 Jingūmae, Shibuya-ku; 6 gyōza ¥290; ⏱11.30am-4.30am; 🚉JR Yamanote Line to Harajuku, Omote-sandō exit; 📖)

Understand
Religion Today

Stroll down Omote-sandō – originally designed as the official approach to Meiji-jingū – and it would seem that Tokyoites have anointed consumption their new religion. The reality is more nuanced: more than three million people visited Meiji-jingū during the first three days of 2013 to ring in the new year in the traditional way.

Rites of Passage

While religion plays little part in the daily lives of most Tokyoites, rites of passage are marked, as for centuries, with a visit to either a shrine or a temple. Japan's two religious institutions – its native Shintō, an animist belief system that sees godliness in trees, rocks and animals, and Buddhism, which arrived via China in the 7th century – have long co-existed.

Generally, Shintō concerns itself with this life: births and marriage, for example, are celebrated at shrines. So is **Shichi-go-san** (七五三; ☺mid-Nov), a ceremony to protect girls aged seven (*shichi*) and three (*san*) and boys aged five (*go*), and **Coming-of-Age Day** (成人の日; Seijin-no-Hi; ☺20 Jan), the collective birthday for all who turned 20 (the age of majority) the previous year. Visit a shrine then and you'll see children and adults dressed in elaborate kimono. Meanwhile, Buddhism deals with the afterlife: funerals and memorial rites take place at temples.

Annual Observances

Ganjitsu, or New Year's Day, is the most auspicious day of the Japanese calendar. Just after midnight on 1 January, crowds begin amassing at temples, where bells are rung 108 times to cast off the worldly desires of the previous year, and at shrines, where people pray for health, happiness and prosperity.

Another important annual event is **O-bon**: three days in mid-August to honour the dead, when their spirits are said to return to the earth. Many Tokyoites return to their hometowns to sweep the graves of their ancestors and to participate in *bon-odori* (folk dances). **Yasukuni-jinja** (靖国神社; ✆3261-8326; www.yasukuni.or.jp; 3-1-1 Kudan-kita, Chiyoda-ku; ®Hanzōmon Line to Kudanshita, exit 1) celebrates O-bon with 30,000 paper lanterns during the **Mitama Matsuri** (みたままつり; Lantern Festival).

Maisen
TONKATSU **$**

12 🍴 Map p92, C4

You could order something else, but almost everyone is here for the *tonkatsu* (deep-fried pork cutlets). Price is determined by grade of meat: you can splurge on the prized *kurobuta* (black pig), but even the cheapest is melt-in-your-mouth divine. The restaurant is in an old public bathhouse. A takeaway window serves delicious *tonkatsu sando* (sandwiches). (まい泉; http://mai-sen.com; 4-8-5 Jingūmae, Shibuya-ku; lunch/dinner from ¥995/1680; ☉11am-10pm; 🚇Ginza Line to Omote-sandō, exit A2; 🍴🅿)

246 Common
STREET FOOD **$**

13 🍴 Map p92, D4

246 Common looks like a fairground plunked into a vacant lot in Aoyama. A ragtag collection of vendors – housed in freight containers, shacks, campers and tents – offer up treats such as baked goods, noodles, *takoyaki* (octopus dumplings) and ice cream. Seating is on picnic tables. (http://246common.jp/; 3-13 Kita-Aoyama, Minato-ku; varies; ☉11am-10pm; 🚇Ginza Line to Omote-sandō, exit A4; 🍴)

A to Z Cafe
CAFE **$**

14 🍴 Map p92, C5

Artist Yoshitomo Nara teamed up with design firm Graf to create this spacious and only slightly off-kilter cafe. Along with wooden schoolhouse chairs, whitewashed walls and a small cottage, you can find a few scattered examples

of Nara's work. The Japanese-style diner food – think fried chicken with *yuzu* (citrus) sauce – is delicious, too. (http://atozcafe.exblog.jp; 5th fl, 5-8-3 Minami-Aoyama, Minato-ku; mains ¥500-1500; ☉noon-11.30pm; 🚇Ginza Line to Omote-sandō, exit B3; 🅿)

Marukaku
JAPANESE **$**

15 🍴 Map p92, B4

The lunchtime *sakana teishoku* (fish set meal) has a loyal following; it's fresh, filling and a steal – especially considering the location on top of Chanel. Options change daily, depending on what's in season. The dinner menu expands to include sashimi, small dishes and skewers of grilled meat and vegetables. Look for the white *noren* (curtains). (丸角; 4th fl, Gyre Bldg, 5-10-1 Jingūmae, Shibuya-ku; lunch set ¥900, small dishes ¥380-700; ☉11.30am-11pm; 🚇JR Yamanote Line to Harajuku, Omote-sandō exit; 🅿)

Mominoki House
ORGANIC **$$**

16 🍴 Map p92, C3

Boho Tokyoites have been coming here for tasty and nourishing macrobiotic fare since 1976. The casual, cosy dining room has seen some famous visitors too, like Paul McCartney. Chef Yamada's menu is heavily vegetarian, but also includes free-range chicken and *Ezo shika* (Hokkaidō venison; ¥4800). (もみの木ハウス; http://omotesando.mominokihouse.net; 2-18-5 Jingūmae, Shibuya-ku; lunch/dinner set from ¥800/3200; ☉11.30am-10pm; 🚇JR Yamanote Line to Harajuku, Takeshita exit; 🍴🖊🅿)

RACHEL LEWIS / GETTY IMAGES ©

Takeshita-dōri (p93)

Sakura-tei

OKONOMIYAKI $

Grill your own *okonomiyaki* (savoury pancakes) at this funky place inside the gallery Design Festa (see 7 Map p92, C3). During lunch (11am–3pm) you can get 90 minutes of all-you-can-eat plus a drink for just ¥1060. *Okonomiyaki* is usually stuffed with meat or shellfish, but Sakura-tei caters well to vegetarians. (さくら亭; ☎3479-0039; www.sakuratei.co.jp; 3-20-1 Jingūmae, Shibuya-ku; okonomiyaki ¥950-1350; ☺11am-11pm; ☒JR Yamanote Line to Harajuku, Takeshita exit; ☝☷)

Pariya

INTERNATIONAL $

17 ☒ Map p92, C5

Pariya is a favourite lunchtime spot for the local fashion crowd. Food is served cafeteria-style here: grab a tray and choose a main, salad and side dish. It's not cheap slop though; typical dishes include avocado and *hijiki* (seaweed) with sesame dressing and curried potato salad with chorizo and egg. (パリヤ; 3-12-14 Kita-Aoyama, Minato-ku; meals from ¥1000; ☺11.30am-11pm; ☒Ginza Line to Omote-sandō, exit B2; ☝☷)

Kinokuniya

SUPERMARKET $

18 ☒ Map p92, C4

Kinokuniya carries expat lifesavers such as Marmite and peanut butter, Belgian chocolate, wholegrain bread and cheeses galore, along with flawless produce. (紀ノ国屋; ☎3409 1231; www.super-kinokuniya.jp; Basement fl, AO Bldg, 3-11-7 Kita-Aoyama, Minato-ku; ☺9.30am-9pm; ☒Chiyoda, Ginza, Hanzōmon lines to Omote-sandō, exit B2)

Agaru Sagaru Nishi Iru Higashi Iru
KAISEKI $$

19 Map p92, B3

The young, unpretentious chefs here serve up a procession of artful dishes that are Kyoto-inspired but tweaked for Tokyoites' been-there-done-that tastes. The restaurant looks like a cave – even from the street. There's only a counter and a few tables, so call ahead on weekends. Sitting at the counter is more fun. (上ル下ル西入ル東入ル; ☑3403-6968; www.agaru-sagaru.com; Basement fl, 3-25-8 Jingūmae, Shibuya-ku; set menu ¥3990; ⊙5.30-10pm Mon-Sat; ◉JR Yamanote Line to Harajuku, Takeshita exit)

Drinking

Two Rooms
BAR

20 Map p92, C5

With its sleek contemporary design, this restaurant and bar, popular with expats, could be anywhere – save for the sweeping view towards the Shinjuku skyline from the terrace. Expect a crowd dressed like they don't care that wine by the glass starts at ¥1400. You can eat here too, but the real scene is at night by the bar. (トゥールームス; ☑3498-0002; www.tworooms.jp; 5th fl, AO Bldg, 3-11-7 Kita-Aoyama, Minato-ku; ⊙11.30am-2am Mon-Sat, to 10pm Sun; ◉Ginza Line to Omote-sandō, exit B2; 🖭)

Harajuku Taproom
PUB

21 Map p92, B3

Come here to sample over a dozen different beers on tap from respected local craft brewer Baird's Brewery. That this bar, off teeny-bopper Takeshita-dōri, is crowded nightly with grown-ups is testament to Baird's popularity. Take a left after Cafe Solare; the bar is at the end of the lane on the right. (原宿タップルーム; http://bairdbeer.com/en/taproom; 2nd fl, 1-20-13 Jingūmae, Shibuya-ku; ⊙5pm-midnight Mon-Fri, noon-midnight Sat & Sun; ◉JR Yamanote Line to Harajuku, Takeshita exit; ⊝🖭)

Omotesando Koffee
CAFE

22 Map p92, C4

Tokyo's most *oshare* (stylish) coffee stand is a minimalist cube set up inside an old traditional house. Be prepared to circle the block trying to find it, but know that an immaculate macchiato and a seat in the garden await you. (http://ooo-koffee.com; 4-15-3 Jingūmae, Shibuya-ku; espresso ¥250; ⊙10am-7pm; ◉Ginza Line to Omotesandō, exit A2; 🖭)

Montoak
CAFE, BAR

23 Map p92, B4

This smoky cube is a calm, dimly lit retreat from the busy streets. It's perfect for holing up with tea or a carafe of wine and watching the crowds go by. Or, if the weather is nice, go for a seat on the terrace. (モントーク; 6-1-9 Jingūmae, Shibuya-ku; ⊙11am-3am; ◉JR Yamanote Line to Harajuku, Omote-sandō exit; ⊝🖭)

Local Life
Yoyogi-kōen Festivals
On most weekends during summer, the plaza across the street from **Yoyogi-kōen** (p94) hosts festivals for Tokyo's ethnic communities with food vendors and live music. Flea markets are also held here from time to time year-round.

Toraya Cafe

TEAHOUSE

24 Map p92, B4

Nevermind the 'cafe' in the name, Toraya excels at tea – Chinese varieties and classic *sencha* (green leaf tea) – which go perfectly with the Japanese sweets served here. (トラヤカフェ; Basement fl, Omotesandō Hills, 4-12-10 Jingūmae, Shibuya-ku; tea from ¥525; ⏰11am-11pm, to 10pm Sun; 🚇Ginza Line to Omotesandō, exit A2; ☺🍴)

Las Chicas

BAR, CAFE

25 Map p92, B5

Urbane and relaxed, Las Chicas draws an international crowd with its inviting terrace. It's popular day and night, with occasional evening events such as swing dance workshops and masquerade parties in the basement lounge. (ラスチカス; ☎3407 6865; www.vision.co.jp; 5-47-6 Jingūmae, Shibuya-ku; cocktails from ¥900; ⏰11.30am-11pm, to 11.30pm Fri & Sat; 🚇Ginza Line to Omotesandō, exit B2; ☺🍷🍴♿)

Le Baron

CLUB

26 Map p92, D4

A swank import from Paris, Le Baron is Tokyo's latest it venue for the partying jet set. It's at the end of an alley, right before the Poplar convenience store. (www.lebaron.jp; 3-8-40 Minami-Aoyama, Minato-ku; admission ¥3000-4000; ⏰Wed-Sun; 🚇Ginza Line to Omotesandō, exit A4)

Anniversaire Café

CAFE

27 Map p92, C4

Anniversaire is an Omote-sandō landmark – look for the red awnings on the left side of the street. Grab a patio seat for some the city's best people-watching, and don't pass up a slice of cake. (アニヴェルセルカフェ; ☎5411-5988; http://giftcafe.anniversaire.co.jp/about_cafe.php; 3-5-30 Kita-Aoyama, Minato-ku; ⏰10am-11.30pm; 🚇Ginza Line to Omote-sandō, exit A2; 🍴)

Entertainment

Jingū Baseball Stadium

BASEBALL

28 ⭐ Map p92, D2

Home to the Yakult Swallows, Tokyo's number two team, Jingū Baseball Stadium was originally built in 1926. You can buy tickets from the booth in front of the stadium; same-day outfield tickets (¥1500) are available at the booth by gate 17. Night games start at 6pm; on Saturdays and Sundays games start from 2pm.

(神宮球場; Jingū Kyūjō; ☎3404-8999; www.jingu-stadium.com; 3-1 Kasumigaoka, Shinjuku-ku; tickets adult/child from ¥1500/500; ⊠Ginza Line to Gaienmae, north exit)

National Nō Theatre
TRADITIONAL THEATRE

29 ⭐ Map p92, C1

This theatre stages the traditional music, poetry and dances that *nō* (stylised Japanese dance-drama) is famous for, as well as the interludes of *kyōgen* (short, lively comic farces) as comic relief. Each seat has a small screen that can display an English translation of the dialogue. Tickets go fast, so you'll want to book well in advance. (国立能楽堂; Kokuritsu Nō-gakudō; ☎3423-1331; www.ntj.jac.go.jp/english; 4-18-1 Sendagaya, Shibuya-ku; tickets from ¥2600; ⊠JR Sōbu Line to Sendagaya)

Blue Note Tokyo
JAZZ

30 ⭐ Map p92, D5

The serious cognoscenti roll up to this, Tokyo's prime jazz spot in Aoyama, to take in the likes of Maceo Parker, Herbie Hancock and Doctor John. Like its sister acts in New York and Milan, the digs here are classily decorated with dark wood and deep velvet, making this the perfect spot for a slow night of cool sounds. (ブルーノート東京; www.bluenote.co.jp; 6-3-16 Minami-Aoyama, Minato-ku; admission ¥6000-15,000; ⏱5.30pm-1am Mon-Sat, 5pm-12.30am Sun; ⊠Ginza Line to Omote-sandō, exit B3)

Crocodile
LIVE MUSIC, COMEDY

31 ⭐ Map p92, A4

This casual, if not slightly grungy, subterranean venue hosts all sorts of music acts as well as a popular English comedy night, with stand-up, sketch and improv from the Tokyo Comedy Store on the last Friday of the month. (クロコダイル; www.crocodile-live.jp; 6-18-8 Jingūmae, Basement fl, Shibuya-ku; ⊠Chiyoda Line to Meiji-jingūmae, exit 1)

Shopping

Takeshita-dōri
VARIETY

This teaming alley (see **1** ◎ Map p92, B3) is where aspiring goths, Lolitas and punks come to shop, and you'll spot some pretty wild wears. Even if you're not in the market for a dress inspired by the Victorian-era, there is still plenty to pull out your wallet for here, such as funky tights and mobile-phone charms. (竹下通り; ⊠JR Yamanote Line to Harajuku, Takeshita exit)

KiddyLand
CHILDREN

32 🔒 Map p92, B4

This multistorey toy emporium is packed to the rafters with character goods, from Hello Kitty to Studio Ghibli. It's not just for kids either; you'll spot plenty of teens and adults indulging their love of *kawaii* (cute). (キデイランド; www.kiddyland.co.jp/en/index.html; 6-1-9 Jingūmae, Shibuya-ku; ⏱10am-9pm; ⊠JR Yamanote Line to Harajuku, Omote-sandō exit)

Laforet
FASHION

Laforet (see **8** 🔒 Map p92, B3) has been a beacon of cutting-edge Harajuku style for decades. It's been looking a little mainstream lately (see Topshop on the ground floor) but you can still find plenty inside here to turn your head. And guys: don't let the gaggle of girls put you off, there's stuff for you too. (ラフォーレ; www.laforet.ne.jp; 1-11-6 Jingūmae, Shibuya-ku; ⏰11am-8pm; 🚇JR Yamanote Line to Harajuku, Omote-sandō exit)

🔍 Local Life

Ura-Hara

Ura-Hara (literally 'behind Harajuku') is the nickname for the maze of backstreets behind Omotesandō. You'll find the eccentric shops and secondhand stores from which Harajuku hipsters cobble together their head-turning looks. Club kids and stylists love the showpiece items at **Dog** (ドッグ; Map p92, B3; www.dog-hjk.com/index.html; Basement fl, 3-23-3 Jingūmae, Shibuya-ku; ⏰noon-8pm; 🚇JR Yamanote Line to Harajuku, Takeshita exit), which stocks bold and brash vintage and remake items. Followers of *fairy-kei* – a light and fluffy '80s throwback look – stock up on candy-coloured accessories at **6% Doki Doki** (ロクパーセントドキドキ; Map p92, B3; www.dokidoki6.com; 2nd fl, 4-28-16 Jingūmae, Shibuya-ku; ⏰noon-8pm; 🚇JR Yamanote Line to Harajuku, Omote-sandō exit).

Pass the Baton
VINTAGE

33 🔒 Map p92, B4

This concept store bills itself as a 'curated' consignment shop. From personal castaways to dead stock from long defunct retailers, everything here comes tagged with a profile of its previous owner. It's in the basement of the Omotesandō Hills West Wing, but you enter from a separate street entrance on Omote-sandō. (パスザバトン; www.pass-the-baton.com; 4-12-10 Jingūmae, Shibuya-ku; ⏰11am-9pm Mon-Sat, to 8pm Sun; 🚇Ginza Line to Omote-sandō, exit A3)

Comme des Garçons
FASHION

34 🔒 Map p92, D4

Designer Kawakubo Rei threw a wrench in the fashion machine in the early '80s with her dark, austere designs. That her work doesn't appear as shocking today as it once did speaks volumes for her far-reaching success. This eccentric, vaguely disorienting architectural creation is her brand's flagship store. (コム・デ・ギャルソン; www.comme-des-garcons.com; 5-2-1 Minami-Aoyama, Minato-ku; ⏰11am-8pm; 🚇Ginza Line to Omote-sandō, exit A5)

On Sundays
BOOKSHOP

Attached to the Watari-Um (see **6** 🔘 Map p92, C3), this is one of Tokyo's best bookshops, with an eclectic collection of avant-garde art catalogues, retro postcards, ultra-mod office accoutrements and colourful coffee-table books. (www.watarium.co.jp; 3-7-6 Jingūmae,

Shibuya-ku; ⏱11am-8pm; 🚃Ginza Line to Gaienmae, exit 3)

Sou-Sou
FASHION

35 🔒 Map p92, D5

Details matter to Japanese fashionistas – socks included. *Tabi* (split-toe socks) are sold all over Tokyo in endless patterns and colours, but Sou-Sou sells high-quality ones in fashionable designs. It also produces some serious footwear, such as the steel-toed, rubber-soled *tabi* worn by Japanese construction workers. (そうそう; ☎3407 7877; 5-3-10 Minami-Aoyama, Minato-ku; ⏱11am-8pm; 🚃Chiyoda, Ginza, Hanzōmon lines to Omote-sandō, exit A5)

Oriental Bazaar
SOUVENIRS

36 🔒 Map p92, B4

Stocking a wide selection of souvenirs at very reasonable prices, Oriental Bazaar is an easy one-stop destination. Items found here include fans, pottery, *yukata* (light summer kimono) and T-shirts, some made in Japan, some not (check the labels). (オリエンタルバザー; www.orientalbazaar.co.jp; 5-9-13 Jingūmae, Shibuya-ku; ⏱10am-6pm Mon-Wed & Fri, to 7pm Sat & Sun; 🚃JR Yamanote Line to Harajuku, Omote-sandō exit)

Chicago Thrift Store
VINTAGE

37 🔒 Map p92, B3

Stuffed to the rafters with funky hats, ties and coats, Chicago is a treasure trove of vintage clothing. Don't miss

Aoyama District

the collection of used kimono and *yukata* in the back corner. (シカゴ; 6-31-21 Jingūmae, Shibuya-ku; ⏱10am-8pm; 🚃JR Yamanote Line to Harajuku, Omote-sandō exit)

Condomania
SPECIALITY SHOP

38 🔒 Map p92, B4

This irreverent outpost may be Tokyo's cheekiest rendezvous point. Popular items include *omamori* (traditional good-luck charms) with condoms tucked inside. (コンドマニア; 6-30-1 Jingūmae, Shibuya-ku; ⏱11am-9.30pm; 🚃JR Yamanote Line to Harajuku, Omote-sandō exit)

ALLAN BAXTER / GETTY IMAGES ©

Explore

Shinjuku

Here in Shinjuku, much of what makes Tokyo tick is crammed into one busy district: upscale department stores, anachronistic shanty bars, buttoned-up government offices, swarming crowds, streetside video screens, leafy parks, racy nightlife, hidden shrines and soaring skyscrapers. It's a fantastic introduction to Tokyo today, with all its highs and lows.

The Sights in a Day

The morning – usually the clearest time of day – is the best time to visit the **Tokyo Metropolitan Government Offices** (p109), for breathtaking views over the city from the 45th-floor observatory. Back on the ground, wind your way through the skyscraper district of **Nishi-Shinjuku** (p109). Then head over to **Isetan** (p115), one of the city's finest department stores. Pick up a *bentō* (boxed meal) from the *depachika* (department store basement food hall) for lunch.

Walk to **Shinjuku-gyoen** (p109) for a picnic on the lawn and spend a relaxing hour strolling through the park. Then return to the hustle and bustle for a bit of shopping – in Shinjuku you can get just about anything, including music, electronics and fashion.

Shinjuku is famous for its nightlife. Have dinner at **Donjaka** (p112), a classic *izakaya* (Japanese style pub) with an excellent *ji-zake* (microbrewed sake) list. Depending on whether your tastes run high-brow or low, you can catch a jazz concert at **Shinjuku Pit Inn** (p114) or a cabaret spectacle at **Robot Restaurant** (p115). For a nightcap, visit **Zoetrope** (p113) – the best whiskey bar in the country.

For a local's day in Shinjuku, see p106.

 Local Life

East Shinjuku at Night

 Best of Tokyo

Architecture
Tokyo Metropolitan Government Offices (p109)

Parks & Gardens
Shinjuku-gyoen (p109)

Food
Nagi (p107)

Donjaka (p112)

Nightlife & Live Music
Zoetrope (p113)

Golden Gai (p107)

Gay & Lesbian
Advocates Cafe (p113)

Getting There

🚆 **Train** The JR Yamanote and Chūō-Sōbu Lines stop at Shinjuku Station.

Ⓢ **Subway** The Marunouchi, Shinjuku and Ōedo Lines run through Shinjuku. The Marunouchi, Fukutoshin and Shinjuku Lines stop at Shinjuku-sanchōme, convenient for east Shinjuku. The Ōedo Line stops at Tochōmae.

Local Life
East Shinjuku at Night

East Shinjuku is Tokyo's largest – and liveliest – nightlife district. The size and depth means there is truly something for everyone, from flashy cabarets to bohemian hole-in-the-walls, neon-lit karaoke parlours to bars for every fetish under the sun. Come dark, a motley cast of characters hits the town to shed the day's anxieties and to let loose.

❶ Take the east exit

On a Friday or Saturday night, the world's busiest train station is particularly busy – and just about everyone is heading to the east exit for Shinjuku's infamous nightlife. From the east exit, follow the station signs for Kabukichō. When you emerge, you should see the glowing screen of Studio Alta, Shinjuku's de facto meeting spot.

❷ Bask in the lights of Yasukuni-dōri

This is East Shinjuku's main drag, where *izakaya* (Japanese-style pubs) are stacked several stories high, along with karaoke joints, all-night noodle shops, convenience stores and acres of neon. Touts for bars and restaurants stalk the sidewalks, waving menus and handing out coupons, the cries of: *Izakaya ikaga desu ka*? ('How about an izakaya?') rising above the din.

❸ Tiptoe through Kabukichō

North of Yasukuni-dōri is the neighbourhood of Kabukichō, Tokyo's most notorious red-light district. The entrance is marked by a red electric *torii* (gate). Here, it's wall-to-wall hostess (and host!) clubs – bars where pretty people are employed to heap compliments and expensive drinks on customers – cabarets and love hotels. It's generally safe to walk through, though we don't recommend going alone (or going inside anywhere).

❹ Take a swing at Oslo Batting Centre

An odd oasis of wholesome fun, **Oslo Batting Center** (オスローバッティングセンター; www.oslo.ecweb.jp; 2nd fl, Oslo Bldg, 2-34-5 Kabukichō, Shinjuku-ku; ☺10am-1am; ☒JR Yamanote Line to Shinjuku, east exit) offers another way to blow off steam in Kabukichō. It's ¥300 for 20 pitches if you feel like taking a swing. There's an arcade on the ground floor.

❺ Rummage through Don Quijote

Back on Yasukuni-dōri, you can't miss the fluorescent-lit bargain castle that is **Don Quijote** (ドン・キホーテ; ☎5291-9211; www.donki.com; 1-16-5 Kabukichō, Shinjuku-ku; ☺24hr; ☒JR Yamanote line to Shinjuku, east exit). It's filled to the brink with weird loot. Though it's now a national chain, it started as a rare (at the time) 24-hour store for the city's night workers.

❻ Raise a glass in Golden Gai

This is Tokyo's most ambient cluster of watering halls, a colony of narrow two-storey wooden buildings that was a black market in the post-WWII years. Each closet-sized bar is as unique and eccentric as the 'master' or 'mama' who runs it. While many give tourists the cold shoulder, **Araku** (亜楽; http://www.facebook.com/bar.araku; 2nd fl, G2-dōri, 1-1-9 Kabukichō, Shinjuku-ku; cover charge ¥500; ☺8pm-5am Mon-Sat; ☒JR Yamanote Line to Shinjuku, east exit) is a friendly place with a groovy interior.

❼ Go for late night rāmen

A late-night bowl of *rāmen* is a beloved Tokyo tradition. **Nagi** (凪; www.n-nagi.com; 2nd fl, Golden Gai G2, 1-1-10 Kabukichō, Shinjuku-ku; rāmen from ¥750; ☺11.30am-3pm & 6pm-5am Mon-Sat, to 2am Sun; ☒JR Yamanote Line to Shinjuku, east exit), in Golden Gai, serves highly-addictive noodles in a dark broth deeply flavoured with *niboshi* (dried sardines). Look for the red sign and the treacherous flight of stairs.

For reviews see

⊙	Sights	p109
⊗	Eating	p110
🍷	Drinking	p113
🎭	Entertainment	p114
🛍	Shopping	p115

KITA-SHINJUKU

SHINJUKU-KU

SHINJUKU-NICHŌME

NISHI-SHINJUKU

SHINJUKU

SENDAGAYA

YOYOGI

Shinjuku-gyoen (Shinjuku Park)

Ōme-kaidō

Kōen-dōri

Yasukuni-dōri

Gyoen-dōri

Meiji-dōri

Kōshū-kaidō

Kuyakusho-dōri

Bunka Senta-dōri

Kabukichō Ichibangai Central Rd

Shinjuku-dōri

Kita-dōri

Gijidō-dōri

Season Rd

One Day's St

Hanazono-jinja

Shinjuku-sanchōme

Shinjuku-sanchōme

Mode Cocoon Tower

Shinjuku Main Post Office

Tokyo Metropolitan Government Offices

Shinjuku NS Building

Keiō Plaza Hotel

Sumitomo Building

Century Hyatt Tokyo

Hilton Tokyo

Shinjuku Island Tower

Park Hyatt Tokyo

Tokyo Tourist Information Center

Shinjuku Chūō-kōen

Nishi-Shinjuku

Nishi-Shinjuku

Shinjuku-nishiguchi

Shinjuku

West Exit

East Exit

Central East Exit

New South Exit

Southeast Exit

Shinjuku Highway Bus Terminal

Shinjuku

Yoyogi

Minami-Shinjuku

0.2 miles

400 m

Sights

Tokyo Metropolitan Government Offices
BUILDING

1 Map p108, A3

Tokyo's seat of power is stunning and distinctive – an enormous grey granite complex designed by the city's master modern architect Tange Kenzō. Head to the 202m-high **observatories** on the 45th floors of the twin towers of Building 1 for city views, and on a clear day, a glimpse of Mt Fuji to the west. (東京都庁; Tokyo Tochō; www.metro.tokyo.jp/ENGLISH/TMG/observat.htm; 2-8-1 Nishi-Shinjuku, Shinjuku-ku; admission free; ☉observatories 9.30am-11pm; ⓡŌedo Line to Tochōmae, exit A4)

Shinjuku-gyoen
PARK

2 Map p108, E4

Though Shinjuku-gyoen was designed as an imperial retreat (completed 1906), it's now definitively a park for everyone. The wide lawns make it a favourite for urbanites needing an escape from the hurly-burly of city life. There's also an impressive **greenhouse** and **traditional teahouse**. In spring, Shinjuku-gyoen is a popular *hanami* (cherry-blossom viewing) spot. (新宿御苑; ☎3350-0151; www.env.go.jp/garden/shinjukugyoen; 11 Naito-chō, Shinjuku-ku; adult/6-15yr/under 6yr ¥200/50/free; ☉9am-4.30pm Tue-Sun; ⓡMarunouchi Line to Shinjuku-gyoenmae, exit 1)

Nishi-Shinjuku
NEIGHBOURHOOD

3 Map p108, A2

Nishi-Shinjuku (west Shinjuku) is the rare grid in a city where right angles are few and far between. Come to gawk at skyscrapers, such as the webbed Mode Cocoon Tower. There's also a smattering of public art, including Robert Indiana's *Love* sculpture and the two *Tokyo Brushstrokes* sculptures by Roy Liechtenstein. (西新宿; ⓡJR Yamanote Line to Shinjuku, west exit)

Humax
ARCADE

4 Map p108, C1

Primp for *purikura* (print club or photo stickers), bang away on the *taiko* (drum) game or try your luck with UFO-catchers at this huge and popular arcade. It's not just for school kids: salarymen skipping work can be found playing virtual horse-racing games in smoky corners. (ヒューマックス; 1-20-1 Kabukichō, Shinjuku-ku; ☉10am-11.45pm Sun-Thu, to 12.45am Fri & Sat; ⓡJR Yamanote Line to Shinjuku, east exit)

Hanazono-jinja
SHINTO SHRINE

5 Map p108, D1

During the day merchants from nearby Kabukichō come to this Shintō shrine to pray for the solvency of their business ventures. At night, despite signs asking revellers to refrain, drinking and merrymaking carries over from the nearby bars onto the stairs

Shinjuku-gyoen (p109)

here. (花園神社; 5-17 Shinjuku, Shinjuku-ku; ⏰24hr; 🚇Marunouchi Line to Shinjuku-sanchōme, exits B10 & E2)

Eating

Nakajima

KAISEKI $

6 Map p108, D2

In the evening, this Michelin-starred restaurant serves exquisite *kaiseki* (Japanese haute cuisine). On weekdays it does a set lunch of humble *iwashi* (sardines) for one-tenth the price. In the hands of Nakajima's chefs they're divine; get yours sashimi or *yanagawa nabe* (stewed with egg). The line for lunch starts to form shortly before the restaurant opens. Reservations are necessary for dinner. (中嶋; 📞3356-4534; www.shinjuku-nakajima.com; Basement fl, 3-32-5 Shinjuku, Shinjuku-ku; lunch/dinner from ¥800/8400; ⏰11.30am-2pm, 5.30pm-10pm Mon-Sat; 🚇Marunouchi Line to Shinjuku-sanchōme, exit A1; ✈)

Omoide-yokochō

YAKITORI $

7 Map p108, C2

Since the postwar days, smoke has been billowing night and day from the *yakitori* (skewered barbecue meat and vegetable) stalls that line this alley by the train tracks, literally translated as Memory Lane (and less politely known as Shonben-yokochō or Piss Alley). A few stalls have English menus. (思い出横丁; Nishi-Shinjuku 1-chōme, Shinjuku-ku; skewers from ¥100; ⏰noon-midnight, hours vary by shop; 🚇JR Yamanote Line to Shinjuku, west exit)

CHRISTOPHER GROENHOUT / GETTY IMAGES ©

Understand

Tokyo Today

Tokyo has reinvented itself countless times in the past hundred years: after being levelled during the Great Kantō Earthquake (1923) and again during the firebombing of WWII; following the bursting of the 1980s' economy bubble; and recently after the 2011 triple disaster of earthquake, tsunami and nuclear meltdown that sent the country reeling. Tokyoites are nothing if not pragmatic, carrying on and adapting to – even embracing – the new normal.

Recession Chic

After two decades of economic stagnation, Louis Vuitton is out and Uniqlo, Japan's ubiquitous budget clothing chain, is in. Tokyo may have earned more Michelin stars than any other city in history, but these days Tokyo foodies are more interested in parsing the minutiae of *rāmen*. Closet-sized *tachinomi-ya* (standing bars) and *tachi-gui* (standing restaurants) do away with seats to fit more customers into a small space – passing the savings on to customers – and proving to be incredibly popular.

After the Quake

The 2011 earthquake and its aftermath – particularly the Fukushima nuclear power plant meltdown – had Tokyoites shaken like nothing else in recent memory, although there was scant damage to the city itself. The future of nuclear power and food safety became hot topics, though with time radiation fears subsided significantly. In the months after the quake, Tokyoites invoked the age-old mantra of *ganbaru* (to do one's best) and donated time and money. Two years later, the city is much as it was, though efforts continue to make buildings as quake-resistant as possible.

Onwards & Upwards

As if anticipating the cycle of destruction and reconstruction, Tokyo is always building: In the past decade, Marunouchi has traded in its tired, almost Soviet-style structures for a host of shiny new skyscrapers. Roppongi buried its signature lowbrow nightlife in the shadow of several high-profile commercial and cultural complexes. Shibuya is the next neighbourhood in line for a makeover, a process that started with the opening of Shibuya Hikarie (p78) in 2012 and Tokyo Sky Tree (p144).

Top Tip

Navigating Shinjuku Station

Shinjuku Station is the world's busiest – three million people pass through daily. It's so big that the wrong exit can take you miles from where you want to be. Check the exit signs on the train platform and use the correct stairs – this will save you a lot of trouble above ground.

Shinjuku Asia-yokochō ASIAN $

 Map p108, C1

An indoor night market that spans the Asian continent, Asia-yokochō has vendors dishing out everything from Korean to Vietnamese to Indian. It's noisy, a bit chaotic and particularly fun in a group. The entrance is on a side street (across from a pub called The Hub); take the elevator to the roof. (新宿アジア横丁; 2nd Toa Hall Bldg roof, 1-21-1 Kabukichō, Shinjuku-ku; dishes from ¥480; ☉5pm-5am; 闿JR Yamanote Line to Shinjuku, east exit; 圎)

Donjaka IZAKAYA $$

 9 Map p108, D2

This is a fantastic *izakaya* with a vintage mid-20th century feel. There's no English menu, but it's cheap enough that you can go *omakase* (chef's choice) without fearing the bill. Or go for classics such as *sashimi moriawase* (mixed sashimi) and tempura. There's a tasting set of three varieties of microbrewed sake (ask for *kiki-sake-setto*). Reservations recommended. (呑者家; 2 3341-2497; 3-9-10 Shinjuku, Shinjuku-ku; dishes ¥315-840; ☉5pm-7am; 闿Marunouchi Line to Shinjuku-sanchōme, exit C6)

Tsunahachi TEMPURA $$

 10 Map p108, D2

Tsunahachi has been expertly frying prawns and seasonal vegetables for nearly 90 years. The sets are served in courses so each dish comes piping hot. Sit at the counter for the added pleasure of watching the chefs at work. Indigo *noren* (curtains) mark the entrance. (つな八; 2 3352-1012; www.tunahachi.co.jp; 3-31-8 Shinjuku, Shinjuku-ku; sets ¥1995-3990; ☉11am-10pm; 闿JR Yamanote Line to Shinjuku, east exit; 圎圎)

Chaya Macrobiotics ORGANIC $$

Inside Isetan department store (see 22 Map p108, D2) Chaya serves fusion of an unexpected sort: it's Japanese macrobiotics meets French. Think burdock croquettes, lily bud gratin and soy crème brûlée. (チャヤマクロビオ ティックス; 2 3357-0014; 7F, Isetan Bldg, 3-14-1 Shinjuku, Shinjuku-ku; lunch/dinner course from ¥2100/3675, mains from ¥1890; ☉11am-10pm; 闿Marunouchi Line to Shinjuku-sanchōme, exits B3, B4 & B5; 圎圎圎)

New York Grill STEAK HOUSE $$$

 11 Map p108, A4

Perched on the 52nd floor of the Park Hyatt, this a date spot of the highest order. The food is perfectly executed and the views are divine, but the prices are commensurately steep. Lunch is more reasonably priced: the set course includes an all-you-can-eat spread of entrees and desserts, plus a main dish. On weekends, a glass of sparkling wine is included (bringing the bill to ¥6600); book ahead. (ニューヨークグリル; 📞5322-1234; http://tokyo.park.hyatt.com; 52nd fl, 3-7-1-2 Nishi-Shinjuku; lunch/dinner course from ¥5200/11,000, mains from ¥4800; ⏰lunch & dinner; 🚇Ōedo Line to Tochōmae, exit A4)

Drinking

Zoetrope BAR

12 🍺 Map p108, C1

Attention whiskey drinkers: behind the small counter are more than 300 varieties of Japanese whiskey – more than you'll find anywhere else in the world, and some of them with international laurels. If you tell the barman what you like, he'll help narrow down some choices from the daunting menu. Don't worry: there are plenty of reasonably priced ones. (ゾートロープ; http://homepage2.nifty.com/zoetrope; 3rd fl, 7-10-14 Nishi-Shinjuku, Shinjuku-ku; ⏰7pm-4am Mon-Sat; 🚇JR Yamanote Line to Shinjuku, west exit)

Advocates Café BAR

13 🍺 Map p108, E2

Many a night out in Ni-chōme starts 'on the corner' at this tiny bar that

spills out to the street and turns into a block party during the warmer months. Everyone is welcome, and the staff speak English. (アドボケイツカフェ; http://advocates-cafe.com; 2-18-1 Shinjuku, Shinjuku-ku; ⏰6pm-4am, to 1am Sun; 🚇Marunouchi Line to Shinjuku-sanchōme, exit C8)

New York Bar BAR

You may not be lodging at the Park Hyatt, but you can still ascend to the 52nd floor to swoon over the sweeping nightscape. Live music plays nightly at this bar famed for its appearance in the movie *Lost in Translation*. There's a cover charge of ¥2200 after 8pm (7pm Sunday) and a dress code – no shorts or sandals. (See 11 ❌ Map p108, A4; ニューヨークバー; 📞5323-3458; http://tokyo.park.hyatt.com; 52nd fl, Park Hyatt, 3-7-1-2 Nishi-Shinjuku, Shinjuku-ku; ⏰5pm-midnight Sun-Wed, to 1am Thu-Sat; 🚇Ōedo Line to Tochōmae, exit A4)

Top Tip

Food Courts

Department stores usually have food courts on their top floors, as do the stores in Shinjuku Station. **Lumine** (ルミネ; ⏰11am-11pm) and **Mylord** (ミロード; ⏰11am-11pm) have the most reasonably priced options. It's an easy way to grab a meal without having to brave the crowds on the streets.

Arty Farty

CLUB

14 Map p108, D2

This bar for boys and gals has been the gateway to Tokyo's gay neighbourhood, Ni-chōme, for many a moon. It has a small dance floor that gets packed on Friday and Saturday nights. (アーティ ファーティ; www.arty-farty.net; 2nd fl, 2-11-7 Shinjuku, Shinjuku-ku; ⊙7pm-3am Mon-Thu, to 5am Fri & Sat, 5pm-3am Sun; ®Marunouchi Line to Shinjuku-sanchōme, exit C8)

Bar Goldfinger

BAR

15 Map p108, E2

A sleek little bar, with sociable counter seating, Bar Goldfinger is the most popular of the few ladies-only joints in Ni-chōme. Men are welcome on Fridays only. (http://goldfingerparty.com/bar/top; 2-12-11 Shinjuku, Shinjuku-ku; ⊙6pm-2am Sun, Mon, Wed & Thu, to 4am Fri & Sat; ®Marunouchi Line to Shinjuku-sanchōme, exit C8)

Pasela

KARAOKE

16 Map p108, D1

Pasela boasts decor that is a cut above the other yodelling parlours and has more songs than anywhere else. This Shinjuku outpost has a curious facade

✓ Top Tip

Picnic in the Park

The grassy lawns at **Shinjuku-gyoen** (p109) are perfect for a picnic. Pick up a *bentō* from the *depachika* at **Isetan** (p115) or a convenience store on the way.

meant to evoke a southeast Asian resort. (パセラ; www.pasela.co.jp/shop/shin-juku; 1-3-16 Kabuki-chō, Shinjuku-ku; per 30min before/after 6pm ¥200/400, Fri & Sat after 6pm ¥480; ⊙3pm-8am Mon-Fri, noon-8.30am Sat & Sun; ®JR Yamanote Line to Shinjuku, east exit)

Champion

BAR

17 Map p108, D1

At the entrance to Golden Gai (a neighbourhood of watering holes that was a black market in the post-WWII years), Champion isn't exactly representative of the district, but it's fun. There's no cover charge, drinks are just ¥500 a pop and the karaoke is loud – you can't miss it. (チャンピオン; G2-dōri, 1-1-10 Kabukichō, Shinjuku-ku; ⊙6pm-5am; ®JR Yamanote Line to Shinjuku, east exit)

Cocolo Cafe

CAFE

18 Map p108, E2

This Ni-chōme hub is a good place to take a break, grab a coffee or a light meal and to browse flyers for upcoming events happening within the gay and lesbian community. (コ コロカフェ; 2-14-6 Shinjuku, Shinjuku-ku; ⊙11am-5am Mon-Thu, to 7am Fri, 3pm-7am Sat, 3pm-4am Sun; ®Marunouchi Line to Shinjuku-sanchōme, exit C8; 🖥)

Entertainment

Shinjuku Pit Inn

JAZZ

19 Map p108, D2

This is not the kind of place where you come to talk over the music. Aficionados have been coming here for more than 40 years to listen to Japan's best jazz performers. Weekday matinees feature new artists and cost only ¥1300; the occasional all-night sessions are evocative of another era. (新宿ピットイン; 📞3354-2024; www.pit-inn.com; Basement fl, 2-12-4 Shinjuku, Shinjuku-ku; admission from ¥3000; ⏰matinee 2.30pm, evening show 7.30pm; 🚇Marunouchi Line to Shinjuku-sanchōme, exit C5)

Robot Restaurant   CABARET

20 ⭐ Map p108, C1

This Kabukichō spectacle is part girly show (though with no nudity) and part hilarity, the highlight being giant robots operated by bikini-clad women. There's enough neon and lights in the small theatre to light all of Shinjuku. Trust us, you'll know it when you see it. Reservations recommended, but not necessary. 'Dinner' is a teeny-tiny *bentō*. (ロボットレストラン; 📞3200-5500; www.robot-restaurant.com/top.html; 1-7-1 Kabukichō, Shinjuku-ku; tickets ¥4000; ⏰shows at 7pm, 8.30pm & 10pm; 🚇JR Yamanote Line to Shinjuku, east exit)

Loft   LIVE MUSIC

21 ⭐ Map p108, C1

The chequerboard stage here has hosted the feedback and reverb of many a Tokyo punk over the last 35 years. The music here is loud and usually good. (ロフト; www.loft-prj.co.jp; 1-12-9 Kabukichō, B2 fl; 🚇JR Yama-note Line to Shinjuku, east exit)

Tokyo Metropolitan Government Offices (p109)

Shopping

Isetan   DEPARTMENT STORE

22 🔒 Map p108, D2

Most department stores play to conservative tastes, but this one is an exception. The recently redone 3rd floor has some edgy womenswear, including collections from famous and not-yet-famous Japanese designers. Men get a building of their own (connected by a passageway). The basement food hall here is tops, too. (伊勢丹; www.isetan.co.jp; 3-14-1 Shinjuku, Shinjuku-ku; ⏰10am-8pm; 🚇Marunouchi Line to Shinjuku-sanchōme, exits B3, B4 & B5)

WINHORSE / GETTY IMAGES © ARCHITECT KENZO TANGE

Disk Union

MUSIC

23 Map p108, D2

Scruffy Disk Union is known by local audiophiles as Tokyo's best used CD and vinyl store. Eight storeys carry a variety of musical styles; if you still can't find what you're looking for there are other branches in Shinjuku that stock more obscure genres (pick up a map here). (ディスクユニオン; 3-31-4 Shinjuku, Shinjuku-ku; ⏰11am-9pm; ⓡJR Yamanote Line to Shinjuku, east exit)

ranKing ranQueen

VARIETY

24 Map p108, C2

If it's trendy, it's here. This clever shop stocks only the top-selling products in any given category, from eyeliner and soft drinks to leg-slimming massage rollers. Look for it just outside the ticket gates of the east exit at JR Shinjuku Station. It's a popular meeting spot and usually has a crowd out front. (ランキンランキン; Basement fl, Shinjuku Station, Shinjuku-ku; ⏰10am-11pm; ⓡJR Yamanote Line to Shinjuku, east exit)

Map Camera

ELECTRONICS

25 Map p108, B3

One of the most respected names in the local used camera trade, Map Camera has a huge selection of bodies, lenses and other camera accessories, with all major brands represented. Prices aren't exactly cheap (and there's no bargaining), but the merchandise is good quality and tourists can buy duty free. (マップカメラ; www.map-camera.com/html/worldguide/english_page.html; 1-12-5 Nishi-Shinjuku, Shinjuku-ku; ⏰10.30am-8.30pm; ⓡJR Yamanote Line to Shinjuku, west exit)

Understand
Karaoke
- -

Karaoke (カラオケ; pronounced kah-rah-oh-kay) isn't just about singing: it's an excuse to let loose, a bonding ritual, a reason to keep the party going past the last train and a way to kill time until the first one starts in the morning. When words fail, it's a way to express yourself – are you the type to sing the latest J-pop hit (dance moves included) or do you go in for an Okinawan folk ballad? It doesn't matter if you're a good singer or not (though the tone deaf might sign up for singing lessons – such is the important social function of karaoke), as long as you've got heart.

In Japan, karaoke is sung in a private room among friends. Admission is usually charged per person per half-hour. Food and drinks – ordered by phone – are brought to the room. To choose a song, use the touch screen device to search by artist or title; most have an English function and plenty of English songs to choose from. Then let your inner diva shine.

Marui One   DEPARTMENT STORE

26 Map p108, D2

You can't swing a coat hanger in Shinjuku without hitting a Marui department store as there are several here. Marui One is the most interesting, stocked with boutiques that appeal to Tokyo's fashion subcultures, from *goth-lolis* (Gothic Lolitas) to Harajuku-style hipsters. (マルイワン; 3-18-1 Shinjuku, Shinjuku-ku; ⏰11am-9pm; 🚇Marunouchi Line to Shinjuku-sanchōme, exit A1)

Bicqlo   CLOTHING, ELECTRONICS

27 🔒 Map p108, D2

This mash-up store brings two of Japan's favourite retailers together under one roof: electronics outfitter Bic Camera and budget clothing chain Uniqlo – so you can match your new camera to your hoodie. It's a bright white building. (ビックロ; 3-29-1 Shinjuku, Shinjuku-ku; ⏰10am-10pm; 🚇Marunouchi Line to Shinjuku-sanchōme, exit A5)

Sekaidō   ARTS & CRAFTS

28 🔒 Map p108, D2

An art-student institution, Sekaidō sells pigments, paints, brushes, paper and all the supplies you need to draw your own manga (Japanese comics). Look for the banner with the *Mona*

Top Tip

Coin Lockers

Store your purchases in a **coin locker** (¥300 for 24 hours) in the station before heading out for the night. Just don't forget where you've left them!

Lisa out front. (世界堂; 📞5379-1111; 3-1-1 Shinjuku, Shinjuku-ku; ⏰9.30am-9pm; 🚇Marunouchi Line to Shinjuku-sanchōme, exit C1)

Journal Standard   FASHION

29 Map p108, C3

Tokyoites love Journal Standard's city smart clothes with bohemian flair. Men on the ground floor, ladies on the 2nd, and there's a popular cafe on the 3rd. (ジャーナルスタンダード; 📞5367-0175; http://journal-standard.jp/; 4-1-7 Shinjuku, Shinjuku-ku; ⏰11am-8pm; 🚇JR Yamanote line to Shinjuku, south exit)

Kinokuniya   BOOKS

30 Map p108, C3

The 6th floor here has a broad selection of foreign-language books and magazines, including English-teaching texts. (紀伊國屋書店; www.kinokuniya.co.jp; Takashimaya Times Sq, 5-24-2 Sendagaya, Shibuya-ku; ⏰10am-8pm; 🚇JR Yamanote Line to Shinjuku, south exit)

Explore

Iidabashi & Around

Northwest of the Imperial Palace, Iidabashi is off the major tourist trail, yet has some fascinating sights, including the landscaped garden Koishikawa Kōrakuen and controversial shrine Yasukuni-jinja, plus history and art museums. Nearby Kagurazaka, an old geisha district, now resplendent with shops and cafes, is a wonderful place to wander. And baseball fans will not want to miss the spectacle at Tokyo Dome.

The Sights in a Day

☀ Take the train to Iidabashi and head to **Koishikawa Kōrakuen** (p121) to enjoy the early morning light though the leaves. Then stroll over to **Canal Café** (p123) for an al fresco lunch along the outer moat of the Imperial Palace.

☼ After lunch, head down to the shrine to Japan's war dead, **Yasukuni-jinja** (p121). If history is your thing, check out the **Yūshū-kan** (p122), a war museum with a particular view of history, or the **National Shōwa Memorial Museum** (p121), which depicts the life of ordinary Japanese during WWII. Otherwise, trace the rise of modern art in Japan at the excellent **National Museum of Modern Art** (p121). In the late afternoon, hop on the subway for **Kagurazaka** (p121) to see shadows lengthen along the neighbourhood's atmospheric cobblestone streets.

☾ For dinner, feast on traditional Japanese home-cooking and sake at **Kado** (p123). You could spend a pleasant evening in a cafe or bar here such as **Beer Bar Bitter** (p124). Or, if you're feeling ambitious, catch a baseball game at **Tokyo Dome** (p125) or a concert at the **Nippon Budōkan** (p125).

 Best of Tokyo

Temples & Shrines
Yasukuni-jinja (p121)

Tokyo Dai-jingū (p122)

Parks & Gardens
Koishikawa Kōrakuen (p121)

Galleries & Museums
National Museum of Modern Art (p121)

National Shōwa Memorial Museum (p121)

Crafts Gallery (p122)

Food
Kado (p123)

Spectator Sports
Tokyo Dome (p125)

Getting There

🚃 **Train** The JR Sōbu Line stops at Iidabashi. Rapid-service JR Chūō Line trains, which use the same track, skip Iidabashi but stop at Suidōbashi.

Ⓢ **Subway** The Tōzai Line is the most convenient, stopping at Kagurazaka, Iidabashi, Kudanshita and Takebashi. The Ōedo, Yūrakuchō and Namboku Lines also stop at Iidabashi; The Hanzōmon Line stops at Kudanshita and Jimbōcho.

Sights

Yasukuni-jinja

SHINTŌ SHRINE

1 ◉ Map p120, B3

Literally 'For the Peace of the Country Shrine', Yasukuni is the memorial to Japan's war dead of 2.5 million souls. It's a beautiful shrine, completed in 1869 and with *torii* (gates) made unusually out of steel and bronze. It is also incredibly controversial: in 1978 14 class-A war criminals were enshrined here. See p124 for more information. (靖国神社; ☎3261-8326; www.yasukuni.or.jp; 3-1-1 Kudan-kita, Chiyoda-ku; ⓡHanzōmon Line to Kudanshita, exit 1)

Koishikawa Kōrakuen

GARDEN

2 ◉ Map p120, C1

Established in the mid-17th century as the property of the Tokugawa clan, this 70,000 sq metre formal garden incorporates elements of Chinese and Japanese landscaping, although nowadays the *shakkei* (borrowed scenery) includes Tokyo Dome stadium. The garden is famed for plum trees in February, irises in June and autumn colours. Don't miss the Engetsu-kyō (Full-Moon Bridge), which dates from the early Edo period. (小石川後楽園; 1-6-6 Kōraku, Bunkyō-ku; adult/child ¥300/free; ⓣ9am-5pm; ⓡJR Sōbu Line to Iidabashi, exit C3)

Kagurazaka

NEIGHBOURHOOD

3 ◉ Map p120, B1

Kagurazaka is an old geisha quarter that's worth a visit more for an atmospheric stroll than for any particular sights. From Sotobori-dōri, head up Kagurazaka Hill, turn right at Royal Host restaurant, and wander the lanes. If you're very lucky, in the evening you might catch a glimpse of one of the few geisha who still work in the area. (神楽坂; ⓡJR Sōbu Line to Iidabashi, west exit)

National Shōwa Memorial Museum

MUSEUM

4 ◉ Map p120, C3

This museum of WWII-era Tokyo gives a sense of everyday life for the common people: how they ate, slept, dressed, studied, prepared for war and endured martial law, famine and loss of loved ones. An English audio guide (free) fills in a lot. On the 5th floor, media consoles show film footage shot during the war. (昭和館; Shōwa-kan; ☎3222-2577; www.showakan.go.jp; 1-6-1 Kudan-minami, Chiyoda-ku; adult/student/child ¥300/150/80; ⓣ10am-5.30pm; ⓡHanzōmon Line to Kudanshita, exit 4)

National Museum of Modern Art (MOMAT)

MUSEUM

5 ◉ Map p120, D4

Picking up from the Meiji period, this excellent museum traces the evolution of Japanese art following the introduction of Western-style techniques in the late 19th century through the grim, propaganda years of WWII to the mid-20th century, when Japanese artists embraced modernism and made it their own. (国立近代美術館;

Kokuritsu Kindai Bijutsukan; ☎5777-8600; www.momat.go.jp/english; 3-1 Kitanomaru-kōen, Chiyoda-ku; adult/student ¥420/130, extra for special exhibitions; ⏱10am-5pm Tue-Thu, Sat & Sun, to 8pm Fri; ℝTozai Line to Takebashi, exit 1B)

Tokyo Dai-jingū
SHINTŌ SHRINE

6 Map p120, C2

This is the Tokyo branch of Ise-jingū, Japan's mother shrine in Mie prefecture. It was established in 1880 to allow Tokyoites to worship the deities enshrined at Ise without having to leave the capital. Credited with establishing the Shintō wedding ritual, Tokyo Dai-jingū is also a popular pilgrimage site for young Tokyoites hoping to get hitched. (東京大神宮; ☎3262-3566; www.tokyodaijingu.or.jp/english; 2-4-1 Fujimi, Chiyoda-ku; ⏱6am-9pm; ℝJR Sōbu Line to Iidabashi, west exit)

Yūshū-kan
MUSEUM

7 ◉ Map p120, B3

This contentious war museum, on the ground of Yasukuni-jinja, begins with Japan's samurai tradition and ends with its imperialist aggressions in the first half of the 20th century. There are also some emotionally harrowing exhibits, such as the messages written by kamikaze pilots (and translated into English) to their families just before their final missions. (遊就館; ☎3261-8326; www.yasukuni.or.jp; 3-1-1 Kudankita , Chiyoda-ku; adult/student ¥800/500; ⏱9am-4pm; ℝHanzōmon Line to Kudanshita, exit 1)

Tokyo Dome City Attractions
AMUSEMENT PARK

8 ◉ Map p120, D1

Tokyo Dome is surrounded by the amusement park Tokyo Dome Attractions, which has rides mostly geared for little kids (ages 3 to 5). Anime fans should head to the Geopolis section, with its *Lupin*-themed labyrinth. Tickets are available for individual rides (¥400 to ¥800) with no additional admission charge. (東京ドームシティアトラクションズ; ☎5800-9999; www.tokyo-dome.co.jp/e; day pass adult/child ¥3800/2000, individual rides ¥400-800; ⏱10am-9pm; ℝJR Chūō Line to Suidōbashi, west exit; 👶)

Crafts Gallery
MUSEUM

9 ◉ Map p120, D4

This showcase for the works of contemporary artisans features ceramics, lacquer ware, wood carving, textiles etc from Japan's so-called living treasures. (東京国立近代美術館工芸館; Bijutsukan Kōgeikan; ☎5777-8600; www.momat.go.jp/english/craft/index.html; 1-1 Kitanomaru-kōen, Chiyoda-ku; adult/student ¥500/300; ⏱10am-5pm Tue-Sun; ℝTozai Line to Takebashi, exit 1b)

Eating

Le Bretagne
FRENCH $

10 Map p120, B2

This French-owned cafe, hidden on a cobblestone lane in Kagurazaka, is credited with starting the Japanese rage for crepes. Savoury buckwheat galettes are made with ham and cheese imported from France and farm fresh vegetables; the sweet ones – with the likes of caramelised butter, apple compote and ice cream – are divine. (ル ブルターニュ; ☎3235-3001; www.le-bretagne.com/e/top.html; 4-2 Kagurazaka, Shinjuku-ku; crepes ¥950-1680; ⏱11.30am-11.30pm Tue-Sat, to 9pm Sun; Ⓡ JR Sōbu Line to Iidabashi, west exit; 🖉📖)

Kururi
RĀMEN $

11 🍴 Map p120, A3

The lineup of *rāmen* fanatics outside this cramped, anonymous noodle shop proves its street cred among connoisseurs. The *miso-rāmen* (みそらぁめん) broth is swamp-thick, incredibly rich and absolutely delicious. There's no sign, so look for the lineup next to a liquor shop with a striped awning; buy a ticket inside from the machine and wait for perfection in a bowl. (麺処くるり; 3-2 Ichigaya-Tamachi, Shinjuku-ku; dishes ¥700-950; ⏱11am-9pm; Ⓡ JR Sōbu Line to Iidabashi, west exit)

Kado
TRADITIONAL $$

12 🍴 Map p120, A1

Set in a house built in 1950, Kado serves the best kind of *katei-ryōri* (home-style cooking) – perfectly executed with only the freshest, seasonal ingredients. Dinner is a set course that changes daily, but if you want to order a la carte (or just sample some sake), hop over to the counter bar on

GREG ELMS / GETTY IMAGES ©

Baseball, Tokyo Dome

the right. Reservations recommended for dinner. (カド; ☎3268-2410; http://kagurazaka-kado.com/; 1-32 Akagi-Motomachi, Shinjuku-ku; lunch sets ¥800-1000, dinner sets ¥3150; ⏱11.30am-2.30pm & 5-11pm; Ⓡ Tōzai Line to Kagurazaka, exit 1)

Canal Cafe
ITALIAN $$

13 🍴 Map p120, B2

Along the languid moat that forms the edge of Kitanomaru-kōen, this is one of Tokyo's best al fresco dining spots. The restaurant serves tasty wood-fired pizzas, seafood pastas and grilled meats, while over on the 'deck side' you can settle in with a sandwich, muffin or just a cup of coffee. (カナルカフェ; ☑3260-8068; 1-9 Kagurazaka, Shinjuku-ku; lunch set from ¥1600, dinner mains ¥1500-2800; ☉11.30am-11pm Tue-Sat, to 9.30pm Sun; ® JR Sōbu Line to Iidabashi, west exit;)

Lugdunum Bouchon Lyonnais
FRENCH $$

14 Map p120, A1

Bringing the proud culinary heritage of Lyon to the backstreets of Kagurazaka, this welcoming outpost of French fare does everything imaginable to transport the senses across continents. The emphasis here is on simple, back-to-nature recipes accompanied by one of the best wine lists in town. (☑6426-1201; www.lyondelyon.com; 4-3-7 Kagurazaka, Shinjuku-ku; lunch/dinner from ¥1850/3850; ☉11.30am-2.30pm & 6pm-10pm Tue-Sun; ® Kagurazaka, exit 1; 📖)

Drinking

Beer Bar Bitter
BAR

15 🚇 Map p120, B1

Stylish for a beer bar, this hideaway in Kagurazaka has Belgian beer on tap and a moody, industrial interior. Look for it above a bistro called Viande and take the stairs on the right. (ビアバービタ ー; ☑5261-3087; www.beerbar-bitter.com; 2nd fl, 1-14 Tsukudochō, Shinjuku-ku; ☉5pm-2am Sun-Fri; ® JR Sōbu Line to Iidabashi, west exit)

Mugi Maru 2
CAFE

16 🚇 Map p120, A1

Several fluffy felines call this Kagurazaka cafe home. Warm, squishy *manjū* (steamed buns) are the house speciality. Seating is on floor cushions. The cafe is inside a tangle of alleys just off Ōkubo-dōri – look for a sign with a cat out front. (ムギマル2; ☑5228-6393; www.

Understand
The Yasukuni Controversy

Yasukuni-jinja (p121) was erected by the Meiji government to honour those who died bringing about the Meiji Restoration. It has since become a shrine to all war casualties, including enlisted men, civilians and since 1978, 14 class-A war criminals, among them WWII general Hideki Tōjō. Following the separation of religion and state in 1946 enacted by the American occupation, the management of Yasukuni-jinja was transferred to a private religious organisation.

Leading politicians ocassionally visit the shrine to pay their respects, most often on the anniversary of the end of WWII. This angers Japan's Asian neighbours, who suffered greatly in Japan's wars of expansion of the 20th century. As a result, the decision by a sitting prime minister to visit the shrine or not is seen as a strong political statement, and is watched throughout East Asia. No emperor has visited Yasukuni-jinja since 1978.

mugimaru2.com; 5-20 Kagurazaka, Shinjuku-ku; coffee ¥520; steamed buns ¥140; ☺noon-9pm Thu-Tue; 🚇Tozai Line to Kagurazaka, exit 1)

Entertainment

Tokyo Dome
BASEBALL

17 Map p120, C1

The 'Big Egg' is home to Japan's favourite baseball team, the Yomiuri Giants. Tickets often sell out in advance; get them online at www.e-tix.jp/ticket_giants/en/ticket_pc_en.php. (東京ドーム; ☎5800-9999; www.tokyo-dome.co.jp/e/dome; 1-3-61 Kōraku, Bunkyō-ku; 🚇JR Chūō Line to Suidōbashi, west exit)

Nippon Budōkan
LIVE MUSIC, MARTIAL ARTS

18 Map p120, C3

This octagonal indoor arena was originally designed as the martial arts stadium for the 1964 Tokyo Olympics. After the Beatles performed here in 1966, it became the venue of choice for visiting and local musicians. Martial arts tournaments are held here ocassionally, too. (日本武道館; ☎3216-5100; http://nipponbudokan.web.fc2.com/; 2-3 Kitanomaru-kōen, Chiyoda-ku; 🚇Hanzōmon line to Kudanshita, exit 2; 📱)

Shopping

Baikatei
FOOD

19 Map p120, A1

See (and sample!) humble beans and rice whipped into pastel flowers at

---

Local Life
Book Town Jimbōchō

Jimbōchō is home to more than 100 second-hand bookshops, and it's a favourite destination for local bibliophiles. Worth a visit is **Ohya Shobō** (大屋書房; ☎3291-0062; www.ohya-shobo.com; 1-1 Kanda-Jimbōchō, Chiyoda-ku; ☺10am-6pm Mon-Sat; 🚇Hanzōmon Line to Jimbōchō, exit A7), a splendid, musty old bookshop that specialises in *ukiyo-e* (woodblock prints), vintage – as in Edo-era – *manga*, and antique maps. The staff are friendly and helpful.

---

this award-winning traditional sweets shop, in business since 1935. There are blue door curtains out front. (梅花亭; 6-15 Kagurazaka, Shinjuku-ku; ☺10am-8pm; 🚇Tōzai Line to Kagurazaka, exit 2)

La Ronde D'Argile
HOMEWARES

20 Map p120, A2

If it weren't for the chalkboard out front you'd walk right past this shop: it's on the first floor of an ordinary house. Inside, are changing displays of homewares made by local artisans. It's tricky to find – follow the curves in the road and keep your eyes peeled for the sign. (ラ・ロンダジル; ☎3260-6801; http://la-ronde.com/; 26 Fukuro-machi, Shinjuku-ku; ☺11.30am-6pm Tue-Sat; 🚇Ōedo Line to Ushigome-Kagurazaka, exit A2)

Local Life
An Afternoon in Akihabara

Getting There

🚃 The JR Yamanote and Sōbu Lines stop at Akihabara; Electric Town exit is the most convenient.

Ⓢ The Hibiya Line stops at Akihabara; take exit 3.

Akihabara ('Akiba' to friends) is the centre of Tokyo's *otaku* (geek) subculture. But you don't have to obsess about manga or anime to enjoy this quirky neighbourhood. It's equal parts sensory overload and cultural mind-bender. In fact, as the *otaku* subculture gains more and more influence on the culture at large, Akiba is drawing more visitors who don't fit the stereotype.

❶ Explore 'Electric Town'

Before Akihabara became *otaku*-land, it was Electric Town – the place for discounted electronics and where early computer geeks tracked down obscure parts for home-built machines. **Akihabara Radio Center** (秋葉原ラジオセンター; 1-14-2 Soto-Kanda, Chiyoda-ku; ⏲hours vary; 🚇JR Yamanote Line to Akihabara, Electric Town exit), a warren of stalls under the train tracks, keeps the tradition alive.

❷ Play vintage arcade games

In Akihabara a love of the new is tempered with a deep affection for the old. **Super Potato Retro-kan** (スーパーポテトレトロ館; 1-11-2 Soto-Kanda, Chiyoda-ku; ⏲11am-8pm Mon-Fri, from 10am Sat & Sun; 🚇JR Yamanote Line to Akihabara, Electric Town exit) is a retro video arcade where you can play on some old-school consoles.

❸ Eat at Marugo

Akiba is known for its *b-kyū gurume* (b-grade gourmet) – comfort food done well (think fried dishes that defy the generally healthy image of Japanese food). **Marugo** (丸五; 📞3255-6595; 1-8-14 Soto-Kanda, Chiyoda-ku; meals from ¥1400; ⏲11.30am-3pm & 5-8.20pm; 🚇JR Yamanote Line to Akihabara, Electric Town exit) serves up delicious *tonkatsu* (deep-fried pork cutlet) and has a loyal following.

❹ Visit a maid cafe

Maid cafes – where waitresses dress as french maids and treat customers with giggling deference as *go-shujinsama* (master) – are an Akiba institution.

Pop into **@Home Cafe** (@ほぉ～むカフェ; www.cafe-athome.com; 4th-7th fl, 1-11-4 Soto-kanda, Chiyoda-ku; drinks from ¥500; ⏲11.30am-10pm Mon-Fri, from 10.30am Sat & Sun; 🚇JR Sōbu Line to Akihabara, Electric Town exit) for a game of *moe moe jankan* (rock, paper, scissors), maid-style.

❺ Shop at Mandarake Complex

If you want to get an idea of what *otaku* obsess over, a trip to **Mandarake Complex** (まんだらけコンプレックス; www.mandarake.co.jp; 3-11-2 Soto-kanda, Chiyoda-ku; ⏲noon-8pm; 🚇JR Yamanote Line to Akihabara, Electric Town exit) will do the trick. It's eight storeys of comic books and DVDs, action figures and cel art.

❻ Use a vending machine

Akihabara has a love affair with vending machines. Look for those dishing out canned bread and *rāmen*, while **Gachapon Kaikan** (ガチャポン会館; 📞5209-6020; www.akibagacha.com; 3-15-5 Soto-Kanda, Chiyoda-ku; ⏲11am-8pm Mon-Fri, to 10pm Sat, to 7pm Sun; 🚇Ginza Line to Suehiro-chō, exit 3) has hundreds of *gachapon* (capsule toy vending machines) under one roof.

❼ Shop at Yodobashi Akiba

The modern avatar of Akihabara Radio Center is **Yodobashi Akiba** (ヨドバシカメラ Akiba; www.yodobashi-akiba.com; 1-1 Kanda Hanaoka-chō, Chiyoda-ku; ⏲9.30am-10pm; 🚇JR Yamanote Line to Akihabara, Shōwa-tōriguchi exit), a monster electronics store beloved by camera junkies. But for all the modern conveniences, Yodobashi Akiba feels like an old-time bazaar.

Explore

Ueno

Ueno is the cultural heart of Tokyo and has been the city's top tourist draw for centuries. At the centre of the neighbourhood is a sprawling park, Ueno-kōen, home to numerous museums, including Japan's grandest, the Tokyo National Museum. There are also temples, shrines, century-old restaurants and an open-air market – all of which lend Ueno a classic, traditional atmosphere.

The Sights in a Day

Get an early start and head to Ueno Station on the JR Yamanote Line. From there, walk to the **Tokyo National Museum** (p130). Spend the morning exploring the museum's vast collection of Japanese art and antiquities, allowing at least two hours to cover the highlights. Next stroll through leafy **Ueno-kōen** (p137), with its temples such as **Kiyōmizu Kannon-dō** (p137) and **Benten-dō** (p137). Break for lunch at historic **Izu-ei** (p140), which specialises in barbecued eel – a classic Japanese dish.

After lunch take a walk through the old-fashioned arcade, **Ameya-yokochō** (p137). Then take your pick from some of the excellent smaller museums: the **Shitamachi Museum** (p137), for a taste of pre-war Tokyo; the **National Science Museum** (p138) for the lowdown on the local flora and fauna; or the **Kyū Iwasaki-teien** (p138), for a glimpse into the life of the late-19th-century elite.

Continue up Shinobazu-dōri to neighbouring Nezu, a quiet residential neighbourhood with some hidden gems in the form of boutiques, restaurants and cafes. Have dinner at **Hantei** (p139), an ambient restaurant in a century-old heritage house.

For a local's day in Yanaka see p134.

Getting There

🚃 **Train** The JR Yamanote Line stops at Ueno, Nippori and Nishi-Nippori. Keisei Line trains to Narita Airport leave from Keisei Ueno Station.

S **Subway** Hibiya and Ginza Lines stop at Ueno. The Chiyoda Line stops at Yushima, Nezu, Sendagi and Nishi-Nippori.

Top Sights
Tokyo National Museum

Holds the world's largest collection of Japanese art including pottery, sculpture, samurai swords, *ukiyo-e* (wood-block prints) and exquisite kimono. There are several buildings; the most important is the Honkan (Main or Japan Gallery), built in the imperial style of the 1930s with art deco flourishes throughout. Exhibitions here are designed to give visitors an overview of Japanese art history throughout the past millennia. Highlights include the 7th century Buddhist relics inside the Gallery of Hōryū-ji Treasures and the Asian artefacts in the Tōyōkan (Gallery of Eastern Antiquities).

東京国立博物館

Map p136, C3

www.tnm.jp

13-9 Ueno-kōen, Taitō-ku

adult/student/child ¥600/400/free

🕑9.30am-5pm Tue-Sun

🚃JR Yamanote Line to Ueno, Ueno-kōen exit

Gallery of Hōryū-ji Treasures, Tokyo National Museum

Don't Miss

Ancient Japanese Art
HONKAN ROOM 1-1

The Honkan is the first port of call for first-time visitors. On the 2nd floor, exhibitions are arranged chronologically, starting with the ancient era. Here you'll see clay works from the centuries before the rise of the imperial court and the arrival of Buddhism – two historic milestones that forever changed the Japanese aesthetic.

National Treasure Gallery
HONKAN ROOM 2

A single, superlative work from the museum's collection of 88 National Treasures – perhaps a painted screen, or a gilded, hand-drawn *sutra* (Buddhist scripture) – is displayed here in a serene, contemplative setting. National Treasure is the highest distinction awarded to a work of art in Japan. Keep an eye out for others, labeled in red, on display around the museum.

Art of the Imperial Court
HONKAN ROOM 3-2

The poetry scrolls and ornately decorated objects on display here – such as gilded hand-mirrors and lacquer boxes – allude to the life of louche elegance led by courtesans a thousand years ago.

Art of the Tea Ceremony
HONKAN ROOM 4

Contemplate the aesthetic of *wabi-sabi* – an aesthetic that favours simplicity, imperfection and a kind of flawed, raw beauty – in the vessels and utensils of the traditional tea ceremony.

Samurai Armour & Swords
HONKAN ROOMS 5 & 6

Glistening swords, finely stitched armour and imposing helmets bring the samurai – those iconic

☑ Top Tips

▶ Allow two hours to take in the highlights, a half-day to do the Honkan in depth or a whole day to take in everything.

▶ For a tour of the highlights, start with the 2nd floor of the Honkan.

▶ Stow your coat and bag in the lockers just inside the entrance to the Honkan.

▶ Be sure to pick up a copy of the brochure *Highlights of Japanese Art*, found in room 1-1 on the 2nd floor of the Honkan.

✕ Take a Break

On the ground floor of the Tōyōkan, the **Hotel Ōkura Yurinoki** (ホテルオークラレストランゆりの木; Map p136, C3; meals ¥800-2500, coffee ¥550; ⏰10.30am-4.30pm) restaurant and cafe has terrace seating and a varied menu.

The charming tea-house **Torindō** (p140) is a 5-minute walk northwest of the museum.

Understand
Rotating Exhibitions

Exhibitions at the Tokyo National Museum (Tokyo Kokuritsu Hakubutsukan) are changed about once a month, both for preservation reasons (many, such as those made of paper, are incredibly fragile) and to create seasonal displays (the seasons being important in the Japanese aesthetic). So there's no guarantee that any one work will be on display when you visit. On the flip side, there's always something new. Most items in the collection were never intended for static display: lacquer boxes, tea bowls, kimono and folding screens, for example, were all used in daily life.

warriors of Japan's medieval age – to life. Kids in particular will love the displays here.

Ukiyo-e & Kimono
HONKAN ROOM 10

Lavish silken kimono are displayed along lushly coloured *ukiyo-e* (woodblock prints). Both are icons of the Edo-era (1603–1868) *ukiyo* (literally the floating world) – a world of fleeting beauty and pleasure inhabited by kabuki actors, courtesans and merchants who set the fashions of the day.

Japanese Religious Sculpture
HONKAN ROOM 11

Back on the first floor, exhibitions are organised by craft (lacquerware or ceramics, for example), rather than time period. Don't miss the excellent exhibition of religious sculpture. Many of Japan's most famous statues are locked away in temple reliquaries, and this is a rare chance to see some up close.

Minority Folk Art
HONKAN ROOM 15

Contrast the works of Japan's dominant culture with artefacts from its historical minorities – the indigenous Ainu of Hokkaido, the Kirishitan (persecuted Christians of the Middle Ages) and the former Ryūkyū Empire, now Okinawa.

Garden & Teahouse

For a few weeks in spring and autumn the garden behind the Honkan, which has five vintage teahouses, opens to the public. If you're visiting then, make time for a stroll; otherwise you can catch a glimpse from the windows when you pass between rooms 15 and 16 in the Honkan.

Gallery of Hōryū-ji Treasures

Another must-see is the Gallery of Hōryū-ji Treasures, which displays masks, scrolls and gilt Buddhas from Hōryū-ji – located in Nara Prefecture, and said to be the first Buddhist temple in Japan (founded in 607). The gallery is in a separate building, a spare, elegant box by Taniguchi Yoshio, who also designed New York's Museum of Modern Art (MoMA).

Gardens, Tokyo National Museum

Kuro-mon

The Kuro-mon (Black Gate), to the west of the main gate and near the Gallery of Hōryū-ji Treasures, was transported from the Edo-era mansion of a feudal lord. On weekends it opens for visitors to pass through.

Buddhist Sculpture from China & India
TŌYŌKAN GALLERIES 1 & 3

The Tōyōkan, which reopened in 2013 after a lengthy renovation, has an excellent collection of art and artefacts from around Asia. Compare and contrast the buddhas of Japan with those that came before in India, China and Central Asia.

Chinese Decorative Arts
TŌYŌKAN GALLERY 5

On the 3rd floor is a fine survey of a thousand years of Chinese ceramics, from the sea-coloured celadon works of the Song dynasty (960–1279) to the delicate painted porcelain of the Ming dynasty (1368–1649).

Fortune-Telling in Asia
TŌYŌKAN GALLERY 6

This neat little hands-on exhibit allows you to try out three different ways of traditional fortune-telling, including *shagai*, the Mongolian divination technique using ankle bones. Explanations are in English and this is another corner that kids will enjoy.

Local Life
A Stroll Through Historic Yanaka

In a city where the sentiment 'new is better' goes almost unquestioned, Yanaka stands out for having a profound connection to the old. Having survived, miraculously, the Great Kantō earthquake and the allied firebombing of WWII, Yanaka has a high concentration of vintage wooden structures and temples. The neighbourhood has long been popular with artists and many live and work here.

❶ Stroll Yanaka Ginza

Yanaka Ginza is pure vintage mid-20th-century Tokyo, a cluttered cluster of street stalls that feels like a bustling village thoroughfare. Stop by butcher shop **Niko-no-sato** (肉のサトー; 3-13-2 Yanaka, Taitō-ku; croquettes from ¥90; ⏰10am-7.30pm Tue-Sun) for one of its famous *menchi* (minced meat) croquettes. Hunker down on a milk crate with the locals and wash it all down with a beer.

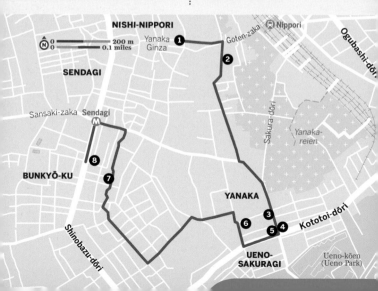

② Explore an artist's home

Sculptor Asakura Fumio (artist name Chōso; 1883–1964) designed this fanciful house and studio himself. It's now the **Asakura Chōso Museum** (朝倉彫塑館; www.taitocity.net/taito/asakura; 7-16-10 Yanaka, Taitō-ku; adult/student ¥400/150; ⊘9.30am-4.30pm Tue-Thu, Sat & Sun; 🚇JR Yamanote Line to Nippori, north exit), with a number of the artist's signature realist works on display. At the time of research the museum was closed for renovation, but should reopen in autumn 2013.

③ See art in a bathhouse

For 200 years, this graceful structure with a sloping tile roof was a public bathhouse. In 1993, it became **Scai the Bathhouse** (☎3821-1144; www.scaithebathhouse.com; 6-1-23 Yanaka, Taitō-ku; ⊘noon-6pm Tue-Sat; 🚇Chiyoda Line to Nezu, exit 1), a contemporary art gallery. There are still plenty of reminders of its original use, like the wooden lockers at the entrance and the vaulted ceiling.

④ See a 100-year-old shop

Shitamachi Museum Annex (2-10-6 Uenosakuragi, Taitō-ku; ⊘9.30am-4.30pm Tue-Sun; 🚇Chiyoda Line to Nezu, exit 1) preserves an old liquor shop that operated from 1910 to 1986, complete with old sake barrels, weights, measures and posters.

⑤ Hangout at Kayaba Coffee

Across the street from the Shitamachi Museum Annex is local hangout **Kayaba Coffee** (カヤバ珈琲; http://kayaba-coffee.com; 6-1-29 Yanaka, Taitō-ku; drinks from ¥400; ⊘8am-11pm Mon-Sat, to 6pm Sun; 🚇Chiyoda Line to Nezu, exit 1), which has been in business since the 1930s (the building itself dates to 1916) and still has many vintage fixtures.

⑥ Peek inside a working studio

A long-time Yanaka resident, Allan West paints gorgeous screens in the traditional Japanese style, making his paints from scratch just as local artists have done for centuries. Visitors are welcome to peek inside his **studio** (えどころアランウエスト; ☎3827-1907; www.allanwest.jp; 1-6-17 Yanaka, Taitō-ku; ⊘1-5pm, from 3pm Sun, closed irregularly; 🚇Chiyoda Line to Nezu, exit 1) when he's there.

⑦ Go shopping on Hebi-dōri

Earning its nickname from its dizzying curves (*hebi* means 'snake'), quiet, residential **Hebi-dōri** is slowly being colonised by boutiques. Shoppers who prefer a slower pace than, say, Harajuku come here to trawl for antiques or one-of-a-kind homewares made by local artisans.

⑧ Grab a cocktail and a book at Bousingot

It's fitting that Yanaka, which refuses to trash the past, would have a bar that doubles as a used book store – **Bousingot** (ブーザンゴ; ☎3823-5501; www.bousingot.com; 2-33-2 Sendagi, Bunkyō-ku; espresso ¥300, beer ¥550; ⊘5pm-11pm Wed-Mon; 🚇Chiyoda Line to Sendagi, exit 1). Sure, the books are in Japanese but you can still enjoy soaking up the atmosphere with some resident book lovers.

NISHI-NIPPORI

ARAKAWA-KU

Nishi-Nippori

Nippori

Yanaka Ginza ✕14

Ogubashi-dōri

🔒20

Otakebashi-dōri

Sakura-dōri

Ⓜ Sendagi
🅟18

Yanaka-reien ⊙8

13 ✕

NEGISHI

BUNKYŌ-KU

YANAKA

Kototoi-dōri

Uguisudani

Kototoi-dōri

🔒19

15 🅟

Gallery of Hōryū-ji Treasures

NEZU

UENO-SAKURAGI

Heiseikan

Tokyo National University of Fine Arts & Music

Honkan

Tokyo National Museum ⊙

TAITŌ-KU

Iriya Ⓜ

Nezu Ⓜ
11

Kuro-mon

Tōyōkan

Shuto Expwy No 1

IKE-NO-HATA

9⊙

Ueno Zoo

Ueno-kōen

National Science Museum

1⊙

⊙7

KITA-UENO

17🅟

UENO

Shinobazu-dōri

Kiyōmizu Kannon-dō ⊙2

HIGASHI-UENO

Tokyo University Branch Hospital

3⊙

Bōto-ike

Benten-dō

Keisei Ueno

🚉 Ueno

Ⓜ Ueno

Asakusa-dōri

Inarichō Ⓜ

Shinobazu-ike

Shitamachi Museum 5⊙

⊙6

12

Chūō-dōri

✕10

HONGŌ

Kyū Iwasaki-teien

Nakamachi-dōri

Ⓜ Yushima

Ueno-hirokōji Ⓜ

Ameya-yokochō

16✕

HIGASHI-UENO

Okachimachi Ⓜ

Kasuga-dōri

Ⓜ Ueno-Okachimachi

Naka-Okachimachi

Shin-Okachimachi

Sights

Ueno-kōen   PARK

1   Map p136, C4

Not a park in the grassy Western sense, Ueno-kōen has pathways that wind past temples and shrines, several museums and a pond, Shinobazu-ike, choked with lily-pads. On weekends look for buskers, acrobats and food vendors. Navigating the park is easy, thanks to large maps in Japanese and English. (上野公園; ⏰5am-11pm; 🚉JR Yamanote Line to Ueno, Ueno-kōen & Shinobazu exits)

Take a Break Stop for a coffee at **Parkside Cafe** (p141).

Kiyōmizu Kannon-dō   BUDDHIST TEMPLE

2   Map p136, C4

Inside Ueno-kōen, this red temple is one of Tokyo's oldest original structures: established in 1631 and in its present position since 1698, it has survived every disaster come its way. It's a miniature of the famous Kiyomizu-dera in Kyoto and is a pilgrimage site for women hoping to conceive. (清水観音堂; 1-29 Ueno-kōen, Taitō-ku; admission free; ⏰9am-4pm; 🚉JR Yamanote line to Ueno, Shinobazu exit)

Benten-dō   BUDDHIST TEMPLE

3   Map p136, B4

Take a stroll down the causeway in Ueno-kōen leading to the island on which Benten-dō stands. The temple is dedicated to Benzaiten, the Buddhist goddess of the arts, wisdom, the sea and the protector of children. From here you can also get a good look at the birds and botany that thrive around the pond. (弁天堂; ☎3821-4638; 2-1 Ueno-kōen, Taitō-ku; admission free; ⏰9am-5pm; 🚉JR Yamanote line to Ueno, Shinobazu exit)

Ameya-yokochō   MARKET

4   Map p136, C5

The gravelly welcome of the clothing vendors and fishmongers at this open-air market couldn't be further from Ginza or Shibuya. Ameya-yokochō started as a black market, post WWII, when American goods were sold here. You can still find the jeans and Hawaiian shirts that were in vogue at the time. (アメヤ横町; Ueno, Taitō-ku; ⏰10am-7pm; 🚉JR Yamanote Line to Ueno, Ueno-kōen exit)

Shitamachi Museum   MUSEUM

5   Map p136, C5

This museum re-creates life in the plebeian quarters of Tokyo during the Meiji and Taishō periods (1868–1926) through an exhibition of typical wooden buildings from that era. Take off your shoes and look inside an old tenement house or sweet shop while soaking up the atmosphere of long-gone *shitamachi* (the low-lying, less affluent parts of Tokyo). Ask for an English-language leaflet; English speaking guides are available, too. (下町風俗資料館; ☎3823-7451; www.taitocity.net/taito/shitamachi; 2-1 Ueno-kōen, Taitō-ku; adult/child ¥300/100; ⏰9.30am-4.30pm Tue-Sun; 🚉JR Yamanote to Ueno, Shinobazu exit; 👪)

YOSHIKAZU TSUNO / GETTY IMAGES ©

Ueno Zoo

Kyū Iwasaki-teien   HISTORIC BUILDING

 6 ⊙ Map p136, B5

This grand residence was once the villa of Hisaya Iwasaki, son of the founder of Mitsubishi, and is now a fascinating example of how the cultural elite of the early Meiji period tried to straddle east and west. Built in 1896, it has been open to the public since 2001. (旧岩崎邸庭園; ☎3823-8340; http://teien.tokyo-park.or.jp/en/kyu-iwasaki/index.html; 1-3-45 Ike-no-hata, Taitō-ku; adult/child ¥400/free; ⊙9am-5pm; ☒Chiyoda Line to Yushima, exit 1)

National Science Museum   MUSEUM

7 ⊙ Map p136, C4

Of particular interest here is the Japan Gallery, which showcases the rich and varied wildlife of the Japanese archipelago, from the bears of Hokkaido to the giant beetles of Okinawa. Also: a rocket launcher, a giant squid, an Edo-era mummy, and a digital seismograph that charts earthquakes in real time. There's English signage throughout, plus an English-language audio guide (¥300). (国立科学博物館; Kokuritsu Kagaku Hakubutsukan; www.kahaku.go.jp; 7-20 Ueno-kōen, Taitō-ku; adult/child ¥600/free; ⊙9am-5pm Tue-Thu, Sat & Sun, to 8pm Fri; ☒JR Yamanote Line to Ueno, Ueno-kōen exit; ☷)

Yanaka-reien   CEMETERY

8 ⊙ Map p136, B2

One of Tokyo's largest graveyards, Yanaka-reien is the final resting place of more than 7000 souls, many of whom were quite well known in their day, such as Japan's most famous modern female novelist Higuchi Ichiyō (you'll find her portrait on the ¥5000 bill). This is also where you'll find the **tomb of Yoshinobu Tokugawa**. (徳川慶喜の墓), the last shōgun. (谷中霊園; 7-5-24 Yanaka, Taitō-ku; 🚈 JR Yamanote Line to Nippori, west exit)

Ueno Zoo   ZOO

9 Map p136, B4

Japan's oldest zoo was established in 1882, and is home to animals from around the globe, but the biggest attractions are two giant pandas that arrived from China in 2011 – Rī Rī and Shin Shin. Ueno Zoo is larger than you'd think, given the obvious space constraints of Tokyo. (上野動物園; Ueno Dōbutsu-en; www.tokyo-zoo.net; 9-83 Ueno-kōen, Taitō-ku; adult/child ¥600/free; ⏰9.30am-5pm Tue-Sun; 🚈 JR Yamanote Line to Ueno, Ueno-kōen exit; 👶)

Eating

Yabu Soba   NOODLES $

10 🍴 Map p136, C5

Near the Ameya-yokochō shopping arcade, this busy place rustles up top-class *soba*; from the simple *zaru soba* (plain, cold buckwheat noodles to dip in broth) to the richly filling *tenseiro* (noodles with shrimp and vegetable tempura). There's a picture menu to help choose. Look for the black-granite sign in front that says in English 'Since 1892'. (上野やぶそば; ☎3831-4728; 6-9-16 Ueno, Taitō-ku; ⏰11.30am-8.30pm Thu-Tue; 🚈 JR Yamanote line to Ueno, Hirokōji exit)

Hantei   JAPANESE $$

11 🍴 Map p136, A3

Housed in a beautifully maintained, nearly 100-year-old wooden building, Hantei is a local landmark. Delectable skewers of seasonal *kushiage* (fried

Understand
Ueno-kōen

Established in 1873, Ueno-kōen is known as Japan's first public park (in the Western sense), but it's much older than that. Structures here date as far back as the 17th century. There's a Kiyōmizu Kannon-dō (p137) modelled after the landmark temple in Kyoto and a **Tōshōgū** (Shintō shrine) similar to the shrine in Nikkō (under reconstruction until January 2014). **Shinobazu-ike** (pond;不忍池), where couples now paddle swan-shaped boats, was likened to the country's central Lake Biwa and Ueno-kōen was billed as a mini-Japan – a sort of prototypical Disney World. During the Edo period, when travel was heavily restricted, Tokyoites could 'see' the country without having to leave home. The park's reputation as the most famous *hanami* (cherry-blossom viewing) spot in the city dates to this era.

meat, fish and vegetables) are served with refreshing side dishes. Lunch courses include eight sticks and dinner courses start with six, after which additional rounds (¥210 for one skewer) will continue to appear until you say stop. (はん亭; ☎3828-1440; www.hantei.co.jp/nedu.html; 2-12-15 Nezu, Bunkyō-ku; lunch/dinner course from ¥3150/2835; ☺noon-3pm & 5-10pm Tue-Sun; ℞Chiyoda Line to Nezu, exit 2)

Izu-ei UNAGI **$$**

 12   Map p136, C5

Izu-ei has been specialising in *unagi* (eel) for more than 260 years. It's served a number of different ways, but purists would insist upon getting it charcoal-grilled, sauced and then laid on a bed of steamed rice – a dish called *unajū*. Izu-ei has an appropriately traditional atmosphere but is hardly stuffy. Kid-friendly (read: eel-free) meals are available, too. (伊豆栄;; 2-12-22 Ueno, Taitō-ku; set meals ¥2520-4725; ☺11am-9.30pm; ℞JR Yamanote Line to Ueno, Hirokōji exit; 🅿 🚼)

Sasa-no-Yuki TOFU **$$**

13   Map p136, C2

Sasa-no-Yuki opened its doors in the Edo period and has been serving the same signature dishes ever since. Tofu is made fresh every morning with water from the shop's own well. The best seats overlook a tiny garden with a koi (carp) pond. Vegetarians should not assume everything is purely vegie: ask before ordering. There's bamboo out front. (笹乃雪; ☎3873-1145; 2-15-10 Negishi, Taitō-ku; dishes ¥350-1000, set meals ¥2600-4500; ☺11.30am-8pm Tue-Sun; ℞JR Yamanote Line to Uguisudani, north exit; 🅿 🅿)

Nagomi YAKITORI **$$**

14   Map p136, B2

On Yanaka Ginza, Nagomi deals in juicy skewers of *ji-dori* (free range chicken). There are plenty of grilled vegie options, too. Wash it all down with a bowl of chicken *rāmen*. It's a stylish place that is popular with locals. Look for the sake bottles in the window. (和味; ☎3821-5972; 3-11-11 Yanaka, Taitō-ku; skewers from ¥180; ☺5pm-midnight; ℞JR Yamanote Line to Nippori, north exit; 🅿)

Drinking

Torindō TEAHOUSE

15   Map p136, B3

Sample a cup of paint-thick *matcha* (powdered green tea) at this tiny teahouse on the edge of Ueno-kōen. Tradition dictates that the bitter tea be paired with something sweet, so choose from the *mochi* (pounded rice) cakes in the counter, then pull up a stool at the communal table. It's a white building with persimmon-coloured door curtains. (桃林堂; 1-5-7

Top Tip

Megurin Bus

The Tōzai Megurin bus (¥100) does a loop around Ueno and neighbouring Yanaka. Get a map at the **Tourist Information Center** (☺9.30am-6.30pm) at Keisei Ueno Station.

Ueno-Sakuragi, Taitō-ku; tea set ¥800; ⏱9am-5pm; 🚇Chiyoda Line to Nezu, exit 1)

Warrior Celt
PUB

16 Map p136, C5

A long-running, thoroughly authentic pub, the Warrior Celt is the rare expat hangout on the east side of town, with a tight-knit crowd of loyal customers and a finely-tuned selection of local and imported beers. There's live music most weekends, ranging from rock to celtic folk. (www.warriorcelt.jp; 3rd fl, 6-9-22 Ueno, Taitō-ku; ⏱5pm-midnight; 🚇JR Yamanote Line to Ueno, Hirokōji exit; 📖)

Parkside Cafe
CAFE

17 Map p136, C4

With an enviable location in the middle of Ueno-kōen, this terrace cafe serves espresso, pots of tea made with fresh herbs and light meals, such as open-faced sandwiches. (パークサイドカフェ; 8-4 Ueno-kōen, Taitō-ku; drinks from ¥540; ⏱10am-9pm, from 9am Sat & Sun; 🚇JR Yamanote Line to Ueno, kōen exit; 🍽📖)

Shopping

Isetatsu
CRAFT

18 Map p136, A2

Dating back to 1864, this venerable stationery shop specialises in *chiyogami*: gorgeous, colourful paper made using wood-blocks. These decorative creations, incorporating traditional Japanese and modern motifs, are beau-

Top Tip

Snack Time

Ameya-yokochō (p137) has a number of venders selling snacks such as skewered fruit and *taiyaki* (grilled cakes shaped like fish and stuffed with bean paste). **Ueno-kōen** (p137), too, has snack carts, especially around Shinobazu-ike.

tiful enough to be framed. (いせ辰; ☏3823-1453; 2-18-9 Yanaka, Taitō-ku; ⏱10am-6pm; 🚇Chiyoda Line to Sendagi, exit 1)

Sekka
ARTS & CRAFTS

19 Map p136, A3

A rotating line-up of Japanese artists and artisans show at this Nezu gallery-cum-shop. Much of the wares, which might be earthy pottery or pen-and-ink drawings, come in under ¥10,000. (汐花; ☏5815-8280; www.sekka-jp.com/index.html; 2-24-3 Nezu, Bunkyō-ku; ⏱11.30am-6.30pm Tue-Sun; 🚇Chiyoda Line to Nezu, exit 1)

Nippori Fabric Town
FABRICS

20 Map p136, C1

If you've got a notion to sew, these shops east of Nippori Station will hit you like a proverbial bolt. Dozens of shops sell buttons, brocade used for kimono and contemporary fabrics. Head out the station's north gate to the east exit and look for maps in the station. (日暮里布の街; Nippori Nuno-no-Machi; Nippori Chūō-dōri, Arakawa-ku; ⏱varied; 🚇JR Yamanote Line to Nippori, east exit)

Explore

Tokyo Sky Tree & Asakusa

Asakusa (ah-saku-sah) is home to Tokyo's oldest attraction, the centuries-old temple Sensō-ji. Just across the river is the city's newest: the 634m tall Tokyo Sky Tree. The neighbourhoods surrounding these sights are known as *shitamachi* (the low city), where the spirit of old Edo (Tokyo under the shōgun) proudly lives on in an atmospheric web of alleys, artisan shops and mum-and-dad restaurants.

The Sights in a Day

☼ Begin your journey through this historic district at Asakusa Station, on the Ginza Line. Follow the signs to Kaminarimon (Thunder Gate), the magnificent entrance to the Nakamise-dōri shopping arcade that leads to the temple **Sensō-ji** (p146). Spend a few hours exploring the temple, neighbouring **Asakusa-jinja** (p149) and the alleys that surround the sights.

☀ Stop for a lunch of tempura at **Daikokuya** (p150), then visit **Chingo-dō** (p149), the **Traditional Crafts Museum** (p149) and, if you're in the mood for old-school thrills, the amusement park **Hanayashiki** (p149). From here take a taxi or walk – it takes about 25 minutes – to **Tokyo Sky Tree** (p144), across the river. Take the lift from the 4th floor up to the observatories at 350m for views that stretch as far as the eye can see.

☽ Back on land, head over to the **Asahi Sky Room** (p154), about a 15 minute walk away, for more views; time your visit for sunset and see the lights go on at Tokyo Sky Tree. Splurge on a dinner of premium-grade beef at **Asakusa Imahan** (p153).

◉ Top Sights

Tokyo Sky Tree (p144)

Sensō-ji (p146)

♥ Best of Tokyo

Architecture
Asahi Flame (p149)

Temples & Shrines
Asakusa-jinja (p149)

Eating
Asakusa Imahan (p153)

Sentō & Onsen
Jakotsu-yu (p150)

Traditional Theatre & Dance
Asakusa Engei Hall (p154)

Drinking & Nightlife
Kamiya Bar (p153)

Getting There

S **Subway** The Ginza Line stops at Asakusa and Tawaramachi. The Asakusa Line also stops at Asakusa at a separate station south of the Ginza Line, and the Hanzōmon Line stops at Oshiage for Tokyo Sky Tree.

⚓ Ferry Azuma-bashi is the starting point for Tokyo Cruise water buses heading to Hama-rikyū Onshi-teien.

Top Sights
Tokyo Sky Tree

Even if you don't go in for heights, Tokyo Sky Tree is an engineering marvel. It opened in May 2012 as the world's tallest 'free-standing communication tower' at 634m. There are two observation decks, at 350m and 450m, which offer jaw-dropping views of the city and vertiginous thrills. At night the exterior of steel mesh is illuminated, turning the tower into an otherworldly beacon in relatively undeveloped east Tokyo.

東京スカイツリー

◉ Map p148, E3

www.tokyo-skytree.jp

Oshiage, Sumida-ku

admission to 350m/450m observation decks ¥2000/3000

🕗 8am-10pm

🚇 Hanzōmon Line to Oshiage, Sky Tree exit

Tokyo Sky Tree

Don't Miss

The Tower

Wedged in the tight space of a former freight yard, Tokyo Sky Tree morphs from a triangle at its base to a circle at 300m. At its centre is a *shinbashira* – a core pillar, part of the structural design that makes the traditional five-storey pagoda so sturdy and gives Tokyo Sky Tree its quake-resistant strength.

Tembō Deck

High-speed elevators leaving from the 4th floor whisk you up to the lower deck in just 50 seconds. From here, at a height of 350m, the panorama is spectacular. At peak visibility you can see up to 70km away.

The Glass Floor

The Tembō Deck is actually three floors, and if you spiral down to the floor at 340m there is a small section of glass floor panels, where you can see – dizzyingly – all the way to the ground.

Tembō Galleria

Another set of elevators takes visitors the rest of the way, from the Tembō Deck to the the Tembō Galleria – the upper deck at 450m. Here, beneath the digital broadcasting antennas, there is a spiraling glass corridor with more extreme views.

Sky Tree Mural

Back on the first floor, this 40m long digital mural of Tokyo by local techno-creatives Team Lab portrays the city in vivid, animated and hilarious detail. It's a contemporary take on the traditional *edozubyōbu* – scenes of Edo depicted on folding screens.

☑ Top Tips

▶ The ticket counter is on the 4th floor; if the line is long for the elevators, the waiting time will be posted there.

▶ Try to avoid visiting on the weekend, when crowds are largest.

▶ To increase your chances of spotting Mt Fuji, go in the early morning or during the winter months.

▶ Just east of the tower, Solamachi Square has the best views of the tower from the ground.

✕ Take a Break

On the 6th floor of the Solamachi building under the tower, **Rokurinsha** (p151) serves delicious *rāmen*.

Head to the **Asahi Sky Room** (p154), a ten-minute walk away, for a beer and unobstructed views of the tower, day or night.

Top Sights
Sensō-ji

Founded more than 1000 years before Tokyo got its start, Sensō-ji is the capital's oldest temple and the spiritual home of its ancestors. According to legend, in AD 628 two fishermen brothers pulled a golden image of Kannon (the Buddhist Goddess of Mercy) out of the nearby Sumida-gawa. The temple was built to enshrine it. Today Sensō-ji stands out for its old-world atmosphere – offering a glimpse of a bygone Japan that can be difficult to find in contemporary Tokyo.

浅草寺

Map p148, B2

http://www.senso-ji.jp/about/index_e.html

2-3-1 Asakusa, Taitō-ku

admission free

⏱24hr

🚇Ginza Line to Asakusa, exit 1

Sensō-ji

Don't Miss

Kaminarimon

The temple precinct begins at the majestic Kaminarimon, which houses a pair of ferocious protective deities: Fūjin, the god of wind, on the right; and Raijin, the god of thunder, on the left.

Nakamise-dōri

Straight on through the gate is the bustling shopping street known as Nakamise-dōri. There are stalls selling all sorts of things – from souvenirs to genuine Edo-style crafts to sweet *age-manjū* (deep-fried buns stuffed with *anko* – bean paste).

Five-storey Pagoda

This 53m-high, five-storey pagoda is a 1973 reconstruction of the one built by Tokugawa Iemitsu in the 17th century. It's the second-highest pagoda in Japan.

Main Hall

In front of the grand main hall is a large incense cauldron. The smoke is said to bestow health, and you'll see people rubbing it into their bodies through their clothes. The ancient image of Kannon is not on public display (and admittedly may not exist at all), but this doesn't stop a steady stream of worshippers from paying their respects.

Getting your Fortune

Before the main hall, plunk down ¥100 for an *omikuji* (fortune). Shake the silver canister and extract a stick, noting its number (in kanji). Find the matching drawer and withdraw a paper fortune (there's English on the back). If you get a bad one just tie the paper on the nearby rack, ask the gods for better luck and try again.

☑ Top Tips

▶ The main hall and its gates are illuminated every day from sunset until 11pm. The minutes just before the sun sinks make for some of the best pictures of this photogenic sanctuary.

▶ Consider the crowds part of the experience, as there doesn't seem to be a time of a day when Senso-ji isn't packed.

✖ Take a Break

Just off of Nakamise-dōri, **Daikokuya** (p150) serves delicious tempura in an unpretentious setting that is typical of Asakusa.

Afterwards, treat yourself to a beer – or better yet, a *denki-bran* (herbal liquor made in-house) – at **Kamiya Bar** (p153), one of Tokyo's oldest western-style bars. It's just steps away from Kaminarimon.

Sights

Asakusa-jinja
SHINTŌ SHRINE

1 ◉ Map p148, B2

Asakusa-jinja was built in honour of the brothers who discovered the Kannon statue that inspired the construction of Sensō-ji. The current building, painted a deep shade of red, dates to 1649 and is an impressive example of an early-Edo architectural style called *gongen-zukuri* – a building with an H-shaped footprint (浅草神社; ☎3844-1575; http://www.asakusajinja.jp/english/; 2-3-1 Asakusa, Taitō-ku; ⌚9am-4.30pm; 🚇Ginza Line to Asakusa, exit 1)

Asahi Flame
LANDMARK

2 ◉ Map p148, C3

Designed by Philippe Starck and completed in 1989, the Asahi Beer Hall, with its tell-tale golden plume, is a Tokyo landmark. The golden bit – which weighs more than 300 tonnes – is open to interpretation: Asahi likes to think it is the foam to the building's beer mug. Locals call it the 'golden turd'. (フラムドール; Flamme d'Or; 1-23-1 Azuma-bashi, Sumida-ku; 🚇Ginza Line to Asakusa, exit 4)

Taiko Drum Museum
MUSEUM

3 ◉ Map p148, A3

There are hundreds of drums from around the world here, including several traditional Japanese *taiko*. The best part is that you can play most of them (those marked with a music note). (太鼓館; Taiko-kan; http://www.miyamoto-unosuke. co.jp/taikokan/; 2-1-1 Nishi-Asakusa, Taitō-ku; adult/child ¥500/150; ⌚10am-5pm Wed-Sun; 🚇Ginza Line to Tawaramachi, exit 3; 👶)

Chingo-dō
BUDDHIST TEMPLE

4 ◉ Map p148, B2

This small, peaceful and unjustifiably overlooked temple pays tribute to the *tanuki*, (raccoon-like, folkloric characters), who figure in Japanese myth as mystical shape-shifters and merry pranksters. They are also said to protect against fire and theft, which is why you'll often see *tanuki* figurines in front of restaurants. (鎮護堂; 2-3-1 Asakusa, Taitō-ku; ⌚6am-5pm; 🚇Ginza Line to Asakusa, exit 1)

Traditional Crafts Museum
MUSEUM

5 ◉ Map p148, B1

Asakusa has a long artisan tradition and changing exhibitions of local crafts are held here. Demonstrations are held on Saturdays and Sundays (between 11am & 5pm). If you see anything that strikes your interest, staff can direct you to the artisans or to shops selling their work. (江戸下町伝統工芸館; Edo Shitamachi Dentō Kōgeikan; http://www.city. taito.lg.jp/index/kurashi/shigoto/jibasangyo/ kogeikan/; 2-22-13 Asakusa, Taitō-ku; ⌚10am-8pm; 🚇Ginza Line to Asakusa, exit 1)

Hanayashiki
AMUSEMENT PARK

6 ◉ Map p148, B2

Japan's oldest amusement park has creaky old carnival rides and heaps of vintage charm. Don't miss the hilariously old-school 'Bikkuri Hausu' ('Surprise House'), which dates from 1949, and the Bee Tower, Hanayashiki's landmark. Once you're inside, you can buy tickets for individual rides, which cost a few hundred yen each. (花やしき; www.hanayashiki.net/index.html; 2-28-1 Asakusa, Taitō-ku; admission ¥900; ◷10am-6pm; ⊠Ginza Line to Asakusa, exit 1)

Kappabashi-dōri STREET

 7 ◉ Map p148, A2

Kappabashi-dōri supplies many a Tokyo restaurant with all the necessities, such as matching sets of chopsticks, crockery, uniforms and neon signs. However, it is most famous for its shops selling those eerily realistic plastic food models that you've been seeing in front of restaurants around town. (合羽橋通り; ⊠Ginza Line to Tawaramachi, exit 3)

Jakotsu-yu BATHHOUSE

 8 ◉ Map p148, B3

This welcoming *sentō* (public bathhouse), with English signage and no policy against tattoos, is the perfect place to dip into Japan's bathing

Top Tip

Tokyo Sky Tree View

Head to the 8th floor of the **Asakusa Tourist Information Center** (p196) for perfect (and free!) views of Tokyo Sky Tree.

culture. Unlike most *sentō*, the tubs here are filled with pure hot spring water, naturally the color of weak tea. Another treat: the lovely, lantern-lit, rock-framed *rotemburo* (outdoor bath). The sauna is an extra ¥200. (蛇骨湯; ☎3841-8645; www.jakotsuyu.co.jp; 1-11-11 Asakusa, Taitō-ku; admission ¥450; ◷1pm-midnight Wed-Mon; ⊠Ginza Line to Tawaramachi, exit 3)

Eating

Daikokuya TEMPURA $

 9 ✕ Map p148, B2

The long queues around the building should give you something of a clue about this much-loved tempura place – even before you catch the unmistakable fragrance wafting from within. Sneak off to the other **branch** (大黒家別館; ☎3844-1111; www.tempura.co.jp/english/index.html; 1-31-9 Asakusa, Taitō-ku; meals ¥1500-2050; ◷11.10am-8.30pm, to 9pm Sat & Sun; ⊠Ginza Line to Asakusa, exit 6) around the corner if the line seems to be putting too much distance between you and your *ebi tendon* (tempura prawns over rice). (大黒家; http://www.tempura.co.jp/english/index.html; 1-38-10 Asakusa, Taitō-ku; meals ¥1500-2050; ◷11am-8.30pm Mon-Fri, to 9pm Sat; ⊠Ginza Line to Asakusa, exit 6; 📷)

Sometarō OKONOMIYAKI $

 10 ✕ Map p148, A3

Sometarō is a fun and funky place to try *okonomiyaki* (savoury Japanese-

GREG ELMS / GETTY IMAGES ©

Plastic food, Kappabashi-dōri

style pancakes filled with meat, seafood and vegetables that you cook yourself). This historic, vine-covered house has seating on tatami mats with low tables and a menu that includes a how-to guide for making the house dish. (染太郎; 2-2-2 Nishi-Asakusa, Taitō-ku; mains ¥390-880; ⏰noon-10pm; 🚇Ginza Line to Tawaramachi, exit 3; 📖)

Rokurinsha

RĀMEN $

11 🍴 Map p148, E3

Rokurinsha's specialty is *tsukemen* – egg noodles served with a bowl of concentrated soup for dipping. The noodles here are thick and perfectly al dente, the soup is a rich *tonkotsu* (pork bone) base with pork, hard-boiled egg and bamboo shoots – an addictive combination that draws lines to this outpost under Tokyo Sky Tree. (六厘舎; www.rokurinsha.com; 6th fl, Solamachi, 1-1-2 Oshiage, Sumida-ku; rāmen from ¥850; ⏰11am-11pm; 🚇Hanzōmon Line to Oshiage, Sky Tree exit)

Chōchin Monaka

SWEETS $

12 🍴 Map p148, B2

Traditionally, *monaka* are wafers filled with sweet bean jam. At this little stand on Nakamise-dōri, they're filled with ice cream instead – in flavours such as *matcha* (powdered green tea) and *kuro-goma* (black sesame) – and shaped like lanterns (*chōchin*). Yum! (ちょうちんもなか; 2-3-1 Asakusa, Taitō-ku; ice cream ¥280; ⏰10am-5.30pm; 🚇Ginza Line to Asakusa, exit 1; 📖)

Understand

Old Edo & Shitamachi

Before Tokyo there was Edo – literally 'Gate of the River' – named for its location at the mouth of the Sumida-gawa. This small farming village rose from obscurity in 1603 when Tokugawa Ieyasu established his shōgunate (military government) here. The new capital quickly transformed into a bustling city and by the late 18th century was the largest city in the world with a population of one million.

Life in Old Edo

Under Tokugawa rule, society was rigidly hierarchical. At the top were the *daimyō* (feudal lords) and their samurai. Then came the peasants – the farmers and fishermen – and at the bottom were the *chōnin*, the townspeople. The layout of Edo, too, was divided: On the elevated plain to the west of the castle was the *yamanote* (literally mountain's hand), where the feudal elite built its estates. In the east, along the banks of the Sumida-gawa, merchants and artisans – the *chōnin* – lived elbow to elbow in wooden tenement houses in *shitamachi* (the low lying parts of Tokyo).

 Wealth, however, didn't follow such neat lines; in reality, some *chōnin* grew fabulously wealthy and enjoyed a lifestyle that thumbed its nose at the austerity prescribed by the ruling class. It was they who patronised the kabuki theatre, sumō tournaments and the pleasure district of Yoshiwara, to the north of Asakusa.

Shitamachi Today

While official class distinctions were laid to rest along with feudalism in the 19th century, the old city patterns remain. Former *shitamachi* districts to the east, such as Asakusa, are still a tangle of alleys and tightly packed quarters, with more traditional architecture, old-school artisans and small businesses.

 Even today, the word *shitamachi* is used to describe such neighbourhoods that come closest to approximating the spirit of old Edo. Those who've lived in such districts for generations can call themselves *Edokko*, or children of Edo. Get to know them and you'll find them down-to-earth and with a droll sense of humour. And even some who don't qualify are finding themselves increasingly drawn to such neighbourhoods, which offer the human connections and warmth lacking in newer parts of the city.

Komagata Dojō TRADITIONAL $$

13 Map p148, B4

For six generations, Komagata Dojō has been simmering and stewing *dojō* (Japanese loach, which looks something like a miniature eel). *Dojō nabe* (loach hotpot), served here on individual *hibahchi* (charcoal stoves) was a common dish in the days of Edo, but is rarely seen on menus today. The open seating around wide, wooden planks heightens the traditional flavour. (駒形どぜう; ☑3842-4001; 1-7-12 Komagata, Taitō-ku; mains from ¥1500; ☺11am-9pm; ⓡGinza Line to Asakusa, exit A2 or A4; ⓐ)

Irokawa UNAGI $$

14 Map p148, B3

This tiny restaurant has a real old Edo flavour and is one of the best, unpretentious *unagi* restaurants in town. The menu is simple: a small gets you two slices of charcoal-grilled eel over rice, a large gets you three. The chef grills everything right behind the counter. Look for the light green building. (色川; ☑3844-1187; 2-6-11 Kaminarimon, Taitō-ku; sets from ¥2500; ☺11.30am-1.30pm & 5-8.30pm Mon-Sat; ⓡGinza Line to Asakusa, exit 2; ⊝ⓐ)

Vin Chou YAKITORI $$

15 Map p148, A3

Tucked away on an Asakusa side street, Vin Chou is an odd bird: it's *yakitori* meets French and there are foie gras and imported cheeses on the menu along with traditional *tori negi* (chicken and spring onion). If

you're hungry, the set-price menu is good value. (萬鳥; ☑3845-4430; www.vinchou.jp/r-asakusa/asakusa.html; 2-2-13 Nishi-Asakusa, Taitō-ku; skewers from ¥190, set-price menu ¥2900; ☺5pm-11pm Thu-Tue; ⓡGinza Line to Asakusa, exit 1; ⓐ)

Asakusa Imahan SHABU-SHABU $$$

16 Map p148, A2

Founded in 1895, this famous restaurant serves memorable courses of *shabu-shabu* (thinly sliced, marbled beef simmered briefly in broth at the table). Prices rise according to the grade of meat, up to Kobe beef – if you're in the mood to splurge. There's both table and tatami seating; reservations recommended. (浅草今半; ☑3841-1114; www.asakusaimahan.co.jp/index.html; 3-1-12 Nishi-Asakusa, Taitō-ku; lunch/dinner set menu from ¥3675/6300; ☺11.30am-9.30pm; ⓡGinza Line to Tawaramachi, exit 3; ⓐ)

Drinking

Kamiya Bar BAR

17 Map p148, B3

One of Tokyo's oldest Western-style bars, Kamiya opened in 1880 and is still hugely popular – though probably more so today for its enormous, cheap draft beer (¥1020 for a litre). Its real speciality, however, is *Denki Bran* (liqueur). Order at the counter, then give your tickets to the server. (神谷バー; ☑3841-5400; www.kamiya-bar.com; 1-1-1 Asakusa, Taitō-ku; ☺11.30am-10pm Wed-Mon; ⓡGinza Line to Asakusa, exit 3)

Asahi Sky Room

BAR

18 Map p148, C3

Spend the day at the religious sites and end it at the Asahi altar, on the 22nd floor of the golden Asahi Super Dry Building. The decor is minimal, but the views over the river and of Tokyo Sky Tree are spectacular, and there are several Asahi brews on tap. (アサヒスカイルーム; ☎5608-5277; 22F, Asahi Super Dry Bldg, 1-23-1 Azuma-bashi, Sumida-ku; ⊙10am-9pm; ☒Ginza Line to Asakusa, exit 4; 🖺)

Ef

BAR

19 Map p148, B3

Set in a wobbly wooden house that beat the 1923 earthquake and WWII, this wonderfully unpretentious space serves coffee and, in the evening, beer and cocktails. Ef doubles as a small gallery showcasing local artists. (エフ; ☎3841-0442; www.gallery-ef.com; 2-19-18 Kaminarimon, Taitō-ku; ⊙11am-midnight Mon, Wed & Thu, to 2am Fri & Sat, to 10pm Sun; ☒Ginza Line to Asakusa, exit 2; 🖺)

Cafe Meursault

CAFE, BAR

20 Map p148, B3

With a large window and a terrace looking over the Sumida-gawa, this cake shop with views serves coffee (from ¥630), tea and light lunches. You can sip beers here at night and watch the ferry boats roll by. (カフェムルソー; ☎3843-8008; http://cafe-meursault.com; 2-1-5 Kaminarimon, Taitō-ku; ⊙11am-10pm; ☒Toei Asakusa Line to Asakusa, exit A3)

Entertainment

Asakusa Engei Hall

COMEDY

21 ⭐ Map p148, B2

Asakusa was once full of theatres such as this one, where traditional *rakugo* (comedic monologue) and other forms of comedy were performed along with jugglers and magicians. It's all in Japanese but the lively acts are fun all the same, and form the foundation for a lot of what you see on Japanese TV. (浅草演芸ホール; ☎3841-6545; www.asakusaengei.com; 1-43-12 Asakusa, Taitō-ku; adult/child ¥2500/1100; ⊙shows 11.40am-4.30pm & 4.40-9pm; ☒Ginza Line to Tawaramachi, exit 3)

Shopping

Solamachi

SOUVENIRS

22 🔒 Map p148, E3

It's not entirely cheesy Sky Tree swag at this mall under the tower. Shops on the 4th floor offer a better-than-usual selection of Japanese-y souvenirs, including pretty trinkets made from kimono fabric. Also look for items by Minä Perhonen, the Japanese fashion brand responsible for the Sky Tree employees' cute uniforms. (ソラマチ; 1-1-2 Oshiage, Sumida-ku; ⊙10am-9pm; ☒Hanzōmon Line to Oshiage, Sky Tree exit)

Yonoya Kushiho

ACCESSORIES

23 🔒 Map p148, B2

Even in a neighbourhood where old is not out of place, Yonoya Kushiho stands out: it's been selling handmade

Understand
Traditional Festivals

Throughout the warmer months, Tokyo's shrines host riotous *matsuri* (festivals) that seem to turn back the clock a few centuries. Men don *happi* (short sleeve coats) and *fundoshi* (the traditional loincloths worn by sumō wrestlers) to carry *mikoshi* (portable shrines) through the streets, chanting as they push through the crowds. These celebrations have their roots in Shintō tradition, but they also serve to renew age-old community bonds. Asakusa's **Sanja Matsuri**, held the 3rd weekend of May, is Tokyo's biggest, drawing some 1.5 millions spectators annually; however, there are festivals throughout the year. Check for listings on Go Tokyo (www.gotokyo.org/en/index.html).

boxwood combs since 1717. Yonoya also sells old-fashioned hair ornaments (worn with the elaborate up-dos of Edo-era courtesans) and modern trinkets, such as key chains. (よのや櫛舗; 1-37-10 Asakusa, Taitō-ku; ◔10.30am-6pm Thu-Tue; ◴Ginza Line to Asakusa, exit 1)

Maizuru
ACCESSORIES

24 Map p148, A3

This fascinating plastic food emporium on Kappabashi-dōri has hundreds of samples on display – from rice balls to king crabs to ice cream that looks real enough to eat. You can get souvenirs here too, such as sushi-shaped key chains. (まいづる; www.maiduru.co.jp; 1-5-7 Nishi-Asakusa, Taitō-ku; ◔9am-6pm; ◴Ginza Line to Tawaramachi, exit 3)

Bengara
CRAFT

25 Map p148, B3

On the sides streets around Nakamise-dōri are dozens of shops specialising in local crafts, including Bengara,

which sells *noren*, the curtains that hang in front of shop doors, as well as other indigo-dyed goods. (べんがら; www.bengara.com; 1-35-6 Asakusa, Taitō-ku; ◔10am-6pm, to 7pm Sat & Sun, closed 3rd Thu of the month; ◴Ginza Line to Asakusa, exit 1)

Kanesō
HOMEWARES

26 Map p148, B3

Kanesō has been selling knives since the early Meiji period. In a country where knives are a serious business, this shop is known as a favourite of the pros. (かね惣; ☏3844-1379; www.kanesoh.com; 1-18-12 Asakusa, Taitō-ku; ◔11am-7pm; ◴Ginza Line to Asakusa, exit 1)

Fujiya
CRAFT

27 Map p148, B2

The *tenugui* (dyed, cotton hand towels) sold here come in traditional Edo-era designs and clever modern ones. Light to pack, they make excellent souvenirs. (ふじ屋; 2-2-15 Asakusa, Taitō-ku; ◔10.30am-6.30pm Fri-Wed; ◴Ginza Line to Asakusa, exit 1)

Top Sights
Ōedo Onsen Monogatari

Getting There

🚃 Take the Yuri-kamome Line from Shiodome to Telecom Centre, south exit.

🚃 Take the Rinkai Line from JR Ōsaki Station to Tokyo Teleport and transfer to the free shuttle bus.

Ōedo Onsen Monogatari proves that Tokyo really does have it all, even a natural hot spring. The water is pumped from a spring 1400m below Tokyo Bay. But Ōedo Onsen Monogatari not solely about bathing. Billed as an 'onsen theme park' – a fantastically Japanese concept – it's done up to resemble a Disneyland-style version of an Edo-era town, with games and food stalls. Touristy, yes, but for visitors making their first foray into Japanese-style communal bathing, the light and kitschy atmosphere makes the actual bathing part that much less intimidating.

Ōedo Onsen Monogatari

Don't Miss

The Bathing Pools

Ōedo Onsen Monogatari has both indoor and outdoor tubs, called *rotemburo*, separated by gender. Part of the fun is hopping from bath to bath trying out the different temperatures and styles. There are jet baths, pools of natural rock and, on the ladies' side, personal bucket-shaped baths made of cedar. The water, rich in sodium chloride, is said to be good for aches and pains.

Wearing a Yukata

The first thing you'll do when you arrive is change into a *yukata*, a light, summer kimono. You'll have your pick from a variety of colours; rental is included in the admission price. It's worn with the left side over the right, tied at the waist for women and at the hips for men.

The Garden & Foot Bath

Outside is a Japanese-style garden with a 50m long *ashi-yu* (foot bath) snaking through the centre. Visitors dressed in *yukata* stroll through the ankle deep water, keeping their feet warm no matter how chill the air. On the bottom are stones designed to stimulate the pressure points on the soles of the feet.

The Town

At the centre of the complex you'll find carnival-style games and food vendors, intended to re-create the feel of an old-time street festival – an atmosphere enhanced by the fact that everyone is in *yukata*. This is your chance to try your luck slinging *shuriken* (ninja throwing stars).

大江戸温泉物語

www.ooedoonsen.jp/ higaeri/english/index. html

2-6-3 Aomi, Kōtō-ku

adult/child from ¥1980/900, after 6pm from ¥1480/900

🕐 11am-8am

☑ Top Tips

▸ Visit on a weekday afternoon, when it is less likely to be crowded.

▸ Visitors with tattoos will be denied admission.

✕ Take a Break

Nothing complements a long soak better than a cold beer. Take the Rinkai Line one stop to **TY Harbor Brewing** (📞5479-4555; www. tyharborbrewing.co.jp; 2-1-3 Higashi-Shinagawa, Shina-gawa-ku; lunch set ¥1200-1700, dinner mains from ¥1700; 🕐 11.30am-2pm, 5.30-10pm), a waterfront restaurant with an on-site brewery in an old warehouse. There are also plenty of eating options within Ōedo Onsen Monogatari.

Top Sights
Mt Fuji

Getting There

🚌 During the climbing season, **Keiō Dentetsu buses** (📞5376-2222; www.highwaybus.com) depart from the Shinjuku Highway Terminal (p191) for Kawaguchi-ko Fifth Station (¥2600, 2½ hours; reservations necessary).

Catching a glimpse of Mt Fuji (Fuji-san; 3776m), Japan's highest and most famous peak, will take your breath away. Climbing it, and then watching the sunrise from the summit, is one of Japan's superlative experiences. The official climbing season runs from 1 July to 31 August. From mid-April to early December, you can take a bus to the Kawaguchi-ko Fifth Station to stand in awesome proximity of the snowcapped cone. Throughout the year, you can hunt for views from the foothills around the lake, Kawaguchi-ko.

Mt Fuji

Don't Miss

The Mountain
Of the iconic images of Japan, Mt Fuji is the real deal. Admiration for the mountain appears in Japan's earliest recorded literature, dating from the 8th century. Then the now dormant volcano was prone to spewing smoke, making it all the more revered. Mt Fuji continues to captivate; some 300,000 people climb it every season.

The Climb
The Japanese proverb 'He who climbs Mount Fuji once is a wise man, he who climbs it twice is a fool' remains valid. While reaching the top brings a sense of achievement, it's a gruelling climb, often packed and the apocalyptic landscape is world's away from Fuji's beauty when viewed from afar.

The Kawaguchi-ko Trail
Of the four trails, Kawaguchi-ko Trail from Kawaguchi-ko Fifth Station (2305m) is the most popular route. It has the most mountain huts and is the easiest to reach by public transport from Tokyo.

Timing Your Hike
Many climbers opt to start at night around 10pm, to arrive at the top for dawn. *Goraikō* (the rising sun) will leave you speechless (unless it's cloudy). This is the most time- and money-efficient way, but also when you'll encounter the most people. Otherwise you can start in the afternoon, spend the night in a mountain hut and begin again before dawn.

The Summit
At the summit, the crater has a circumference of 4km and it takes about 1½ hours to complete

☑ Top Tips
▶ Weekdays see fewer climbers, except during the week-long O-bon holiday, in mid-August.

▶ Climbing info and a map is at www.city. fujiyoshida.yamanashi. jp/div/english/html/ climb.html

▶ Check weather at www.snow-forecast. com/resorts/Mount-Fuji

▶ Descending can be harder on the knees than ascending; bring hiking poles.

✖ Take a Break
You can spend the night at **Fujisan Hotel** (富士山 ホテル; ☎0555-22-0237; www.fujisanhotel.com; per person without/with 2 meals from ¥5700/7900), a mountain hut at the Eighth Station. Reservations are essential. Other huts, offering simple meals and spartan sleeping facilities, are located at stations five through eight. Most huts will let you rest inside if you buy something, and have toilets you can use for a fee (usually ¥100).

o-hachi meguri, the circling of the top. The highest point (3776m) is on the opposite side from the trail, and there's a post office to send a postcard back home. There are also a handful of humble restaurants. Trust us: a hot bowl of noodles never tasted so good.

The History
The trails up the mountain are centuries-old, dating to the time when reaching the summit was a spiritual endeavor. Many of the mountain huts have long histories, too, having got their start as pilgrim inns.

Nearby: Kawaguchi-ko
Nearby lake Kawaguchi-ko acts as a natural reflecting pool for the mountain's cone. The eponymous lakeside town offers year-round activities including hiking and onsen-soaking. Keiō Dentetsu buses run daily from the **Shinjuku Highway Bus Terminal** (p191) to Kawaguchi-ko town (¥1700, 1¾ hours).

Nearby: Fuji Sengen-jinja
During the era of the pilgrim a necessary preliminary to the Mt Fuji ascent was a visit to the deeply wooded, atmospheric Shintō shrine, **Fuji Sengen-jinja** (富士浅間神社; ☏0555-22-0221; http://sengenjinja.jp/index.html; 5558 Kami-Yoshida, Fuji-Yoshida; ⏰grounds 24hr; staffed 9am-5pm), in the neighbouring town of Fuji-Yoshida. In fact, the top of Mt Fuji (from the Eighth Station up) is part of its sacred precinct; look for a small 'branch' shrine at the summit.

Understand
Climbing Mt Fuji

- -

Know Before You Go
Although children and grandparents regularly summit Fuji-san, it is
a serious mountain. It's high enough for altitude sickness and the
weather can be volatile. You can count on it being close to freezing in
the morning, even in summer. Bring clothing appropriate for cold and
wet weather, including a hat and gloves. If you're climbing at night, bring
a torch (flashlight) or headlamp and spare batteries. On the mountain,
water costs around ¥500 for 500ml; make sure to bring enough of your
own, or enough cash.

The Trails
Mt Fuji is divided into 10 'stations' from base (First station) to summit
(Tenth). The original pilgrim trail starts from the base, but most climbers
begin from one of the four Fifth stations, accessible via bus. If, like most
travellers, you're taking the Kawaguchi-ko Trail, allow five to six hours to
reach the top and about three to descend, plus time to enjoy the summit.

    The three other trails – Subashiri, Fujinomiya and Gotemba – see
less people traffic, but have little to no public transportation access. All
routes converge at the Eighth Station, so you need to take care to make
sure you take the right path on the way down.

Off-season Advisory
Authorities strongly caution against climbing outside the regular season, when the weather is highly unpredictable and first-aid stations are
closed. Mountain huts on the Kawaguchi-ko Trail stay open through
mid-September when weather conditions may still be good; none open
before July, when snow still blankets the upper stations. Once snow or
ice is on the mountain, Fuji becomes a very serious and dangerous un-
dertaking and should only be attempted by those with winter mountain-
eering equipment and plenty of experience. Check weather conditions
carefully before setting out and do not climb alone. Off-season climbers
should register with the local police department; fill out the form at the
Kawaguchiko Tourist Information Center next to Kawaguchi-ko Station.

The Best of
Tokyo

Shinjuku-gyoen (p109)
TOM BONAVENTURE / GETTY IMAGES ©

Best Walks
Contemporary Architecture in Omote-sandō

🏃 The Walk

Omote-sandō, a broad, tree-lined boulevard between Harajuku and Aoyama, is known for its upmarket boutiques designed by the who's who of (mostly) Japanese contemporary architects. This stretch of prime real estate functions as a design showroom and is full of architectural eye candy. All of the buildings on the route are contemporary, though the final stop Nezu Museum is a modern take on the traditional Japanese villa.

Start Omotesandō Hills; 🚉 Harajuku

Finish Nezu Museum; 🚉 Omote-sandō

Length 1.5km; one hour

✖ Take a Break

On Omote-sandō, between Harajuku and Aoyama, **Anniversaire Café** (p100) has an attractive patio that is perfect for people-watching.

Omote-sandō, Harajuku (p94)

❶ Omotesandō Hills

Andō Tadao's deceptively deep **Omotesandō Hills** (2003) is a high-end shopping mall spiralling around a sunken central atrium. It replaced an ivy-covered pre-WWII apartment building (to considerable protest); the low horizontal design pays homage to the original structure.

❷ Dior Building

Across the street from Omotesandō Hills, the flagship boutique for **Dior** (2003), designed by Pritzker Prize winner SANAA (composed of Sejima Kazuyo and Nishizawa Ryūe), has a filmy, white exterior that seems to hang like a dress. The exterior is made entirely of glass and a thin grey sheath, which acts as a semipermeable veil protecting the refined interior from the urban tangle outside.

❸ Japan Nursing Association

The glass cone of the **Japan Nursing Association** (2004) is classic Kurokawa Kishō, the architect who later designed the undulating glass facade of the **National Art Center Tokyo** (p54).

❹ Louis Vuitton Building

Evoking a stack of clothes trunks, Aoki Jun's design for **Louis Vuitton** (2002) features offset panels of tinted glass behind sheets of metal mesh.

❺ Tod's Building

Climb onto the elevated crosswalk to better admire Itō Toyō's construction for **Tod's** (2004). The crisscross-

ing strips of concrete take their inspiration from the zelkova trees below; what's more impressive is that they're also structural.

❻ Spiral Building

Maki Fumihiko's postmodernist **Spiral Building** (p95) is worth a detour down Aoyama-dōri. Constructed in 1985, it predates everything else on this walk. The patchwork, uncentred design is a nod to Tokyo's own mismatched landscape. Inside, a spiralling passage doubles as an **art gallery**.

❼ Prada Building

The most internationally famous structure on this strip is the convex glass fishbowl that Herzog and de Meuron designed for **Prada** (2003).

❽ Nezu Museum

Finish the walk at the **Nezu Museum** (p93), remodelled in 2009 by Kuma Kengō. The bamboo-lined entrance is likened by the architect to the pathway that leads to a traditional teahouse, which gives the visitor time to adjust his or her mood.

Best Walks
Asakusa Shitamachi

🏃 The Walk

Shitamachi is the word used to describe the Tokyo that comes close to approximating the spirit of old Edo. Not only does Asakusa have important temples and shrines dating to the Edo era (1603–1868), it also has the narrow lanes and wooden shop fronts that characterise Shitamachi today. This walk will take you past the main sights, and also along lanes that ooze old-Tokyo atmosphere.

Start Azuma-bashi; 🚇 Asakusa

Finish Ef; 🚇 Asakusa

Length 3km; two hours

🍴 Take a Break

Stop for tempura at **Daikokuya** (p150) on Dembō-in-dōri. You'll also find snack vendors along Nakamise-dōri, such as **Chōchin Monaka** (p151).

Sensō-ji (p146)

❶ Azuma-bashi

Originally built in 1774, **Azuma-bashi** was once the departure point for boat trips to the Yoshi-wara pleasure district, just north of Asakusa. Today, **tourist boats** leave from a nearby pier, going towards Hama-rikyū Onshi-teien and Odaiba (in Tokyo Bay).

❷ Nakamise-dōri

Most shops along the pedestrianised **Nakamise-dōri** sell tour-ist trinkets, but there are also a few that sell authentic artisan crafts. Check out **Kanesō** (p155), purveyors of hand-made knives since 1873.

❸ Sensō-ji

At the end of Nakamise-dori is the ancient temple **Sensō-ji** (p146), which has been drawing pilgrims to Asakusa for centuries. Also worth a visit is nearby **Asakusa-jinja** (p149), a rare early-Edo Shintō shrine, dating to the early 17th century.

❹ Dembō-in-dōri

Dembō-in-dōri is lined with shops fronted by

wooden signboards and sliding doors, providing a historic atmosphere. Stop in **Yonoya Kushiho** (p154), a shop that has been producing box-wood combs since 1717. At the end of the street is **Chingo-dō** (p149), a tiny Buddhist temple dedicated to the *tanuki*, the Japanese raccoon dog.

5 Traditional Crafts Museum

The **Traditional Crafts Museum** (p149) show-cases the crafts still produced locally in Asakusa, and it's free to enter. On the way, you'll pass **Hanayashiki** (p149), Japan's oldest amusement park.

6 Asakusa Engei Hall

Lantern-lit **Asakusa Engei Hall** (p154) is reminiscent of the vaudeville halls that were once common here. The theatre is part of the Rokku district of Asakusa, a famous (and famously bawdy) entertainment district during the century before WWII.

7 Covered Passages

More Shōwa period (1926–1989) than Shi-tamachi, the **covered shopping arcades** around Asakusa have a retro feel. Among the more modern shops are some oldies, such as those specialising in *geta*, the traditional sandals worn with kimono.

8 Ef

Finish at **Ef** (p154), a gallery and cafe in an old wooden building originally built in 1868 as a warehouse.

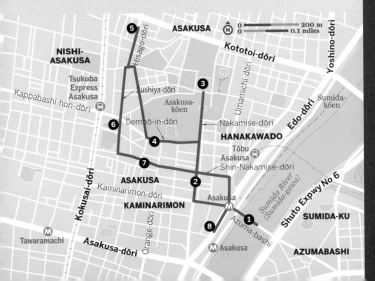

Best Walks
Historic Marunouchi & Ginza

🏃 The Walk

Neighbouring Marunouchi and Ginza were the first Tokyo neighbourhoods to modernise (in the western sense) after Japan opened its doors to foreign influence at the end of the 19th century. Many reminders of this fascinating, turbulent time still exist. This is also where you'll find top sights, such as the Imperial Palace and Kabuki-za, and the city's most expensive real estate.

Start Tokyo Station; 🚇Tokyo

Finish Ginza Lion; 🚇Ginza

Length 2.5km; 90 minutes

✗ Take a Break

Cafe 1894 (p29) in Marunouchi Brick Square, does light lunches, coffee and cake. There are also plenty of treats to be sourced from the *depachika* (department store food hall) in **Mitsukoshi** (p44).

ULTRA.F / GETTY IMAGES ©

Tokyo Station (p27)

❶ Tokyo Station

Head out the Marunouchi exit to see the recently restored domes of **Tokyo Station** (p27). Conceived as the city's first rail hub, the European-style brick station opened in 1914.

❷ Marunouchi Building

Walking west from the station, you'll pass the **Marunouchi Building**, first erected in 1923 when Marunouchi was taking shape as the city's first modern business district. The building emerged 30 storeys taller after a renovation in 2001, but the street level facade evokes the original structure. From the **lounge** on the 35th floor you can see all the way to the Imperial Palace.

❸ Imperial Palace

After the Meiji Restoration brought the emperor from Kyoto to Tokyo, the **Imperial Palace** (p24) was built to replace the shōgun's castle, Edo-jō. Walk along the moat and look in the distance to see some of the old castle keeps that still remain.

❹ Brick Square

Brick Square, one of Marunouchi's newest shopping and dining complexes, contains a faithful reproduction of the neighbourhood's first office building, now the **Mitsubishi Ichigōkan Museum** (p27), and a bank, now **Cafe 1894** (p168). From here, take a gambol south along pretty, tree-lined **Naka-dōri** to Ginza.

❺ Ginza

Ginza was the city's first modern retail district, where department stores introduced the latest fashions from the west. **Mitsukoshi** (p168), which was a kimono store before it became a department store, is the oldest on the block, founded in 1904 – though it just had a facelift. There are others along Ginza's main drag, **Chūō-dōri** (p39).

❻ Kabuki-za

Kabuki is the rare traditional art form that survived the onslaught of western culture throughout the 20th century. Tokyo's premier kabuki theatre, **Kabuki-za** (p36), has stood on this spot since 1889 and recently drew headlines for the completion of a lengthy renovation. Stop by to see the contemporary take on the traditional kabuki theatre facade.

❼ Ginza Lion

Finish the walk with a toast at **Ginza Lion** (p43). It dates to the 1930, when such beer halls were the height of fashion, and has a fabulous retro interior.

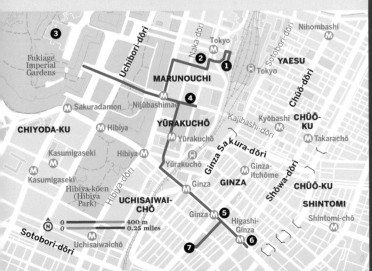

Best
Architecture

WAYNE FOGDEN / GETTY IMAGES ©

Tokyo is forever under construction; there is always something new going up that is taller, sleeker, and generally more dazzling than what existed before. It's fertile ground for the country's architects, many of whom are among the most feted in their world. The city's soaring towers, stunning museums and fanciful boutiques will make architecture fans swoon.

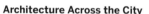

Architecture Across the City

During the construction boom in the decades following WWII, Tokyo expanded to the west and this is where you'll see more contemporary structures and the riot of neon that has come to symbolise modern Tokyo. The east side is considered the old city, though few truly old buildings remain. Still, in small pockets, such as around Ueno and Asakusa, you can see some examples of the traditional wooden structures that once defined Tokyo.

Contemporary Design

Tange Kenzō was the most prominent architect of the post-WWII years, creating landmark structures such as the National Gymnasium in Yoyogi-kōen and the Tokyo Metropolitan Government Offices (p109). Among Kenzō's contemporaries were the Metabolists Kurokawa Kishō and Maki Fumihiko, whose design philosophy championed flexible spaces over fixed form.

A second wave of architects arrived in the 1980s and 1990s, who continue to explore both modernism and post-modernism, pushing forward while also drawing on Japan's rich heritage. Names to know include Kuma Kengō and Pritzker Prize winners Andō Tadao, SANAA (Sejima Kazuyo and Nishizawa Ryūe) and Itō Toyō.

☑ Top Tip

▶ **Omote-sandō** is the best place in the city to see contemporary architecture. Here you'll find works from most of the rising stars, all on one strip so that you can easily compare styles. For a walk through the neighbourhood, see p164.

Best Structural Statements

Tokyo Metropolitan Government Offices Iconic skyscrapers by Tange Kenzō. (p109)

Roppongi Hills Ambitious, utopian micro-city. (p50)

Tokyo Sky Tree Tokyo's newest sky-high landmark. (p144)

Tokyo Metropolitan Government Offices (p109)

Tokyo International Forum Soaring glass vessel in the heart of downtown. (p27)

Asahi Flame Phillipe Starck's curious golden plume. (p149)

Tokyo Tower Beloved symbol of post-WWII Tokyo. (p55)

Best Museum Architecture

National Art Center Tokyo Sculptural structure of curving glass by Kurokawa Kishō. (p54)

Gallery of Hōryū-ji Treasures Modernist home of ancient Buddhist sculpture, designed by Yoshio Taniguchi. (p132)

Nezu Museum Kuma Kengō's contemporary take on traditional Japanese design. (p93)

21_21 Design Sight Concrete clam shell by Andō Tadao. (p54)

Best East Meets West

Kyū Iwasaki-teien 19th-century estate with both western- and Japanese-style wings. (p138)

Tokyo Metropolitan Teien Art Museum Art deco former princely residence. (p68)

Takashimaya Opulent 1930's department store filtered through Japanese sensibilities. (p31)

Kabuki-za Traditional theatre superimposed on a modern skyscraper, designed by Kuma Kengō. (p36)

Worth a Trip

On the grounds of a sprawling park, the **Edo-Tokyo Open Air Architectural Museum** (江戸東京たてもの園; http://tatemonoen.jp/english/index.html; 3-7-1 Sakura-chō, Koganei; adult/child ¥400/free; ⊙9.30am-5.30pm Tue-Sun Apr-Sep, to 4.30pm Tue-Sun Oct-Mar; ♿; 🚃JR Chūō Line to Musashi-Koganei) preserves a number of original structures from the Edo period (1603–1868) to the early post-WWII years, all rescued from Tokyo's modernising zeal.

Best **Temples & Shrines**

Tokyo is home to countless Buddhist temples and Shintō shrines, honouring Japan's two entwined religions. The grounds are free to enter and open to all – so long as the gate is open. The grandest ones are simply stunning, but just as enchanting are the tiny temples and shrines tucked among buildings that you're likely to stumble upon as you explore the city.

DAVID CLAPP / GETTY IMAGES ©

Visiting Etiquette

Shrines and temples don't have strict rules (there are no dress codes, for example). However, there are some prescribed manners. Since the *torii* gates in front of a Shintō shrine indicate the entrance to sacred space, you'll often see Japanese visitors bowing upon entering and exiting. Before approaching the main shrine, it is customary to wash your hands at the font, since Shintō prizes purity.

Temples often have a slightly raised threshold, which you should step over – not on. Taking pictures on the grounds is fine, but many temples do not want you taking photos – especially flash photos – of the inside.

☑ **Top Tips**

▶ Temples and shrines host festivals throughout the year. For event listings, see **Go Tokyo** (www.gotokyo.org/en/index.html).

▶ It is customary to make a small offering at both temples and shrines. Fortunately for budget travelers, a five yen coin is considered the luckiest (10 yen coins are unlucky).

Best Temples

Sensō-ji Beloved symbol of Tokyo for centuries. (p146)

Zōjō-ji A sprawling temple, home to the tombs of former shōguns. (p56)

Kiyōmizu Kannon-dō Modeled after Kyoto's famous Kiyōmizu-dera. (p137)

Best Shrines

Meiji-jingū Tokyo's grandest shrine, set in a wooded grove. (p90)

Asakusa-jinja Edo-era structure that survived earthquakes, fire and war. (p149)

Yasukuni-jinja Beautiful and controversial shrine to Japan's war dead. (p121)

Tokyo Dai-jingū Tokyo branch of Japan's 'mother' shrine, Ise-jingū. (p122)

Nogi-jinja The scene of General Nogi's famous ritual suicide. (p56)

Best
Parks & Gardens

Apartment-dwellers of Tokyo may not have the luxury of backyards, but they have hectares of open space in the city's many parks – almost all of which are free to enter. Most of the city's sprawling, manicured gardens, which cost just a few hundred yen, once belonged to the imperial family or the former feudal elite.

Cherry Blossoms

Tokyo's parks and gardens really come to life during *hanami* (cherry blossom viewing), which usually happens in late March or early April. Blue tarps are spread on the ground and groups of friends and co-workers gather under the *sakura* (cherry blossoms) for sake-drenched picnics. It's a centuries-old tradition, to celebrate the fleeting beauty of life, symbolised by the blossoms which last only a week or two.

Ueno-kōen (p137) has long been Tokyo's most famous *hanami* spot. Yoyogi-kōen (p94) is the destination for serious party-people, who come armed with barbecues, karaoke machines and even turntables. Shinjuku-gyoen (p109) is a grassy, family-friendly spot for lazing under the blossoms. Naka-Meguro (p67), with its tree-lined canal, is another local favourite; come in the evening for *yozakura* (night-time cherry blossoms), when the canal is lit with lanterns.

Best Parks

Yoyogi-kōen The city's biggest, liveliest swath of green and a popular gathering spot, especially on weekends. (p94)

Shinjuku-gyoen An imperial garden turned glorious park. (p109)

Ueno-kōen A pond full of waterlilies, plus temples and shrines. (p137)

TOM BONAVENTURE / GETTY IMAGES ©

☑ **Top Tip**

▶ Pick up a *bentō* (boxed meal) from a *depachika* (department store food hall) or convenience store for a picnic lunch in the park.

Institute for Nature Study What Tokyo would look like with no people. (p68)

Best Gardens

Hama-rikyū Onshi-teien A manicured garden with a centuries-old tea house. (p39)

Koishikawa Kōrakuen A classic Edo-era landscaped garden. (p121)

Imperial Palace East Garden On the palace grounds, with the ruins of an old stone keep. (p25)

Best
Galleries &
Museums

TRAVELASIA / GETTY IMAGES ©

Tokyo is a city enamored with museums. Not only does it have many excellent established institutions, it is constantly building new ones. These include both grand repositories of art and antiquities, and tiny centres of devotion to one particular thing. Tokyo is also the centre of Japan's contemporary art scene and has numerous galleries to show for it.

Contemporary Art Scene

Tokyo's contemporary art scene is broad, dynamic and scattered – much like the city itself. Ginza is Tokyo's original gallery district, and a good place to get started. In the last decade, Roppongi, with its three big museums – Mori Art Museum (p51), National Art Center Tokyo (p54) and Suntory Museum of Art (p54) – has emerged as an art centre. As a result, many galleries, such as those in the Piramide Building (p56) have moved into the neighbourhood. Yanaka, with its proximity to the city's top art school, Geidai, has long been an artist's neighbourhood and there are galleries and studios there, too.

Access & Admission

Many museums close one day a week, often on Mondays (or, if Monday is a national holiday, then the following Tuesday). Museums in Tokyo tend to close early, around 5pm or 6pm, and last admission is 30 minutes before closing. Take advantage of the free lockers (¥100 deposit) to stow your coat and bag. Permanent exhibits at national museums are the most economical; expect to pay more for admission to temporary exhibits or private museums. Commercial galleries are free to enter.

☑ Top Tip

▶ See p193 for information on museum discounts.

▶ Check out **Tokyo Art Beat** (www.tokyoartbeat.com) for exhibition listings and reviews. The site also produces a printed guide every other month to the best shows around town; look for it at museums and galleries.

Best for Traditional Art

Tokyo National Museum Hands-down the best collection of Japanese art and antiquities anywhere. (p130)

Ukiyo-e Ōta Memorial Art Museum Woodblock prints by masters of the medium. (p93)

Nezu Museum Asian antiquities in a striking contemporary building. (p93)

Best for Modern & Contemporary Art

Mori Art Museum Blockbuster, large-scale contemporary exhibits. (p51)

Tokyo Metropolitan Museum of Photography The city's best photography museum. (p67)

National Museum of Modern Art A crash course in Japanese modernism. (p121)

National Art Center Tokyo Venue for contemporary exhibitions, such as the Japan Media Arts Festival. (p54)

Best for Decorative Arts

Musée Tomo Stunning collection of contemporary ceramics. (p54)

Suntory Museum of Art Ceramics, glassware, lacquerware etc from Japan and abroad. (p54)

Best History Museums

Shitamachi Museum Recreation of a wooden, Edo-era tenement neighbourhood. (p137)

National Shōwa Memorial Museum Exhibitions on daily life for the Japanese during WWII. (p121)

Best Galleries

SCAI the Bathhouse Cutting-edge contemporary art in a converted bathhouse. (p135)

Tokyo Gallery Long-running, influential gallery showing mostly Japanese and Chinese artists. (p40)

Piramide Building Several fine-art galleries under one roof. (p56)

Design Festa Funky locus of the DIY art movement. (p95)

Best Quirky Museums

Beer Museum Yebisu A concise history of beer in Japan. (p67)

Meguro Parasitological Museum Internal creepy-crawlies on display. (p69)

Kite Museum Colourful traditional kites in the old Edo style. (p28)

Worth a Trip

The excellent **Edo-Tokyo Museum** (江戸東京博物館; ☎3626-9974; www.edo-tokyo-museum.or.jp; 1-4-1 Yokoami, Sumida-ku; adult/child ¥600/free; ☉9.30am-5.30pm Tue-Sun, to 7.30pm Sat; 🚃JR Sōbu Line to Ryōgoku, west exit) documents Tokyo's epic transition from old Edo to its modern avatar. Highlights include real examples of Edo-era infrastructure and impeccably detailed scale models of markets and shops during the era of the shōgun.

Best
Food

When it comes to Tokyo superlatives, the city's eating scene takes the cake. At the top of the dining hierarchy is sushi – best eaten in Tokyo's posh Ginza neighbourhood or fresh from Tsukiji Central Fish Market – and *kaiseki*, Japan's traditional haute cuisine. Tokyo also has some wonderful traditional restaurants that have been turning out excellent renditions of classic dishes for decades.

SHYMAN / GETTY IMAGES ©

Tokyo Dining Scene

Tokyo is a food lover's paradise and wherever you are in the city, you're rarely more than 500m from a good, if not great, meal. Fine-dining is most heavily concentrated in and around Ginza and Roppongi; Roppongi, where expats tend to congregate, also has the most diverse spread of international cuisines. Stylish Harajuku has stylish restaurants, naturally, and is particularly good for lunch. Shibuya, with its nightlife, has lots of low-price dinner options aimed at the young crowd who party here. Ebisu is stocked with hip, casual restaurants that draw fashionable 20 and 30-somethings. Ueno and Asakusa are a good bet for classic Japanese cuisine in a traditional setting. Shinjuku, as a major transit hub, has something for just about everyone.

Izakaya

Izakaya (居酒屋) translates as drinking house – the Japanese equivalent of a pub. Here food is ordered for the table a few dishes at a time and washed down with plenty of beer or sake. *Izakaya* come in all stripes, from stripped down working-class joints to *oshare* (fashionable) date spots. Either way, it's a classic local experience.

☑ **Top Tips**

▶ Reservations are necessary at high-end restaurants and a good idea at midrange places, especially on weekends or if your party is larger than two.

▶ Traditional or smaller restaurants may not accept credit cards.

▶ Check out **Tokyo Food Page** (www.bento.com) for dining listings and reviews in English.

Best Japanese

Tonki *Tonkatsu* (pork cutlets) as art. (p69)

Agaru Sagaru Nishi Iru Higashi Iru Creative *kaiseki* in a subterranean cave. (p99)

Kado Classic home cooking in a classic old house. (p123)

d47 Shokudō Regional specialities from around the country. (p79)

Best Local Eating

Shirube Wildly popular *izakaya* with inventive dishes. (p87)

Nagi Late night *rāmen* in Golden Gai. (p107)

Yanaka Ginza Old-fashioned alley lined with takeout counters. (p134)

Ebisu-yokochō Hip retro dining arcade. (p69)

Best Old Tokyo Flavour

Hantei Grilled skewers in a hundred-year-old heritage house. (p139)

Komagata Dojō One of few restaurants that still serves stewed eel, an Edo-era dish. (p153)

Omoide-yokochō Atmospheric *yakitori* stalls near the train tracks. (p110)

Daikokuya Down-home tempura, an old Tokyo specialty. (p166)

Best Sushi

Daiwa Sushi Ultra fresh fish served inside Tsukiji Fish Market. (p42)

Sushi Kanesaka Rarefied Ginza sushi at its finest. (p42)

Sushi-no-Midori Popular joint selling reasonably-priced, filling sets. (p80)

Best Noodles

Tokyo Rāmen Street Mini-branches of the country's best *rāmen* shops. (p28)

Narutomi Classic soba (buckwheat noodle) dishes in a sophisticated setting. (p40)

Tsurutontan Huge bowls of udon (thick wheat noodles) with oodles of toppings. (p56)

Best *Izakaya*

Jōmon Lively counter joint serving delicious grilled skewers. (p58)

Gonpachi Tokyo landmark that inspired a set in the film *Kill Bill*. (p58)

Donjaka Classic *izakaya*. (p112)

Best Splurge

Tofuya-Ukai Handmade tofu becomes haute cuisine. (p59)

Kikunoi Gorgeous *kaiseki* in the classic Kyoto style. (p59)

Asakusa Imahan Kobe beef *shabu-shabu* (simmered in broth). (p153)

Bird Land Exquisite *yakitori* from free-range, heirloom birds. (p42)

Best Sweets

Ouca Ice cream in only-in-Japan flavours. (p69)

Kyō Hayashi-ya Decadent *matcha* parfaits. (p56)

Worth a Trip

A 10-minute walk from Naka-Meguro Station and all but hidden in a swank residential enclave, **Higashi-Yama** (ヒガシヤマ; ☎5720-1300; www.higashiyama-tokyo.jp; 1-21-25 Higashiyama, Meguro-ku; lunch/dinner course from ¥2100/4000; ⏰11.30am-2pm & 6pm-1am Mon-Sat; ⓇHibiya Line to Naka-Meguro) serves up gorgeous modern Japanese cuisine in a stark, minimalist setting. Look for the concrete building with the small, illuminated sign.

Best
Sentō & Onsen

DAJ / GETTY IMAGES ©

Don't be shy! Many Japanese would argue that you couldn't possibly understand their culture without taking a dip, and the blissful relaxation that follows can turn a sceptic into a convert. Onsen is pure hot spring water – believed to have therapeutic powers. *Sentō* are old-school public bathhouses dating from the era when Tokyo housing didn't have private baths.

Bathing Etiquette

Getting naked with strangers is scary enough, so relax. There's really only one hard and fast rule you need to remember: wash yourself *before* you get in the bath.

When you enter a bathhouse, put your shoes at a locker at the entrance. Then pay your admission fee and head to the correct – check the characters on the door curtains – changing room. Leave your clothes in a locker or basket and enter the bathing room with just your toiletries and a small hand-towel. Park yourself on a stool in front of one of the taps and give yourself a thorough wash, making sure to rinse off all the suds.

That little towel performs a variety of functions: you can use it to wash (but make sure to give it a good rinse afterwards) or to cover yourself as you walk around. It is not supposed to touch the water though, so leave it on the side of the bath or – as many Japanese do – folded on top of your head. Before heading back to the changing room, use it to wipe yourself down, so as not to drip on the changing room floor.

Note that many bathhouses refuse entry to persons with tattoos because of their association with the *yakuza* (Japanese mafia).

☑ **Top Tips**

▸ *Sentō* don't provide soap and towels, so bring your own (or buy some from the counter).

▸ Know your kanji: 女 means women and 男 means men.

Best Baths

Ōedo Onsen Monogatari 'Onsen theme park' with real hot spring water and a variety of tubs. (p157)

Jakotsu-yu A classic *sentō* with pure hot spring water and no policy against tattoos. (p150)

Shimizu-yu Sparkling modern *sentō*, with jet baths and saunas. (p95)

Best
Traditional
Theatre & Dance

WILL ROBB / GETTY IMAGES ©

Tokyo, when it was Edo (1600–1868), had a rich theatre culture. Above all, there was kabuki – captivating, occasionally outrageous and beloved. Ribald *rakugo* (comedic monologue) was another favourite diversion in Edo times, and still draws audiences today. Other classic forms include *nō* (stylised dance-drama), *gagaku* (music of the imperial court) and *bunraku* (classic puppet theatre).

☑ **Top Tips**

▶ Purchase kabuki tickets from http://www.kabuki-bito.jp/eng/top.html.

▶ Get kabuki *makumi* tickets an hour before the show from the counter in front of the theatre.

▶ Rent a headset (¥700, plus ¥1000 deposit) at Kabuki-za for explanations of the plays and translations of the dialogue into English. It's impossible to follow along without it!

Kabuki

A day at the theatre is a popular pastime. In Tokyo, kabuki performances are held at Kabuki-za (p36) in Ginza. Shows run 25 days a month and ticket sales begin on the 12th of the preceding month. A whole performance lasts several hours. If you're on a tight schedule you can opt instead for a '*makumi*' ticket (¥800–2000) for just one act, which usually lasts about an hour. These tickets are only good for 4th-tier seats.

Rakugo

While kabuki tickets now fetch a handsome price and carry an air of sophistication, *rakugo* is wonderfully unpretentious. The performer sits on a square cushion on stage, using only a fan and hand towel as props. A typical show lasts hours and features more than a dozen performers. A number of famous comedians, including movie director Kitano Takeshi have studied *rakugo* as part of their development.

Best Traditional Theatres

Kabuki-za *The* place for the full kabuki experience. (p36)

National Nō Theatre
Ancient *nō* on a sparse stage. (p101)

Asakusa Engei Hall An old-fashioned vaudeville stage for *rakugo* comedians, jugglers and more. (p154)

Best Shopping & Markets

(TRAVELASIA / GETTY IMAGES ©)

Tokyo is the trendsetter for the rest of Japan, and its residents shop – economy be damned – with an infectious enthusiasm. From quirky fashion to cutting-edge electronics, antiques to traditional crafts, Tokyo has many ways to tempt your wallet. Merchandise is generally of excellent quality, and not as wildly expensive as you might think.

Shopping Tokyo

Tokyo is famous for its fashion tribes, each of whom has a preferred stomping grounds. Ginza has long been Tokyo's premier shopping district and is home to many high-end department stores and boutiques. Rival Harajuku, on the other side of town, has boutiques that deal in both luxury fashion and street cred. Shibuya is the locus of the teen fashion trend machine, while nearby Shimo-Kitazawa has the city's highest concentration of vintage clothing stores. Ebisu and Meguro are known for small one-off shops selling artsy fashions and homewares.

For one-stop shopping, Shinjuku is your best bet: here you'll find department stores, electronics outfitters, book stores, record shops and fashionable boutiques. Akihabara is the place to go to source anime and manga related goods. Ueno and Asakusa have many stores selling artisan crafts, both traditional and contemporary.

Antiques & Flea Markets

Tokyo's biggest and best antique market is the Ōedo Antique Market (p30), held on the 1st and 3rd Sunday of the month. Some shrines and temples also host regular flea markets; for listings, see **Metropolis** (http://metropolis.co.jp/listings/).

☑ Top Tip

▶ Department stores and other large retailers have tax-free exemption counters for foreign tourists spending more than ¥10,000; you'll need to show your passport.

Best for Fashion

Dover Street Market Comme des Garçons and other avant-garde Japanese labels. (p44)

Sister Hipster boutique with the latest labels and vintage finds. (p84)

Laforet Harajuku landmark filled with kooky clothes. (p102)

Okura Beautiful indigo-dyed clothing and accessories. (p72)

Mitsukoshi department store (p44)

Best Local Shopping

Don Quijote An all-night treasure trove of miscellaneous oddities. (p107)

Meguro Interior Shops Community Interior-design district. (p72)

Best for Souvenirs

Tōkyū Hands Cute stationery, gadgets and beauty products. (p84)

Souvenir from Tokyo One-of-a-kind local artists and designers. (p63)

Best Department Stores

Mitsukoshi Classic department store with an excellent food hall. (p44)

Isetan Tokyo's most fashion forward department store. (p115)

Best Traditional Shops

Kamawanu Colourfully dyed cotton. (p72)

Isetatsu Gorgeous, printed paper. (p141)

Best Shopping Streets

Ameya-yokochō Vintage market in Ueno. (p137)

Takeshita-dōri Trend-setting fashion alley. (p101)

Best Bookstores

Daikanyama T-Site Designer digs for books. (p73)

On Sundays Art books galore and artsy stationary, too. (p102)

Worth a Trip

For proof that Tokyo's centuries-old artisan tradition is still alive and kicking, take a trip to **2K540 Aki-Oka Artisan** (アキオカアルチザン; www.jrtk.jp/2k540; 5-9 Ueno, Taitō-ku; ⏰ hours vary; 🚇 Ginza Line to Suehirochō, exit 2). In this minimalist bazaar, set up under the JR Yamanote Line tracks between Akihabara and Okachimachi Stations, you'll find young creators peddling all kinds of handmade wares.

Best
Nightlife & Live Music

Tokyo's nightlife is one of the city's highlights. Whatever stereotypes you may have held about Japanese people being quiet and reserved will fall to pieces after dark. Tokyo is a work hard, play hard kind of place and you'll find people out any night of the week. There is truly something for everyone here, from sky-high lounges to grungy hole-in-the-walls.

What's Hot Now

In the last few years, the craft beer scene has exploded in and around Tokyo, producing a number of respected breweries and beer bars, such as **Harajuku Taproom** (p99) and **Craftheads** (p82). Another recent trend is the rise of the *tachinomi-ya* (literally 'standing bar'), small, lively joints where patrons crowd around the bar. Karaoke remains ever popular in the land of its birth; to learn more about this very Japanese pastime, see p116.

Clubbing & Live Music

Tokyo has a healthy club scene, centred mostly around Shibuya and Roppongi. Friday and Saturday are the big nights out, though most clubs have something going on nearly every night. Discount flyers can be downloaded from most club websites. While bars don't ask for ID, clubs do: you must be 20 to enter and you *must* have a picture ID – even if you are decades beyond 20.

Tokyo's home-grown live music scene has turned out some good acts, often found playing around Shibuya, Ebisu and Shimo-Kitazawa. To find out what club and live music events are happening when you're in town, check out **Metropolis** (p180) and **Time Out Tokyo** (www.timeout.jp/en/tokyo).

CHRIS MELLOR / GETTY IMAGES ©

☑ **Top Tip**

▶ Get tickets for concerts at **Ticket Pia** (チケットぴあ; ☎0570-02-9111; http://t.pia.jp/; ⏰10am-8pm), on the 4th floor of **Shibuya Hikarie** (p78) and inside the **Asakusa Tourist Information Center** (p196).

Best Bars

Buri The *tachinomi-ya* that started the trend. (p70)

Zoetrope The best selection of Japanese whiskey in the world. (p113)

Beat Cafe Grungy haven for music lovers. (p81)

Pink Cow Funky wine bar with regular art events. (p60)

Kinfolk Lounge Cocktails in an old wooden house. (p71)

Best Local Drinking

Golden Gai A cluster of tiny bars in a former black market. (p107)

Mother Shimo-Kitazawa's groovy hideaway. (p87)

These Cocktails and books in posh enclave Nishi-Azabu. (p60)

Nonbei-yokochō Atmospheric alley near the train tracks in Shibuya. (p83)

Best Drinks with a View

New York Bar Sophisticated perch on top of the Park Hyatt Hotel. (p113)

Mado Lounge Glass boîte in Roppongi. (p60)

Two Rooms Comfy sofas on a terrace overlooking Harajuku. (p99)

Asahi Sky Room Views of Tokyo Sky Tree and the Sumida-gawa. (p154)

So Tired Cocktail lounge with a terrace in Marunouchi. (p30)

Best Historic Bars

Kamiya Bar One of Tokyo's first Western-style bars. (p153)

Ginza Lion Once fashionable, now wonderfully kitsch, beer hall from the 1930s. (p43)

Best Clubs

Womb It's all about the music – house and techno – at Tokyo's most famous club. (p81)

SuperDeluxe Artsy lounge with live music and DJ'd events. (p59)

Sound Museum Vision Cavernous space with a blockbuster roster of international DJs. (p81)

Best for Live Rock & Pop

Unit Basement venue with consistently great

indie bands, local and international. (p72)

Club Quattro Slick space for local and overseas artists playing pop, rock and world music. (p83)

Abbey Road Spot-on Beatles covers from the Japanese house band. (p61)

Loft Grungy, long-running launch pad for new bands. (p115)

Best for Live Jazz

Shinjuku Pit Inn Straight-up Tokyo's best jazz club. (p114)

Alfie Classy joint with a solid line-up of local musicians. (p62)

Best for Karaoke

Festa Iikura Good food, lots of English songs and free costume rentals. (p60)

Lovenet The most outlandish karaoke suites in the city. (p61)

Worth a Trip

Jicoo The Floating Bar (ジークザフローティングバー; ☏0120-049-490; www.jicoofloatingbar.com; admission ¥2500; ◷8-10.30pm Thu-Sat; ☒Yurikamome Line to Hinode or Odaiba Kaihin-kōen) cruises around Tokyo Bay after dark in a boat straight out of a sci-fi flick – it's designed by manga artist Leiji Matsumoto. DJs and the occasional live act lend a clubby vibe. Naturally, space is limited; reservations recommended.

Best
Pop Culture

From giant robots to saucer-eyed schoolgirls to a ubiquitous kitty, Japanese pop culture is a phenomenon that has reached far around the world. At the centre of the manga and anime vortex is the neighbourhood of Akihabara. For eye-popping street fashion, look to Shibuya and Harajuku.

DIGITAL VISION / GETTY IMAGES ©

Akihabara Otaku

Otaku gets translated as 'geek', but means someone who is passionately obsessed with something. More often than not that passion is anime (Japanese animation) or manga (Japanese comics), but it can also be used to describe a devoted fan of a pop idol or a collector of model trains. The *otaku*'s natural habitat is Akihabara, where comic bookstores, cosplay (costume play) cafes and electronics outfitters come together in a blaze of neon.

Shibuya Pop

Shibuya is the centre of Tokyo's teen culture. Here, the latest fashion trends grow legs, pop stars perform on giant TV screens and nightclubs and karaoke parlours glow all night long.

Harajuku Fashion

Harajuku continues to turn out fascinating fashion tribes, from *goth-loli* (think zombie Little Bo Peep) of the last decade to today's *doli-kei* (doll-style) girls, who model their look after cherub-cheeked dolls.

Best Pop Culture Experiences

Shibuya Crossing Intersection at the heart of Shibuya lit by giant TV screens. (p78)

@Home Cafe Akihabara's most famous maid cafe, where the waitresses dress like french maids. (p127)

Super Potato Retro-kan Old-school video arcade in Akihabara. (p127)

Robot Restaurant Shinjuku cabaret co-starring giant robots. (p115)

Humax Shinjuku arcade full of *purikura* (print club) photo booths. (p109)

Best Pop Culture Shopping

Takeshita-dōri Harajuku's famous subculture bazaar. (p93)

Mandarake Complex Mammoth anime and manga shop. (p127)

Shibuya 109 Teen fashion trend factory. (p84)

Gachapon Kaikan Hundreds of *gachapon* (capsule vending machines). (p127)

KiddyLand Four-storey emporium of cute character goods. (p101)

Best
Gay & Lesbian

Tokyo is more tolerant of homosexuality and alternative lifestyles than most of its Asian counterparts, though you won't see public displays of affection, or even hand-holding. Shinjuku-nichōme (nicknamed 'Ni-chōme') is the city's gay and lesbian enclave, where hundreds of establishments, including bars, dance clubs, saunas and love hotels, are crammed into a space of a few blocks.

AFP / STRINGER / GETTY IMAGES ©

Parties & Events

Shangri-La (www.ageha.com/gn/ja/events/index.html) is arguably the city's best gay party, held roughly every other month at bayside super club Ageha. **Fancy Him** (www.fancyhim.com) is the city's most fashion-forward party, with a mixed straight and gay crowd arriving in often over-the-top handmade costumes. **Goldfinger** (www.goldfingerparty.com), hosted by the bar of the same name, is Tokyo's sexiest women-only party. But for something totally 'only-in-Tokyo', check out monthly event **Dept H** (http://ameblo.jp/department-h), where you'll find drag queens rubbing shoulders with cosplayers watching *shibari* (Japanese-style bondage) shows – it's Tokyo at its most out-there and open-minded.

Tokyo Rainbow Pride (http://tokyorainbowpride.com/en/parade), Japan's largest GLBT festival, takes place in April and includes a colourful parade through the streets of Harajuku and Shibuya. The **Tokyo International Lesbian & Gay Film Festival** (www.tokyo-lgff.org), which has been going strong for more than two decades, usually hits screens in July.

Cosy neighbourhood hub **Cocolo Cafe** (p114) is a good place to browse flyers for upcoming parties and events.

☑ Top Tips

Not all Ni-chōme bars welcome foreigners – ask around or check out **Utopia Asia** (www.utopia-asia.com) for a list of friendly places (and a handy map).

Best Bars & Clubs

Advocates Cafe A Ni-chōme landmark and the best place to start the night. (p113)

Arty Farty Popular, foreigner-friendly dance club for guys and gals alike. (p114)

Bar Goldfinger Fun, friendly girls-only bar. (p114)

Kingyo Irreverent drag revue in Roppongi. (p62)

Best
For Kids

TRAVEL INK / GETTY IMAGES ©

In many ways, Tokyo is a parent's dream: clean, safe, with all mod-cons. The downside is that most of the top attractions aren't that appealing to little ones. Older kids and teens should get a kick out of Tokyo's pop culture and neon. Shibuya and Harajuku in particular are packed with the shops, restaurants and arcades that local teens love.

Travelling with Children

Since few families can afford to live downtown, most restaurants don't see many young children. Large chains (such as Jonathan's, Royal Host and Gusto) are the exception: catering for families with booths, non-smoking sections and children's menus (that usually include western food). You'll also find more child-friendly eateries around major tourist attractions. Most hotels can offer a cot for a small fee, however it is near impossible to find a room with two double beds (that isn't an expensive suite). Ryokan (traditional inns) usually have rooms that can accommodate four or five people on futons; otherwise try a rental.

Best Kid-Friendly Museums

National Science Museum Filled with natural wonders and hands-on activities. (p138)

Tokyo National Museum Samurai armour and swords. (p130)

Shitamachi Museum Edo-era games and buildings to explore. (p137)

Taiko Drum Museum Play drums. (p149)

Best Family Fun

Ōedo Onsen Monogatari A festival atmosphere with the chance to try on a *yukata* (a light, cotton kimono). (p157)

Tokyo Dome See baseball, Japanese-style. (p125)

☑ Top Tips

▶ Children under 12 get in for free at most city museums and gardens.

▶ Under six, they ride for free on public transport; under-12s are charged half the adult fare.

▶ Try to limit your subway time to the hours between 10am and 5pm, when they're free of pushing crowds.

▶ For nursing and nappy-changing stations, department stores are your best bet.

Hanayashiki Amusement park with retro charm and creaky old rides. (p149)

Survival Guide

Survival Guide

Before You Go

When to Go

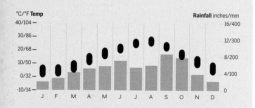

°C/°F **Temp**
40/104 —
30/86 —
20/68 —
10/50 —
0/32 —
-10/14 —

Rainfall inches/mm
16/400
12/300
8/200
4/100
0

J F M A M J J A S O N D

➡ **Winter (Dec–Feb)**
Cold but clear. December is lively with end-of-year celebrations, then the city shuts down for the New Year's holiday (1–3 Jan).

➡ **Spring (Mar–May)**
Gradually warmer days and glorious cherry blossoms from late-March to early April.

➡ **Summer (Jun–Aug)**
Rainy season from June to mid-July, then hot and humid. City gets sleepy during the week-long O-bon (festival of the dead) holiday in mid-August.

➡ **Autumn (Sep–Nov)**
Warm days with the odd typhoon in September, becoming crisp and cool from October.

Book Your Stay

➡ Tokyo accommodation runs the gamut from sumptuous luxury hotels to cheap dorm rooms in converted warehouses.

➡ While boutique hotels haven't really taken off here, ryokan (traditional inns) fill the need for small-scale lodgings with heaps of character; you'll find these in traditional areas such as Ueno and Yanaka.

➡ Asakusa is the *de facto* backpacker neighbourhood, home to the highest concentration of hostels.

➡ For top end, look to upscale districts such as Marunouchi, Ginza and Roppongi.

➡ Business hotels, though bland, fall squarely in the middle and exist in every major hub, including Shinjuku and Shibuya – two neighbourhoods that make convenient bases.

➜ Advanced booking is highly recommended. Not only will you get a better price at most hotels, but even at hostels walk-ins can fluster staff. Note that some midrange and budget options do not accept credit cards.

Useful Websites

JAPANiCAN (www.japanican.com) Compare prices and make booking at this English-language site run by Japan's largest travel agency, JTB.

Jalan (www.jalan.net) Japan-based discount hotel booking site with pages in English.

Japanese Inn Group (http://japaneseinngroup.com/) Nationwide association of inexpensive ryokan.

Tokyo Apartments (www.tokyoapartments.jp) Furnished and serviced apartments in central locations; by the week and by the month.

Lonely Planet (www.lonelyplanet.com/japan) Author-recommendation reviews and online booking.

Best Budget

Nui (http://backpackers japan.co.jp/nui_en) Hipster hostel in a former warehouse near Asakusa.

K's House Tokyo Oasis (http://kshouse.jp/tokyo-oasis-e/index.html) Super-friendly, clean hostel near the sights in Asakusa.

Khaosan Tokyo Kabuki (www.khaosan-tokyo.com/en/kabuki) Quirky, cosy hostel in Asakusa.

Capsule & Sauna Century (http://travel.rakuten.com/hotelinfo/78/104578/) Clean capsules for men only, in central Shibuya.

Best Midrange

Claska (www.claska.com/en/hotel) Tokyo's most stylish boutique hotel, in a quiet residential neighbourhood south of Meguro.

Shibuya Granbell (www.granbellhotel.jp) Funky boutique hotel in the thick of Shibuya.

The B Roppongi (www.theb-hotels.com/the-b-roppongi/en/index.html) Slick, though small, rooms; with Roppongi nightlife just around the corner.

TokHouse (www.tokhouse.com) Vacation rentals in the heart of Yanaka.

Best Top End

Park Hyatt (http://tokyo.park.hyatt.com) Palatial high-rise with otherworldly views in Shinjuku.

ANA Intercontinental Tokyo (www.anaintercontinental-tokyo.jp/e) Fantastic night views, chic design and reasonable rates. Near Roppongi.

Hotel Okura (www.okura.com/domestic/kanto/okura_tokyo) Vintage 1960s Japanese design, a celebrated guest list and gracious service.

Tokyo Station Hotel (www.tokyostationhotel.jp) Classic luxury inside the newly renovated Tokyo Station in Marunouchi.

Best Ryokan

Sawanoya Ryokan (www.sawanoya.com) A gem in quiet Yanaka with wonderful hospitality and traditional baths.

Hōmeikan (www.homeikan.com) Beautifully crafted, 100-year-old wooden ryokan, near Ueno.

Sukeroku no Yado Sadachiyo (www.sadachiyo.co.jp) Gorgeous old-world oasis in Asakusa.

Annex Katsutarō Ryokan (www.katsutaro.com) Minamalist, modern ryokan with friendly managers in Yanaka.

Arriving in Tokyo

☑ **Top Tip** For the best way to get to your accommodation, see p188.

Narita Airport

Narita Airport (成田空港; ☏0476-34-8000; www.narita-airport.jp/en; Narita-shi, Chiba-ken) is 66km east of Tokyo.

➡ **Narita Express** (N'EX; 成田エクスプレス; www.jreast.co.jp/e/nex/index.html) Trains run approximately every half-hour, 7.30am to 9.45pm, to Tokyo Station (¥2940, 53 minutes), with branches heading to Shinjuku, Shibuya or Shinagawa stations (all

¥3110, 1½ hours). Seats are reserved, but tickets can be purchased immediately before departure, if available, from ticket counters near the arrival gate in either terminal.

➡ **Keisei Skyliner** (京成スカイライナー; www.keisei.co.jp) Trains zip twice an hour, 8am to 10.15pm, to Ueno Station (¥2400, 45 minutes), where you can pick up the subway. Trains also stop at Nippori Station for transfers to the JR Yamanote Line. Get tickets from the counter at Narita Keisei Station in either terminal.

➡ **Keisei Main Line** (京成本線) *Tokkyū* (special express) trains run the same route as the Skyliner twice an hour 10am to 9pm. This budget option costs ¥1000 and takes 1½ hours to Ueno or Nippori.

➡ **Limousine Bus** (リムジンバス; www.limousinebus.co.jp/en) Coaches depart regularly from Narita, 7am to 10.30pm, for major hotels and train stations such as Shinjuku (¥3000, 1½ hours). Get tickets from the Limousine Bus counter near the arrival gates at either terminal.

➡ **Taxis** Run at about ¥25,000 from Narita to the city centre – naturally we don't recommend this.

Haneda Airport

Haneda Airport (羽田空港; ☏5757-8111, international terminal 6428-0888; www.tokyo-airport-bldg.co.jp/en; Ōta-ku) On the southern edge of Tokyo and much more convenient than Narita.

➡ **Tokyo Monorail** (東京モノレール; www.tokyo-monorail.co.jp/english) Runs frequently, 5.15am to midnight, to Hamamatsuchō Station (¥470, 25 minutes), where you can transfer to the JR Yamanote Line.

➡ **Keikyū Line** (京急線; www.haneda-tokyo-access.com/en/export/) Airport Express trains run frequently, 5.20am to midnight, from Keikyū Haneda Station to Shinagawa Station (¥400, 16 minutes), where you can transfer to the JR Yamanote Line.

➡ **Limousine Bus** Coaches connect Haneda with major hubs such as Shibuya (¥1000), Shinjuku (¥1200) and Tokyo Station (¥900). Travel time depends on traffic but averages about 45 minutes to most points in the city centre. The last bus of the evening leaves for Shibuya Station at 12.30am; buses start up again around 5am.

➡ A taxi to the city centre, which is your only option if you opt for a flight that gets in before dawn, averages about ¥6000.

Tokyo Station

Tokyo Station is the terminus for the *shinkansen* (bullet train).

➡ Connect here to the JR Yamanote Line or the Marunouchi subway line for points around the city centre, from 5am to midnight.

Getting Around

Bicycle

☑ **Best for...** exploring local neighbourhoods.

➡ Cycling is an excellent way to get around some of the fringe neighbourhoods, though the traffic is not for the faint of heart.

➡ Some budget accommodation (espe-

cially around Ueno and Asakusa) have bicycles to lend or know where you can rent one.

➡ **Sumida-kōen Bicycle Parking Lot** (隅田公園駐輪場; Map p148, C3; 1-1 Hanakawado, Taitō-ku; ¥200; ⏰6am-8pm; 🚇Ginza Line to Asakusa, exit 5), next to the Tokyo Cruise Pier in Asakusa, rents city bikes (¥200/day). Picture ID is required.

Boat

☑ **Best for...** combining sightseeing with transport.

➡ **Tokyo Cruise** (水上バス; Map p148, C3; Suijō Bus; http://suijobus.co.jp) Water buses run up and down the Sumida-gawa (Sumida River), roughly twice an hour between 10am and 6pm, connecting Asakusa with Hama-rikyū Onshi-teien (¥720, 35 minutes) and Odaiba (¥1520, 50 minutes). Tickets can be purchased immediately before departure, if available, at any pier.

Bus

☑ **Best for...** getting around residential neighbourhoods and out of the city.

➡ A ride on a municipal bus costs ¥200; there are no transfer tickets.

➡ The **Megurin Community Bus** (めぐりん; www.city.taito.lg.jp/index/kurashi/kotsu/megurin/index.html; one ride/day pass ¥100/300; ⏰every 15 minutes, 7am-7pm) runs around Ueno and Asakusa.

➡ Highway buses headed to the Mt Fuji area leave from the **Shinjuku Highway Bus Terminal** (新宿高速バスターミナル; Map p108, B2; 📞5376-2222; www.highwaybus.com/html/gp/foreign/en/access/index.html; 1-10-1 Nishi-Shinjuku, Shinjuku-ku; ⏰6am-11.30pm; 🚇JR Yamanote Line to Shinjuku, west exit). Reserve tickets online in advance.

Taxi

☑ **Best for...** late nights and groups sharing the cost.

➡ Flagfall is ¥710. After 2km the meter starts to clock an additional ¥100 for every 350m (and up to ¥100 for every two minutes you sit idly in traffic). It adds up quickly – figure around ¥2500 for a ride from Ginza to Roppongi.

➡ It's best to have cash on you as not all taxis take credit cards.

➡ Look for taxi ranks in front of all major train stations and hotels.

➡ You can also hail a cab from the street – taxis with their indicator in red are free; green means taken.

➡ Cabbies usually don't speak English and have trouble finding all but the most well-known spots. Fortunately many have GPS systems, so have an address or a business card for your destination handy.

Train & Subway

☑ **Best for...** getting around the city efficiently.

➡ Tokyo's train network runs approximately 5am to midnight and includes Japan Rail (JR) lines, 13 subway lines – four operated by Toei and nine by Tokyo Metro – and numerous private commuter lines.

➡ The line you'll probably use the most is the JR Yamanote Line, the city's elevated loop line that runs through many key sightseeing areas.

➡ Try to avoid rush hour (around 8am to 9.30am and 5pm to 8pm), when 'packed in like sardines' is an understatement.

➡ All train stations have English signage and the

Train Passes

Suica (www.jreast.co.jp/e/pass/suica) This is a prepaid train pass fitted with an electromagnetic chip. To use it, swipe it over the card reader on any automatic ticket gates. It works on all city trains, subways and buses, and makes transferring between multiple lines and calculating fares a no-brainer. Get one from a ticket vending machine at any JR station; note that Suica cards require a ¥500 deposit, refundable when you return it to a JR window.

Suica & N'EX (Narita) or **Suica & Monorail** (Haneda) packages, available at either airport from the JR EAST Travel Service Centers (http://www.jreast. co.jp/e/customer_support/service_center.html), are an excellent deal combining a prepaid Suica card with discounted transport to and from the airport.

Day passes Can save you money if you plan to cover a lot of ground in one day. You'll need to get one that covers the rail lines you'll be using, and purchase it from one of the station windows on those lines:

➡ **Tokyo Metro 1-Day Open Ticket** costs ¥710 (child ¥360) and covers Tokyo Metro subway lines.

➡ **Common 1-Day Ticket** costs ¥1000 (child ¥500) and covers both Tokyo Metro and Toei subway lines.

➡ **Tokyo Combination Ticket** costs ¥1580 (child ¥790) and covers JR trains in Tokyo and all subway lines.

ines are conveniently colour-coded.

→ Tickets are sold from vending machines near the automated ticket gates. Look for the newer touch screen ones that have an English option.

→ Fares are determined by how far you ride; there should be a fare chart above the ticket machines. If your journey involves lines run by different operators, you'll need to purchase a transfer ticket.

→ If you can't work out how much to pay, one easy trick is to buy a ticket at the cheapest fare (¥130 for JR; ¥160 for Tokyo Metro; ¥170 for Toei) and use one of the 'fare adjustment' machines, near the exit gates, to settle the difference at the end of your journey.

→ You'll need a valid train ticket to exit the station, so make sure to pick it up when it pops out of the entry gates.

→ Tokyo's competing rail lines can make getting from point A to point B – in the cheapest, most economical way – a little confusing. **Jorudan** (www.jorudan.co.jp/english/nori-

kae), also available as a smart phone app, is a life-saver: it calculates routes by speed and fare.

→ Most train stations have multiple exits. Look for maps in the station that show which exits are closest to major area landmarks.

Essential Information

Business Hours

Exceptions to the following hours are noted in the listings.

Banks 9am to 3pm Monday to Friday

Bars 5pm to late Monday to Saturday

Boutiques noon to 8pm

Clubs 10am to 5am Thursday to Saturday

Department Stores 10am to 8pm

Museums 9am to 5pm

Post Offices 9am to 5pm

Restaurants lunch 11.30am to 2.30pm, dinner 6pm to 10pm; larger restaurants stay open throughout the afternoon.

Discount Cards

→ **Tokyo Handy Guide** (www.gotokyo.org/book/tokyo_handy_guide) offers small discounts (around ¥100) to many museums; pick one up for free at most tourist information centres and many accommodation venues.

→ **Grutt Pass** (www.rekibun.or.jp/grutto; pass ¥2000) is a good deal if you plan to hit a lot of museums. Valid for two months, it offers discounted – and sometimes free – admission to more than 70 museums in greater Tokyo; purchase at any of the affiliated museums.

Electricity

100V/50Hz

Money-Saving Tips

➜ Many of Tokyo's more expensive restaurants are comparatively reasonable at lunch; you'll get better value if you splurge at midday.

➜ Stock up on sundries (and even food and souvenirs) at ¥100 stores. Look for colourful signs proclaiming '¥100'.

➜ After 5pm, grocery stores, bakeries and even department store food halls slash prices on *bentō* (a boxed lunch, usually of rice with a main dish and pickles or salad), baked goods and sushi – an inexpensive dinner-to-go made easy.

Emergency

☑ **Top Tip** Most emergency operators don't speak English, but they will immediately refer you to someone who does.

➜ **Ambulance** (救急車; Kyūkyūsha; ☎119)

➜ **Fire** (消防署; Shōbōsho; ☎119)

➜ **Police** (警視庁; Keishichō; ☎emergency 110, general 3501-0110; www.keishicho.metro.tokyo.jp) 24-hour staffed *kōban* (police boxes) are located near most major train stations.

➜ **Medical Information & Emergency Interpretation** (☎emergency translation 5285-8185, medical information 5285-8181; www.himawari.metro.tokyo.jp/qq/qq13enmnlt.asp; ⏰9am-8pm) in English, Chinese, Korean, Thai and Spanish.

Money

➜ The unit of currency is the Japanese yen (¥).

➜ Tokyo is still largely a cash society, though major hotels, restaurants and stores usually take credit cards. Still, it's a good idea to have cash as back-up.

ATMs

➜ Post offices and 7-Eleven convenience stores have ATMs with English instructions that work with overseas cards; 7-Elevens are open 24hr.

➜ **Citibank** (シティバンク; www.citibank.co.jp/en) is the only bank with ATMs (in English) that accept cards from every country. ATMs are open 24hr and you can find them in Shinjuku, Shibuya, Ginza and Roppongi.

Changing Money

➜ Most banks and some major hotels and department stores can change cash or travellers cheques. US dollars and euros are the easiest to change, and fetch the best rates.

Tipping

➜ Tipping is not standard practice in Japan; however, a service charge (10%) will be added to the bill at upper-end restaurants.

Public Holidays

☑ **Top Tip** When a public holiday falls on a Sunday, the following Monday is taken as a holiday. If a business remains open on a holiday – often the case with museums – then it will usually close the next day.

New Year's Day 1 January

Coming-of-Age Day Second Monday in January

National Foundation Day 11 February

Spring Equinox 21 March

Shōwa Emperor's Day
29 April

Constitution Day 3 May

Green Day 4 May

Children's Day 5 May

Marine Day Third Monday in July

Respect-for-the-Aged Day Third Monday in September

Autumn Equinox Day
22 or 23 September

Sports Day Second Monday in October

Culture Day 3 November

Labour Thanksgiving Day 23 November

Emperor's Birthday
23 December

Safe Travel

➡ For a megalopolis with more than 35 million people, Tokyo is surprisingly safe. Crimes against foreign tourists are exceedingly rare. That said, you should exercise the same caution you would in your home country.

➡ Touts for bars and clubs in Roppongi and Shinjuku's Kabukichō can be aggressive. Be wary of following them; while not common, spiked drinks followed by theft, or worse, beatings, have

occurred. Overcharging is the more likely outcome.

➡ Women should note that *chikan* (gropers) do haunt crowded trains, though they usually prey on local women (who are presumed less likely to make a scene). Yelling *'chikan!'* is often enough to shame the offender into stopping. During rush hour, many express trains heading to the suburbs have women-only cars (marked in pink).

Telephone

Country code 📞81

International access code 📞001

Calling Tokyo

➡ Tokyo's area code is 03, followed by an eight-digit number. You can drop the area code if calling from a landline within Tokyo.

➡ Drop the zero from the area code when calling Tokyo from abroad.

International Calls

➡ Phone cards are available from many convenience stores and newsstands and are the most convenient way to call either locally or internationally. Look for the Brastel cards (www.brastel.com/pages/eng/

home/#location), which have explanations in English.

Mobile Phones

➡ Overseas mobile phones are not compatible with local SIM cards.

➡ Pick up a rental from one of the counters operating out of Narita Airport (www.narita-airport.jp/en/guide/service/list/svc_19.html). Some even offer smart phones, which are invaluable for navigating Tokyo's confusing address system.

➡ There are a few rental shops at Haneda Airport, too (www.haneda-airport.jp/inter/en/premises/service/internet.html).

Pay Phones

➡ Payphones (usually bright green) are still fairly common around train stations; domestic calls cost ¥10 per minute.

Toilets

☑ **Top Tip** Public toilets stocked with toilet paper are easy to come by and are almost always clean. All train stations have them, as do convenience stores (though technically you should buy something).

➡ Traditional squat toilets still exist in Tokyo, but it's

rare to find accommodation, restaurants or public facilities that don't have at least one Western-style toilet.

➜ You'll see people drying their hands on handkerchiefs or small washcloths as most public toilets lack paper towels or hand-dryers; pick one up at a ¥100 shop.

➜ If you encounter one of Japan's state-of-the-art 'washlets' (toilets with bidets), check the control panel for your flush options – 大 means 'big' and 小 means 'small'.

Tourist Information

☑ **Top Tip** Tourist information centres at both terminals at Narita Airport and at the international terminal at Haneda Airport have English-speaking staff who can help you get orientated.

Asakusa Tourist Information Center (浅草文化観光センター; Map p148 C3; http://taitonavi.jp; 2-18-9 Kaminarimon, Taitō-ku; ⏰9am-8pm; 🚇Ginza Line to Asakusa, exit 2) English speaking staff, plus maps and brochures.

JNTO Tourist Information Center (TIC; Map p38, D3; 📞3201-3331; www.jnto.go.jp; 1st fl, Shin-Tokyo Bldg, 3-3-1 Marunouchi, Chiyoda-ku; ⏰9am-5pm; 🚇JR Yamanote Line to Yūrakuchō, Tokyo International Forum exit) Run by the Japan National Tourism Organisation (JNTO) with knowledgeable, English-speaking staff and brochures.

Tokyo Tourist Information Center (東京観光情報センター; Map p38, D4; 📞5321-3077; www.gotokyo.org/en/index.html; 1st fl, Tokyo Metropolitan Government Bldg 1, 2-8-1 Nishi-Shinjuku, Shinjuku-ku; ⏰9.30am-6.30pm; 🚇Ōedo Line to

Dos & Don'ts

➜ Relax. Japan is famous for its hair-splitting etiquette rules, but foreign tourists are given a pass for just about everything.

➜ Pack light. Tokyo hotel rooms tend to be tiny, leaving little room for a big suitcase.

➜ Dress smart if you want to blend in, although for all but the fanciest restaurants, casual clothes are fine.

➜ Wear shoes you can slip on and off easily, as many ryokan and restaurants still ask you to leave your shoes at the door.

➜ Refrain from eating on the subway or while walking down the street – it's considered impolite.

➜ Get in line. The Japanese are famous for forming neat, orderly lines for everything.

➜ Stand to the left on the escalator.

Tochōmae, exit A4) Run by the municipal government, with lots of English language maps and brochures. There's also a branch at the entrance to Keisei Ueno Station.

Travellers with Disabilities

➡ Newer or recently renovated buildings have ramps, elevators and barrier-free facilities. However, there is still a long way to go. Visitors in wheelchairs will find navigating train stations and crowded city streets a challenge.

➡ Though it hasn't been updated in years, **Accessible Tokyo** (http://accessible.jp.org/tokyo/en/) is still the best resource for travellers with disabilities; email them for a copy of their free guide.

➡ For a list of barrier-free hotels, see http://www.gotokyo.org/en/administration/barrier_free/barrierlist.html.

Visas

➡ Citizens of 61 countries, including Australia, Canada, Hong Kong, Korea, New Zealand, Singapore, USA, UK and almost all European nations do not require visas to enter Japan for stays of 90 days or less. Consult http://www.mofa.go.jp/j_info/visit/visa/short/novisa.html for a complete list of visa-exempt countries.

Language

Japanese pronunciation is easy for English speakers, as most of its sounds are also found in English. Note though that it's important to make the distinction between short and long vowels, as vowel length can change the meaning of a word. The long vowels (ā, ē, ī, ō, ū) should be held twice as long as the short ones. All syllables in a word are pronounced fairly evenly in Japanese. If you read our pronunciation guides as if they were English, you'll be understood.

To enhance your trip with a phrasebook, visit **lonelyplanet.com**. Lonely Planet iPhone phrasebooks are available through the Apple App store.

Basics

Hello.
こんにちは。　　　　kon·ni·chi·wa

Goodbye.
さようなら。　　　　sa·yō·na·ra

Yes.
はい。　　　　　　　hai

No.
いいえ。　　　　　　ī·e

Please.
ください。　　　　　ku·da·sai

Thank you.
ありがとう。　　　　a·ri·ga·tō

Excuse me.
すみません。　　　　su·mi·ma·sen

Sorry.
ごめんなさい。　　　go·men·na·sai

How are you?
お元気ですか?　　　o·gen·ki des ka

Fine. And you?
はい、元気です。　　hai, gen·ki des
あなたは?　　　　　a·na·ta wa

Do you speak English?
英語が　　　　　　　ē·go ga
話せますか?　　　　ha·na·se·mas ka

I don't understand.
わかりません。　　　wa·ka·ri·ma·sen

Eating & Drinking

I'd like to reserve a table for (two).
(2人)の　　　　　　(fu·ta·ri) no
予約をお　　　　　　yo·ya·ku o
願いします。　　　　o·ne·gai shi·mas

I'd like (the menu).
(メニュー)　　　　　(me·nyū)
をお願いします。　　o o·ne·gai shi·mas

I don't eat (red meat).
(赤身の肉)　　　　　(a·ka·mi no ni·ku)
は食べません。　　　wa ta·be·ma·sen

That was delicious!
おいしかった。　　　oy·shi·kat·ta

Please bring the bill.
お勘定　　　　　　　o·kan·jō
をください。　　　　o ku·da·sai

Cheers!　　乾杯!　　kam·pai

beer　　ビール　　bī·ru

coffee　　コーヒー　　kō·hī

Shopping

I'd like ...
…をください。　　　... o ku·da·sai

I'm just looking.
見ているだけです。　mi·te i·ru da·ke des

How much is it?
いくらですか? i·ku·ra des ka

That's too expensive.
高すぎます。 ta·ka·su·gi·mas

Can you give me a discount?
ディスカウント dis·kown·to
できますか? de·ki·mas ka

Emergencies

Help!
たすけて! tas·ke·te

Go away!
離れろ! ha·na·re·ro

Call the police!
警察を呼んで! kē·sa·tsu o yon·de

Call a doctor!
医者を呼んで! i·sha o yon·de

I'm lost.
迷いました。 ma·yoy·mash·ta

I'm ill.
私は病 wa·ta·shi wa
気です。 byō·ki des

Where are the toilets?
トイレは toy·re wa
どこですか? do·ko des ka

Time & Numbers

What time is it?
何時ですか? nan·ji des ka

It's (10) o'clock.
(10)時です。 (jū)·ji des

Half past (10).
(10)時半です。 (jū)·ji han des

morning	朝	a·sa
afternoon	午後	go·go
evening	夕方	yū·ga·ta

yesterday	きのう	ki·nō
today	今日	kyō
tomorrow	明日	a·shi·ta

1	一	i·chi
2	二	ni
3	三	san
4	四	shi/yon
5	五	go
6	六	ro·ku
7	七	shi·chi/na·na
8	八	ha·chi
9	九	ku/kyū
10	十	jū

Transport & Directions

Where's the ...?
…はどこ ... wa do·ko
ですか? des ka

What's the address?
住所は何 jū·sho wa nan
ですか? des ka

Can you show me (on the map)?
(地図で)教えて (chi·zu de) o·shi·e·te
くれませんか? ku·re·ma·sen ka

When's the next (bus)?
次の (バス)は tsu·gi no (bas) wa
何時ですか? nan·ji des ka

Does it stop at ...?
…に ... ni
停まりますか? to·ma·ri·mas ka

Please tell me when we get to ...
… に着いたら ... ni tsu·i·ta·ra
教えてください。 o·shi·e·te ku·da·sai

Behind the Scenes

Send Us Your Feedback

We love to hear from travellers – your comments help make our books better. We read every word, and we guarantee that your feedback goes straight to the authors. Visit **lonelyplanet.com/contact** to submit your updates and suggestions.

Note: We may edit, reproduce and incorporate your comments in Lonely Planet products such as guidebooks, websites and digital products, so let us know if you don't want your comments reproduced or your name acknowledged. For a copy of our privacy policy visit lonelyplanet.com/privacy.

Rebecca's Thanks

Thank you to Chikara for his inhuman patience and support; to Julian for his company and bar expertise; to Emi for joining me on dining expeditions; to Jon and Kanna for getting me away from my computer; and to Emily Wolman and everyone at LP who worked on this book.

Acknowledgments

Cover photograph: Shinjuku; Kokoroimages.com/Getty Images.

This Book

This guidebook was commissioned in Lonely Planet's Oakland office, and produced by the following:

Commissioning Editor Emily K Wolman **Coordinating Editor** Amanda Williamson **Senior Cartographer** Diana Von Holdt **Coordinating Layout Designer** Nicholas Colicchia **Managing Editors** Annelies Mertens, Martine Power **Managing Layout Designer** Chris Girdler **Assisting Editor** Sam Trafford **Cover Research** Naomi Parker **Internal Image Research** Kylie McLaughlin **Language Content** Branislava Vladisavljevic **Thanks to** Naoko Akamatsu, Barbara Delissen, Ryan Evans, Larissa Frost, Genesys India, Jouve India, Gerard Jellema, Chris Love, Katie O'Connell, Trent Paton, Kerrianne Southway, Shiyun Tan, Gerard Walker

Index

See also separate subindexes for:

😵 Eating p204
🍸 Drinking p205
🎭 Entertainment p206
🛍 Shopping p206

Sights p000
Map Pages **p000**